BELIEVE IT.
SPEAK IT.
DO IT.

Finding Peace Within Your Purpose

BELIEVE IT.
SPEAK IT.
DO IT.

Finding Peace Within Your Purpose

BEVERLY "COACH BEV" KEARNEY

Books may be purchased in quantity and/or special sales by contacting the publisher.

Published by
Mynd Matters Publishing
715 Peachtree Street NE, Suites 100 & 200
Atlanta, GA 30308
www.myndmatterspublishing.com

978-1-948145-51-0 (pbk)
978-1-948145-52-7 (ebook)

FIRST EDITION

To my mother and my grandmother,
and everyone who has ever dared to have the courage to pursue
peace and purpose

CONTENTS

PREFACE

When I was young, probably in the early stages of elementary school, we lived in Tampa, Florida. Although life was, at times, challenging during the week, the weekends were worse. There was always drinking, fighting, unwanted and undesired sexual episodes, as well as nasty hangovers. But on Sundays, we could always count on family time. It seemed odd that my mother could raise so much hell on Fridays and Saturdays but on Sundays, be almost angelic. There was one very memorable Sunday family outing, which consisted of a rare trip to the beach in nearby Clearwater, Florida.

Although I did not particularly care much for the beach, we were always excited about family time. I didn't like sand or dirt on my feet and I rarely, if ever, wore flip-flops or sandals, preferring tennis shoes and socks to protect my feet. I especially hated how the water moved the sand underneath my toes, given all of the jellyfish and other creatures roaming throughout the ocean's waves. We had never been to a swimming pool before and in the rare times when we did go anywhere near water, it was either a river in Mississippi or the ocean in Florida. So, to say that neither my younger brother Derick nor I could swim, would be an understatement.

On this particular Sunday, my father and my much older brother Howard decided Derick and I needed to learn how to swim. They held us above the water and told us to move our arms and legs. It was so much fun with the kicking and splashing and especially the opportunity to gain special attention, something hard to come by in our family. After a while, my father lifted me onto his shoulders as Howard placed Derick on his shoulders and began to sort of walk/swim us into deeper water. I wasn't afraid because I was holding on tightly and trusted my big brother and father wouldn't allow anything to happen to us. As we moved out farther and into deeper water, they stopped swimming, lifted us from their shoulders, and lowered us into the water around a barge of sand that stood a little higher than the water. They dove into the waters, swimming back to shore. I screamed for them to come back as they retorted for us to swim to them. Derick and I looked at each other as if to say, "They must be crazy. We can't swim and especially not that far." In actuality, it wasn't far but when you're little, everything seems miles away. So, I did what any self-respecting kid would do, I cried.

As we limply stood there, planted on the sand, water splashing around us, they kept encouraging us to swim. Finally, I heard them say, "Okay, stay your asses out there. We're going to McDonald's." We never got to eat out and McDonald's was a rare treat. I looked at Derick and he looked at me and I can't tell you who jumped in first, but we fought and splashed our way back to shore. I doubt we were truly swimming in the formal sense as our movements were pretty ugly. It looked more like two little people playing in the water as opposed to kids swimming.

After what felt like a lifetime, we made it back. I wasn't mad about getting dumped. I wasn't even thinking about how afraid I was of the water, the sea creatures, or drowning. I was too excited about going to McDonald's. All I can recall is enjoying the best hamburger and fries I'd ever had and we didn't even have to share a burger. Everyone was so proud of us that we each got our own meal.

I wish this was the story that led to me becoming a world-class swimmer but it is not. Heck, I looked more like someone refusing to drown than someone learning how to swim. No, this story is about overcoming life's challenges and fears and finding the inner magic that allows each of us to dive into our greatest dreams and passions. It's about having the courage to jump into the depths of murky and unknown waters knowing we will reach the shores of life.

The aforementioned story is symbolic of how I have lived my life by swimming in the depths of the oceans of opportunity, often among sharks and predators, to reach greatness which sits on the other side of failure. I have lived with many fears, but none have been greater than my desire to reach my goals—my McDonald's of life.

When drowning is not an option, you swim! The Power, the Magic, which exists within each of us reveals itself when we allow ourselves to dream big. This book is a journey of discovering that magic and how it not only propels us beyond our obstacles, but more importantly, towards our dreams.

BELIEVE IT.
SPEAK IT.
DO IT.

Finding Peace Within Your Purpose

INTRODUCTION

As I sat in the quiet stillness of the night surrounded by bright lights yet engulfed in the peacefulness of the darkness, I hadn't felt this level of tranquility since finding myself sprawled in the middle of an interstate near death. That moment resulted in a three-month hospital stay. Just as I had been given a slim chance of surviving, with the high impossibility of ever walking again, I now faced the remote possibility of a team, with only seven athletes, winning the Collegiate National Championship at the Outdoor Women's Track and Field Championships.

The odds had not been in our favor all year and now we were faced with competing teams whose roster doubled ours in the hunt for their first, and my sixth, national title. Still suffering from paralysis as a result of the horrific accident, I sat alone on my mobility scooter in the hustle and bustle of television cameras, athletes, coaches, and various college personnel from across the country. Yet, in the midst of it all, for the first time in four long, grueling days of competition, I felt alone.

Although the brightness of the stadium lights blanketed the practice field, it was the brightness of the moon that shown through the darkness of the night, lighting up my heart. I sat awaiting the final event, the women's 4x400 relay, which would determine which of the top four leading collegiate Division I teams would win the coveted 2005 national championship team title. As I stared into the night sky, the moon appeared to glow, creating a sense of serenity. At that moment, I realized my lips were moving, and surprisingly, I heard the sound of my own voice.

I spoke to Ilrey, at least, a vision of Ilrey given she'd died three years earlier in the same car crash that had left me paralyzed. "Ilrey, I feel you and I know it's going to be all right. Ill, this one's for you." I pounded my fist on the left side of my chest to signify how much love and respect I had for her fighting, loving spirit and her strength of character. As I spoke, the power of such a rare moment of clarity and peace surrounded me.

Suddenly, my moment was disrupted by the sounds of chanting behind me. As I drifted back into the present, I saw the opposing team, which had changed from their normal school colors and track and field attire into bright neon pink tennis outfits. Now the favorites to win the championship, there had to be fifteen or more of them chanting. Their vast amount of talent and confidence was on full display as they jogged around the small practice track. Normally I would be inspired into action, ready to fight back against what could easily be perceived as blatant disrespect, but not this time. It only made me smile.

It had been rare moments that such "knowing," such peace, had enveloped me. I knew everything was okay, just as I had known I was okay on that frigid December morning in 2002 while lying in the middle of the interstate after the accident. As I turned my scooter towards our training camp area, my four-person relay team finished their warm-ups. Although we were not fully equipped with the two allowable relay alternates, their faces showed no signs of concern. As I approached them, my calmness connected with their air of confidence and determination, confirming my deepest inner sentiment. They were displaying an identical "knowing" that had arisen within me. I wanted to cry *and* smile. But mostly, it gave me an uncannily sense of peace in the midst of a tense physical and emotional battle.

I thought about what I would say. I knew I could never explain to them what happened just moments prior. So, I decided not to try. As the team gathered around me, I looked into each of their eyes and thought of the unlikelihood of this group of only seven athletes ever contending for the national championship. Yet, here we were, with television cameras surrounding us as we entered the arena for the final curtain in an event with which we had struggled all year. I told each of them how proud I was of them for placing themselves in the position of potentially being national champions. Then, I explained that if they finished fourth, they would finish no lower than third in the nation and if they were second, they would tie for the national championship. But, if they won the race, they alone would be national champions. They were in a no-lose situation and I trusted them. As my message of encouragement continued, I advised them not to focus on the other team parading around the track because it was an intimidation tactic. Before I could finish, collectively, they told me they were resolute to win the relay and the meet. The conversation was over. They calmly and confidently gathered their bags and headed towards the final check-in area, to enter the stadium.

As my staff gathered our gear to walk to the stadium seating and coaching area, members of the media, with their television cameras, looked uncertain about who to follow. Should they follow the favorites or the unlikely story of seven underdog athletes, aiming to win the national championship? It didn't matter to us. We were not there to prove ourselves to anyone. We were in it to finish what we started…WIN! With tremendous pressure, and true to their word, the team carried themselves with the message that they were focused on only one place and it was first.

I made my way into the stadium, finally feeling the magnitude of our challenge. The lights of the stadium shone even brighter than the practice field. When I glanced up at the stadium seats, I saw and heard the rumblings of the crowd as the men's mile relay lined up for their final battle. The rumble grew and erupted into screams and shouts as the gun went off, signaling the start of the men's 4x400 relay.

I can't describe the men's race because my eyes and mind were affixed on the silent entry of the eight women's teams as they lined them up along the wall of the track. In the meantime, the men engaged in their own epic battle as indicated by the roaring noises coming from the stadium. The mile relay is historically a fan favorite and always ends every meet. People rarely leave before that race ends. Unlike the women's race, the men's 4x400 relay would not determine the team title. Arkansas would rein again as the national champions, regardless of the outcome. Their race was for pride and bragging rights. Ours had become an old-fashioned all or nothing brawl, fighting with all of our might.

As I watched our young ladies, three sophomores and a first-year junior college transfer student, enter the stadium, I couldn't help but reflect on the journey that had gotten us there. I watched their faces and as they glanced in my direction. Again I took my fist and pounded it against the left side of my chest, signaling the message to not only run from their hearts, but that I felt them and believed in them. With only stern, focused faces, they simply nodded back as if to say, *we got this.*

They were uncharacteristically locked-in and fixated, staring either straight ahead or at the ground as prizefighters do prior to entering the ring of battle. Each of them entered that night's race with a personal and collective purpose to prove themselves under pressure and as champions. Everyone had doubted them all year and proclaimed Texas weak after the bulk of our history-making team had either graduated or gone professional at the end of the 2004 season. There we stood with a handful of athletes on the verge of doing what we had failed to accomplish with a historically talented team the previous year.

This time, our team had lost every major 4x400 relay race that year, and atypically for The University of Texas teams, had been placing outside the top three finishers. To say the season was difficult is an understatement. In fact, in the most recent indoor national championship, the team had performed so poorly that for the first time in my history as a coach and probably the history of Texas, the team had not made the qualifying standards for the championship. As a result, I refused to take them to a last chance meet to qualify. Thus, for the first time in decades, Texas did not field a mile relay team at the championship. My decision did not go over well with the athletes and it was worse with my administration. I will never forget being in the heart of my practice one day in March, after making the decision and getting a call from my athletic director, Chris Plonsky. Her demeanor was usually a mix of anger and annoyance, but on that day, she was livid. I didn't have to wonder why, without a greeting, she immediately began to tear into me for not taking the mile relay to a last chance-qualifying meet and not telling her. I retorted that she was out of line and being cursed at by her in the middle of my practice was most egregious and out of order. She had the right to tell me what I could spend but not how to coach. I'm certain my final comment about my mother cursing better than her and that she should be ashamed of herself for always hollering and cursing at us, didn't go over well. She had intimidated others but I grew up getting cursed at and my mother was better at it and even then, I didn't like it. I ended with a firm, "So cut that shit out."

If there was any doubt before that moment about the instability of our relationship, that exchange pushed it to non-existent. No matter how hard either one of us would try, we would never or could never have the same meaningful and inspiring relationship I had with my former Texas athletic director, Jody Conradt. It had been only four or five years since Jody stepped down to focus on her position and true passion of women's basketball. She had taken the dual role of coach and women's athletic director upon the departure of the legendary women's activist, Donna Lopiano. Yet, listening and tending to the needs of her basketball athletes was a strain but that, coupled with listening and adhering to the needs of coaches and staff, became overwhelming. Thus, she resigned her position as athletic director to focus solely on her love of coaching women's basketball.

I was Jody's first hire in 1992, and it was a sad day when she left. She had been my protector and advisor for nearly ten years. After her departure, the administrators took advantage of the opportunity to more aggressively attack me. The decision not to run the 4x400 relay in the last chance meet was a decision, although tough, made without a second thought. The team had not been focused, our numbers were low, we "needed" every athlete and they knew it. As the team became more challenging, I preferred to go to nationals with three athletes who were willing to fight than go with ten athletes who were not.

I told my staff we would not be held hostage by need. I favored going down fighting and losing with warriors than clinging to the hope our team would fight. In 2005, we entered the national championship with only three athletes or should I say, warriors. Ironically, all of their names started with an M. There was Marshavet, Michelle, and Malanie—the M & M crew. Even with only three members, we were leading the meet. Eventually, we ran out of events and the larger teams took over. But, we were a threat for the championship until the other coaches figured out we couldn't score any more points.

After returning to campus, my athletic director congratulated us on a great performance and the overall result culminated with the effect I had hoped for, those who were left behind joined together and decided that if they had done what they were supposed to do, we could have won. That team was never the same. My long jumper finished second in the nation and came to me after her competition. Apparently, her competitor from Tennessee, who won the event, had jumped so far early in the competition that she removed her competition shoes and sat and watched as my long jumper and others strained to finish in the top slots behind her. As she boarded the plane at the conclusion of the meet, she pulled me aside and simply said, "Coach, I don't know if I can beat her, but I promise you she will never be able to take her shoes off again in the middle of a competition." Every athlete on our team had a newfound mission to win. Yet, even with their passion and determination came challenges.

As the athletes lined up for the final event, I decided to leave the stability of my mobility scooter and stand. I still suffered from paralysis from my knees down and balance felt nearly impossible. Standing for long periods of time was painful, yet, none of that crossed my mind as I instinctively stood. I rose from the chair feeling my heart pounding in my chest and my breathing became shallow. I was officially nervous. I wondered to myself, how long could I hold on to the "knowing" I had developed. As they adjusted their blocks for the start of the race, there was no looking to the skies for reassurance, just nerves as I stood there and began to notice I was swaying from side to side, too nervous to stand still. What was happening to me?

The words of the legendary elder coach and my mentor, Coach Jim Bibbs, formerly of Michigan State University, came back to me. When I first started coaching, I was a nervous wreck. I was only in my mid-twenties and already vying for national titles and records. Yet, the nerves, then and now, would eat at me. At one particular national championship, while I was coaching at The University of Tennessee in the late 80's, they were particularly bad. I happened to run into coach Bibbs and asked him, as an elder in the sport, if he ever got over the nervousness, because I was tired of feeling like my heart would either jump out of my chest or stop beating.

He grabbed my hand and patted it as he looked into my eyes and lovingly said, "Baby, if you ever stop feeling that way, you need to get out of coaching. So, no, they won't ever go away but those feelings are what makes you a winner and they shouldn't and won't ever go away."

That day, the nerves were front and center making it difficult to breathe, much less speak. Yet, this was the first time, despite their presence in the pit of my stomach, I understood their value and I embraced the sensation. As I rose from my scooter, I scanned the field of female athletes near the starting line. Looking into the faces of the four warriors donned in the burnt orange of Texas, I couldn't help but reflect on the multitude of challenges that each had endured during the season. I prayed for them, knowing every challenge we faced that season, somehow prepared us for the cameras, which followed the top teams, and the massive undertaking of carrying the weight of a race to determine who would walk away as champions.

As the athletes marched to the start of the line, the tension in the air created a silence broken only by the meet's announcer proclaiming the race as the final one of the four-day competition. I stood staring down the track wondering if my athletes were listening to the announcer, hoping, without much success, he'd stop talking. But he did what he had been hired to do, distinguish the relay as the ultimate event.

The eight teams of three remaining athletes stood in the grassy infield of the track as the first legs of the relay were led to the starting line. I could barely watch as the lead off legs entered the blocks and the murmurs in the stadium drifted to a nerve-racking silence. Just as my heart pounded through my chest, the sound of the starting gun and the sight of its smoke shook me from the nerves into my fighting coach mode. The junior lead off fought hard but struggled in the final stretch prior to handing off and wound up somewhere in the middle of the pack. We weren't leading the race, but we weren't out of it either. Our second leg, the junior college transfer, who would go on to become a multiple Olympic gold medalist, fought her way back near the front of the pack, handing off a distance three putting us in a position to at least finish amongst the top four teams. Miami, Tennessee, and South Carolina battled for position as our team closed in on the hand-off to the third leg. As the junior from Houston took off, I held my breath for a moment wanting her to do well after what she had experienced on the national stage just a year prior. As an alternate on our record-breaking world leading 4x400 relay the year before, she had been called in a moment prior to the start of the national championship final to run the first leg. Tragically, after running a great lead-off leg, her feet got tangled with the second leg, sending them both tumbling to the ground and dashing any hopes of defending their title and breaking another record.

Everyone's heart sank for the relay, but especially for her. It had been no one's fault but it had to have been devastating for her. She lived with that memory and now, over eight meters behind the leaders and with higher stakes, she would be the leg to make or break our teams' hope of pulling off a major upset against extreme odds and winning not just the relay, but the coveted team national championship. As she received the baton, she bolted out with an uncharacteristically smooth but blazing pace. This was her moment. It was her redemptive race as she began to close in on the pack.

As the athletes moved into the final turn to hand off the final leg, front-runner South Carolina lost contact with the lead pack and fell off. The crowd erupted into total pandemonium as the race tightened into a four-person battle going into the final handoff. Our anchor leg was a sophomore from Dallas, Texas, who, although one of the most talented athletes I'd ever coached, struggled all season. Yet, I knew from the beginning of the meet that she was the person to run the final leg of the relay. No one had more talent or a competitive heart as big as Jerika Chapel. No matter what the outcome would be, she would fight from wire to wire.

Every team had something to lose and something to prove and as the runners headed around the first turn, they jostled for position without anyone giving ground or space to another. This was an epic dogfight to the end. The crowd screamed and cheered, reacting not only to the battle on the track but the excitement coming from the meet commentator over the loud speakers. I held onto the railing even tighter, maintaining my balance as they battled down the back stretch. Somehow, our Texas anchor with nowhere to go, found a narrow seam and somehow twisted her body without breaking her stride or the stride of her fellow competitors and took a slight lead, blasting towards the finish line. With only eighty meters of a 1600-meter relay remaining, no one was giving up and South Carolina's anchor who was five to ten meters back, began to close the gap on the other teams, while barreling down on our anchor leg.

The crowds' yells elevated as our anchor, still in the lead, showed signs of fatigue, leaving us vulnerable. But they didn't know what I knew about the Texas anchor. Because even in extreme states of pain and weariness, she would not quit. With thirty meters to go, it would be a toss-up as to whether we could get to the finish line before the

South Carolina anchor closed in as she had now passed every team except ours. Shouting at the top of my lungs and drowned out by the collective screams of the crowd cheering equally for Jerika, I encouraged her to keep pushing and get to the finish line before the other runner. Within a few seconds more, it was over. Not only had we won the race against teams we hadn't beaten all year, but we'd also won the Team National Championship.

We held onto the lead by the narrowest of margins and it was in that moment, fist pumping in the air as screams of "YES, YES, YES" emanated from my soul, that I fully understood and now knew the power of "knowing" and the true power of deliberate manifestation.

As we headed onto the field to receive our championship trophy, I was stopped by one of the television executives who requested we gather our entire team for the victory ceremony and interview. To his surprise, I informed him that this *was* our complete team and in fact, there were only seven athletes. I could understand his confusion because we had deliberately made it appear as if we had a larger team. I'd asked the staff and coaches to dress up in team gear to give the impression our numbers were much greater, creating the illusion that we were a massive force with which to be reckoned. The perception was greater than our reality.

Many in the stadium were still in shock and buzzing around the epic battle that had ensued not only in the final event, the 4x400 relay but its impact on the team title. While many may have been excited and probably in shock of the outcome, some were downright angry we had won. I heard one major shoe brand's executive cursed out a coach saying, "How in the hell did you guys let her win, not Texas or the team but her (meaning me), with only seven damn athletes?"

But the victory wasn't about me or for me. It was much greater than anyone could have ever imagined. No one had given us much of a chance at winning just as I hadn't been given much of a chance to ever walk again, keep my job, or coach at a high level. To some degree, the championship meant something special and I wanted every one of them to succeed so badly. Too often, I'd witnessed the painful effects failure had on people, including me. So regardless of the sacrifices, I was determined to never see that look on another athlete's face, thus failure had not been an option.

As I looked back on that moment in that stadium in 2005 and after going on to win another National Championship in 2006, I could have never imagined that by the Olympic year in 2012 I would engage in the biggest career-altering, maybe even career-ending, battle of my life. I wondered throughout those years if I would be able to complete my journey. Would I ever take a stage again? When the possibility of failure was greater than the possibility of success, would failure be my only option?

BELIEVE IT

"My personal beliefs were formed in the early stages of my life. It was while creating ways to cope, not only with life's experiences, but my circumstances, that I finally found what I truly believed in. Then, I was able to not just cope, but embrace those experiences and thrive in different circumstances. Through the process of developing my beliefs, I found my truth."

CHAPTER 1

I may never fully understand the magnitude of my successes or failures or why any of this matters to anyone. There have been many unimaginable experiences in my life—seating next to the President of the United States while dining at the White House, ringing the opening bell on Wall Street, being watched by millions and televised on the world's stage. I didn't understand why or how me, of all people, ended up in those places and how I'd become driven to inspire people to succeed and then be so admired by some yet so scorned by others.

In looking at the various facets of prejudice, I fell under multiple categories: Black, female, gay, and would become, disabled. Yet, I was succeeding. I was confident, at least publicly, and to the annoyance of many, I have always been outspoken and endowed with intelligence and the courage to speak up, even in times when it wasn't my preference. I grew up and worked in a society that did not embrace any of those attributes, especially in women, not to mention Black women. Yet, I personally never saw my attributes as shortcomings or negative factors. I only saw the targeted outcomes. It was always about the bottom line, the end result of finishing what you started to the best of your ability. I encountered many environments and situations that I should have run away from, but running away was never an option for me. My mantra stems not from some inner faith, but my upbringing. It was a message deeply imbedded in my core being.

Although I have been fortunate to celebrate the highs of success and endure the solitude of controversy, my early life never indicated I would be anything but ordinary. I didn't stand out. I wasn't the tallest, the smallest, the dumbest, or the smartest. I was average-looking and had no remarkable talents or traits and nothing that inspired people to say, "Someday, she is going to be somebody."

I was the sixth of seven children, conceived in Springfield, Massachusetts, and born February 25, 1958 in a Franklin County, Mississippi hospital. Given the start of my life, I believed there was nothing special about my conception or my birth.

I did have one distinct characteristic, if that is what you'd call it. I was a perpetual thinker and observer. But, when you think a lot, you feel a lot. You drift off into your own world, which resulted in me being fairly quiet and slightly reclusive. Although I never saw myself as special, and no one ever told me that someday I would make something of my life, I knew from an early age that my life's goal was to achieve more. With few ambitions, I longed to make my family proud–including my mother, grandmother, two brothers and four sisters. I never wanted to disappoint or anger them. I wanted to make them happy because too often, they seemed angry and unhappy.

As the constant observer, I silently noticed everything and everyone. I watched their actions, listened to their conversations, and noticed how they felt or made others feel. I learned some key, life-changing lessons from my family, particularly my mother and grandmother. These lessons not only taught me how to survive but they equally included what *not* to do.

Growing up in an unpredictable home that was equal parts crazy, fun, and dangerous, meant quickly having to learn how to judge the circumstances of a situation and act accordingly. If people were in a bad mood, I stayed clear. If they were having fun or in a loving mood, I joined in, acutely aware that either situation could change in the blink of an eye.

My family spewed curse words effortlessly and you had to use the tone of their words to determine meaning and intent. Profanity was used to convey anger, hurt, details within a funny story, and sometimes, as normal conversation. I had to stay on guard because I was sensitive, and words hurt deeply. I would have preferred a spanking with a switch, shoe, or whatever was handy, as opposed to someone yelling at me. No one ever told us not to drink, smoke, or curse but I chose to refrain because I didn't like the effects on the people in my life or how it made me feel.

In the summer of 1956, my mother, Bertha "Christine" Buie, met my father in Springfield, Massachusetts while at a bar. He had been stationed at the nearby Air Force base. She and her youngest child at the time, Gerettia, had ventured there from Mississippi to visit her only brother, Luther. I'm sure my mother was drinking, dancing, and the focus of everyone's attention when my father walked into the bar that night. She was probably dressed to kill in whatever was the latest tight-fitting style, showing off her small waist, large breasts, and beautiful shapely legs. My mother's smooth caramel skin and flawless legs were her pride and joy. With legs so flawless, she never bothered to wear stockings when she'd don her ever-present high-heeled shoes, which showed off her lean, shapely figure. She was 5'8 and when dressed up, drew the attention of any man in the room with the signature pearls and lips glistening from her trademark ruby red lipstick. She attracted men like bees to honey, enjoying their company before moving on to the next suitor. Many times, she'd leave them without a second thought, as soon as they fell in love with her. For some reason, it was different when she met my father. He proved to be the one, although never the only one.

My father was a shy, well-groomed man from North Carolina named Beverly Beatrice Kearney, Jr. (yep, my dad had a girl's name but thankfully everyone, including my mother, always called him "Kearney" while his family called him "Junior" and yep, his dad had the same name). He had never met anyone like my mother. For the longest time, I didn't know my dad's real name. When I finally found out, I would tease my younger brother that if I had not been born before him, he would have been Beverly Beatrice Kearney III. When my parents met, my mother was already in a relationship with another serviceman, but it was my dad who somehow managed to steal her heart. After a brief courtship, they got married and I was on the way.

My mother had been a loving child who adored her mother, father, and younger brother, Luther. But during her time growing up in Bude, Mississippi, she turned into a wild child focused on partying and drinking. In her teenaged years, she would sneak into my grandmother's bootleg whiskey supply and take a swig. I grew up hearing stories about her fighting and raising hell. She always seemed fearless to us. It was customary for her to give natural birth on my grandmother's living room floor in front of the wood-burning stove. So as my delivery date drew near, she told my father she was going home to her mother in Mississippi to give birth. This was the first time my father realized how many children belonged to my mother. He had seen only one child when he met her. But upon his arrival in Mississippi, he met four more.

My mother had seven children by five different men and each of us knew the identity of our birth fathers. Aside from the one child in her care, my grandmother was raising three of my mom's children and her sister, Aunt Allie, was raising Alice, the oldest. Upon my father's arrival, I can imagine his shock at discovering a house full of children. I can also imagine my mother not giving a damn.

During my delivery, there were complications and the midwife and my grandmother had to rush my mother to the nearby hospital in Franklin County. My soon-to-be born younger brother and I were the only two of my mother's seven children not born on my grandmother's wooden floors. We were born by cesarean. Once my brother was born, my mother was informed that her tubes needed to be tied to preserve her life. It would be a danger for her to have another child.

Growing up wasn't easy for anyone in my family, a bunch of victims and victimizers. Often the victimizers were really just victims lashing out. The lessons I learned growing up weren't taught through the conventional methods of school. They were life's lessons squeezed out of adverse circumstances. However, those lessons shaped who I became and were often contributors to my successes and influenced my decisions throughout my life.

You could say I was what the older people described as an "old soul." But in a way, we were all old souls, not because we were gifted with wisdom or exceptional intelligence, rather because we were overwhelmed with experiences, as youth, that most people see throughout a lifetime. At an early age, we learned how to take care of ourselves. My younger brother Derick always says, "We had to act like adults before we were adults."

My family lived hard and on the edge with too much drinking, cursing, fighting, smoking, and *way* too much sex. In a funny kind of way, we were a loving family that never spoke the words "I love you." We also lacked a lot of cuddly, warm and fuzzy moments. But we all knew we loved one another and were taught to always be there for each other, no matter what. I hated being the sensitive one in the family because I felt everything so deeply. I would cry for the pain of others as much as for myself. I longed to be harder inside, but I just wasn't. I noticed almost everything and everyone and my feelings got hurt too often. But in our home, you couldn't afford to be weak because everyone else was strong and my mother was the strongest of all.

I learned not to show my hurt because it seemed no one cared. I can still remember being quite upset, my mother noticing and saying, as she walked away, "Those same damn drawers you got mad in, you can get glad in. Now straighten up your damn face before I give your ass something to cry about." One warning was always enough for me. She never had to tell me twice. I'd snap right out of any emotional or attitudinal issues I had. I quickly learned it was a waste of time to stay mad about anything, except if I was injured, sick, or bleeding, and even then, I was expected not to be "a big baby" about it.

One day, my older brother Howard told me that when I was small, they would laugh at how upset I'd get. He said they'd look at me and say, "Man, she's mad as hell. If she was any bigger, she'd try to kick our asses." Now, that's funny because there were times when I was younger and thinking the exact same thing. Ultimately, it was clear that if I wasn't going to do anything about the situation that angered or hurt me, the best thing to do was move on and get over it. So that's the method I have lived by my entire life.

I grew up with memories of the good times when life seemed perfect, and the bad times filled with fear, due to not knowing what would happen next. I could never figure out when arguments would erupt into physical violence or fade into more drinking and partying. I really have no idea how my mother managed to take care of all of us and party the way she did. My father would drink and remain quiet. My mother would drink and get louder. She would drink on Fridays and Saturdays while raising hell the entire time, but by Sunday she was back to being calm, loving, and supportive.

There was the sober mother and the mother that showed up at our house filled with liquor. They were as different as night and day. Whether she was drunk or not, we were always well-provided for, never lacking food, clothing, or a roof over our heads. However, while living in Mississippi, there were times when we didn't have a full bathroom. Instead, we heated water on the stove and used a tin tub in the middle of the living room floor for a bath. The tin stove in the middle of my grandmother's living room, which also served, as her bedroom, is where the most amazing meals were cooked and eaten while we warmed ourselves on cold days and nights.

My mother and grandmother were polar opposites. My mother was like fire, warm and inviting, but hot and spicy. She cursed like a sailor, fought like a man, and was adventurous. We were constantly on the move following my father who was stationed all across the country. My mother found work pressing clothes and made friends easily. She never really smoked cigarettes but chewed Days Work tobacco, a stark contrast to her sexy attire and well-groomed hair. Although she only had a fifth-grade education, she was one of the smartest, most resourceful people I've ever known.

On the other hand, my grandmother, Brady Bracie Buie, never raised her voice and I never heard her curse. She'd hum gospel songs as she moved throughout our house or the homes she cleaned and the only two places she ever lived were Mississippi and California. She had two forms of income, an illegal bootleg business in the backwoods of Bude, Mississippi, and cleaning white people's homes in both Mississippi and California. My grandmother was everything you could have desired in a grandmother. Whereas my mother dressed impeccably, my grandmother would roam the house in a colorful muumu or a thin worn-out, faded robe with big pockets stuffed with a little bit of everything.

She was a short, dark-skinned, gray-haired, thickly-built woman who was everyone's idea of a southern grandmother. She was the rock of the family, our matriarch. But more than that, she was my first hero, the person I always wanted to be around and wanted to be most like. My grandmother was resourceful in ways that formally-educated people could never imagine. Grandma was also one of the first in our small town of Bude, Mississippi to have indoor plumbing installed as well as a full bathroom and kitchen. She wanted her children, and especially her grandchildren, to feel comfortable coming home.

I never could imagine being like my mother. She was more of a superhero, and at times seemed somewhat like a villain. I couldn't imagine carrying her strength in my own spirit. I loved and looked up to my mom, but mostly, I wanted her to be proud of me, which is one of the reasons I worked hard in school to get good grades. I loved bringing my report card home and showing it to her. And when we lived near my grandmother, I'd proudly show her as well.

Grandma was the second most important person in my life, aside from my mom. To this day, I'm not sure where my father ranks. I love him because he is my father but after what he did to our family and how distant but friendly he was, it was hard to have a meaningful relationship with him. He is in fact just my dad and I neither have no expectations from him and wish him no ill will.

My dad was a nice man who wore a constant smile, which is likely where Derick and I got our tendency to smile all the time, but I can't remember ever having a conversation with him because if you weren't talking about music or cars, he had little to say. He and my mother were polar opposites, just as she was with my grandmother. He was quiet and smiled a lot and I can't remember him being angry very often. He was from Virginia. She was from Mississippi. He was formally-educated, she was not, though she was smarter than him. She dropped out of school before reaching high school. His family was highly-educated with professional careers. My mother came from a down home, country, under-educated yet hard working family. He was quiet. She was not. He rarely got drunk. She drank too much and too often.

Although he was in the military, he was non-violent. My mother had a hot temper and never backed down from a fight. In fact, truth be told, she started and finished most of them. He wore button-down checkered short-sleeved shirts. When not in uniform, he was in flip-flops or dress shoes with black socks even when he wore shorts. I don't think I ever saw my dad in sneakers. My mother was a *dresser*. When she went to work, everything was pressed, clean, and over the top. You couldn't catch my dad in a baseball cap. Instead, he wore fedoras over his Army crew cut. He seemed small and timid compared to my mother. But I guess opposites attract.

When my mother was drinking, her actions were liable to make anyone nearby angry. In contrast, you couldn't help but love and respect her when she was sober. Aside from my grandmother, she had the greatest impact on our lives. She was the one who taught us all to live, survive, and expect the best from life. We all knew and loved our biological fathers, but none of them were integral parts of our rearing, including my own dad. My mother married my father, but he didn't stay around much. When he was around, he didn't really talk or interact with us. He wasn't mean or anything, he was just into music and cars. I honestly can't remember one impactful decision he ever made. It was always my mother. Whenever we tried to get around asking my mother for anything and go to him, the first thing he would ask was, "What did mama say?"

I loved Mississippi when I was young because it was the place where my grandmother lived and wherever she lived, I loved. Grandma's house was located at the end of the tracks that separated the two neighborhoods, the Blacks and the whites, as well as downtown. We only crossed the tracks to pick up mail or go to the drugstore. Otherwise, you stayed on your side. I rarely saw any white people passing our house. I would stand on the front porch early in the mornings and watch my grandma's driver pick her up and take her across the tracks to clean homes. I loved watching her get ready for work with her freshly pressed maid's uniform and Sunday wig. She always seemed to have money, whether it was from her earlier years selling bootleg whiskey, from land she'd inherited, or from cleaning people's homes. Whatever we needed, she supplied. When she didn't give us money, Derick and I would go to the juke joints with my mom and hustle money by running errands, dancing, or waiting for the adults to get so drunk they'd just hand us money.

In the early days of living in Mississippi, there was only one school and the Black children attended the same school from elementary to high school. My childhood memories of Mississippi were all good, and consisted of playing outside until dark, saw mills, puck wood trucks, juke joints, going to school with my older brothers and sisters and watching them play sports, eating my grandmother's cooking, watching my brother hunt, my grandmother cleaning rabbits and squirrels (I never ate any of that, especially after watching them be skinned and cleaned), and listening to old people's conversations. It was an amazing life, but as soon as I got comfortable in one location, my mother would announce that we were moving.

It didn't take long to figure out that getting comfortable in one place wasn't a smart idea. Because as soon as we made new friends and settled into a new school or new house, my mother would unceremoniously announce an impending move. Sometimes we moved with my dad to whatever Air Force base he was being relocated. When we weren't following my father all around the country, my mother would move us to either Bude, Mississippi, or Monrovia, California, to be near our grandmother. We never asked questions about where we were going or how long we would stay. My mother was the law and whatever she said was the final word.

We drove everywhere so the car was constantly overcrowded with my mom, dad, three to four kids, and a lot of stuff. I never thought about it, but it was crowded because as Black folks traveling through small towns, it wasn't safe for us to stop at most restaurants and stores. So, for long trips, dad's Ford would not only be loaded down with kids, clothes, and personal items, but with food as well. When I was little, moving never bothered me. It became second nature to make the adjustments from living in Mississippi to living in California or up north in Nebraska or Kansas. But the place I grew to love more than all of them was Florida, it felt most like home. My second favorite place was anywhere my grandmother lived because she made everything better. Even when my mother would start drinking and cursing, my grandmother would make her sit down and shut-up. I didn't discover my mom had a drinking problem until we moved to Topeka, Kansas in the mid 1960's.

My mother did not prefer cold weather, so we tended to live in warm states. When my father was stationed in Topeka, Kansas, we moved there to be with him. This is where everything imploded and never again would I have a child-like approach to life. Kansas would fracture our family in ways that would never be repaired.

I was in the second or third grade when we moved. That's when I realized my mother had a serious drinking problem, coupled with violence and infidelity. My dad was rarely around and could usually be found working multiple jobs, outside working on his cars, messing with his extensive music equipment, or out partying. We never really knew what he was doing or where he was, he simply wasn't home. Sunday through Thursday in our house, we lived a fairly normal family life with both parents physically present. But on Fridays and Saturdays, the drinking started. When my mom drank, she was unrecognizable. I couldn't identify the wild woman who showed up at our house on the weekends drunk, cursing, fussing, and fighting. Surely, this wasn't the mother who loved and cared for us all week.

I began to dread weekends. Mama had such extreme mood changes whenever she was drunk. After only one drink, the alcohol took effect. Her speech became altered and her personality shifted within minutes. It usually didn't take a lot of liquor for her to be declared drunk and unsafe. With continued drinking, she would become dangerous, verbally and sometimes physically abusive. My mother wasn't a happy drunk. She was more of the angry and depressed drunk. Our only hope, at that point in her alcohol binges, was for her to either pass out or when my dad or grandma were around, have them come home in time to stop her from hurting us or herself.

While living in Kansas, in an effort to protect us from her weekly fits of rage, my older sisters, Gerettia and Cherry, would take Derick and me up to a small, dark, dingy crawl space in the attic for safety. We would huddle up in that spooky attic for hours listening to her calling our names and cursing. I hated the screaming and profanity and I would try to cover my ears to drown out the noises. We would wait in the attic for what felt like forever, waiting for my mother to pass out or for my dad to come home from the base, whichever came first.

As much as I hated my mother's fits of drunken anger, I equally hated that creepy attic. So, for me, it was double torture. After a while, my sister stopped letting us leave the crawl space even after my father came home. We would tell her it was safe, but she would tell us to shut up and not to move. We were scared of our big sister Gerettia and although she was only three and four years older than Derick and me, we looked to her more like a parent than a big sister. We would sit listening quietly to my father asking where all the children were, as my drunk mother tried to cook dinner for him. At the same time, Gerettia, for some reason, would refuse to allow us to leave the safety of the attic. It would take another fifteen or more years before my sister would reveal the real reason she was afraid to leave the attic, even when all appeared safe.

Just like Kansas had been the place where I learned of my mother's drinking problems, it also was where I learned the meaning of the word infidelity. For the first time, this led to me witnessing domestic violence. My dad was working two jobs at the time. One was in the Air Force and the other, tending bar at night. Whenever he wasn't home, my mother drank with, who I assumed to be, her male "friends." For some reason, one day my dad decided not to go to his second job and came home early.

I don't know why he came home early that day but upon his arrival, he found my mother cozied up on the sofa drinking with another man. Chuck had been at our house many times. We thought he was a family friend. Even when he and my mom would disappear into the bedroom, I never thought anything of it. He was in the Air Force like my dad. So, the assumption was that he was my dad's friend too. I had never seen my quiet, subdued dad get mad or violent until that day, when all hell broke loose in our house.

My dad wasn't just mad. He was *fighting* mad. Dad wasn't a big man, but he was a lot tougher than his size revealed. The moment Chuck saw him walk into the house, he jumped up and tried to make a dash for the door. Before he could escape, my dad jumped on him, tackling him to the floor. The scuffle shocked us all and we stood in the safety of the doorway watching the two men as my mother stood over them screaming my dad's name.

All you could hear her saying repeatedly was, "Kearney! Kearney!" and somehow, Chuck broke loose and dashed out the back door in a full sprint, running for his life. In that moment, standing in the middle of the living room face-to-face with my mother, was the first time I'd ever heard my father curse. He began his tyrant by calling her all types of whores and anything else he could imagine. She stood there, and for some reason, I don't think she truly grasped the full extent of his anger. He had never hit her or gotten angry with her, so she assumed he would back down and walk away. While we watched in horror and then surprise, my mother began to show signs not of remorse, but anger.

So many questions ran through my pubescent mind. Why didn't she shut up? Why didn't she beg for forgiveness? Why didn't she know he was hurt? As well as the biggest question to this day, why did she yell and curse back? There they were, standing in the middle of the room swearing and yelling at each other until finally, my mother crossed an invisible line of no return. She looked at him and said with a straight face, "Kearney, f—k you! This is my motherf—king pussy and I will give it to whoever I motherf—king please."

Dang, did she just say that? As young as I was, I knew this was not going to end well. It's like something went off in his head and he lost what little control he had. He reached out to grab her. Shocked, my mother jumped back and made a dash for the door when my father jumped in the air and kicked her square in the ass with his steel-toed military combat boots. From the sheer force of the kick, my mother went flying across the living room through the glass door and onto our front porch.

It all happened so fast. I don't know who was more shocked, my father, my mother, or us kids. As the fight began, I did my usual, covered my ears and closed my eyes, not wanting to see or hear the violent sounds. As tears welled in my eyes, the glass shattered, screams ensued, and I voluntarily retreated to the only safe place I knew—the attic. But this time, I balled up in a corner alone and cried, not knowing if my mother was dead or alive.

Luckily, my mother lived but suffered extensive injuries, with the most severe being a broken collarbone. My dad picked up my mother and rushed her to the base hospital where I later overheard them laughing about her explanation of the events, telling the military doctors she was running through the house playing with her kids and accidently ran through a glass door. Later, I found out my mother lied to protect my father because had he been responsible for her injuries, the military would have immediately dishonorably discharged him. After they returned home from the hospital, my father was still angry. So, the next day, unbeknownst to my mother, he put in for an overseas transfer.

My mother was now in a body cast and with the severity of her pain, my father and older sisters became her caretakers. They lovingly nursed her back to health. I could never imagine the pain she suffered because I never saw her cry or even heard her complain. If anything, she would moan and rock. I had witnessed her extreme hangovers, which always included a bucket for vomit and a request for us to run to the local store for B.C. Powder for the headaches and body aches and even then, she never cried or complained.

My mother may not have cried from her injuries, but each time I left her room, seeing her in that body cast, I wept. She was a mean drunk but to me, she was still the greatest mom ever and none of us wanted to see her injured. I couldn't help but wonder why she had cursed back that day instead of apologizing. It wasn't as if my father wasn't cheating as well, they both were. I hated the violence and I now attributed every part of our dynamic to drinking and thus, I hated alcohol.

I am not sure how my dad felt about catching my mother cheating but whatever they both felt about it, they never spoke about it again and they never separated. He was home for the next several months, nursing her back to health and everyone continued as if nothing happened. Moving on from each traumatic episode we experienced became our family trademark. Having a short memory was mandatory because so much occurred so often and you never knew what might happen next, therefore focusing on what had already happened was not a healthy option.

My mother had often sustained injuries while drinking but she always healed quickly, and that was no exception. Within no time, she was back on her feet and that's when my dad finally told her he'd put in the transfer request. Within days, he was gone.

The winters in Kansas were brutal. It snowed all the time and my mother hated cold weather, especially snow. I guess it was harder to party and have fun in a blizzard. We had survived the snow and the tornados the previous year. Despite it being the middle of the school year, my mother decided we were leaving. I am not sure if it was my sister getting into a fight that led to my mother's final frustration with Kansas, or just the weather. But, the fight was definitely a factor.

It had been snowing more than usual and walking home from elementary school seemed like miles as my younger brother and I trudged through the heavy, overwhelming snow. When we finally made it home, wet and cold, we joined our older sisters around the heater to try to warm our chilled bones. Just as my body regained a sense of normalcy, my older sister, Cherry, burst through the door screaming that some girls had jumped on her and my other sister Ernestine down the street.

Without hesitation, my mother demanded we go and get her, and we had better not come home until we not only found Ernestine, but "took care" of anyone who fought her. I was scared and nervous and chose not to ask if her command included me. So, as my older sisters pulled on their boots and coats and sprinted out of the house, I fell in right behind them.

As we raced down the street, we could see a crowd gathering and watching as a group of girls punched and buried my sister in the snow. We all jumped in: Cherry, Gerettia, Alice, and me. I might have been the youngest and the smallest, but if you had heard the tone in my mother's voice, there was no way I was going home, and they tell her I didn't participate in the fight. I might not have actually helped, but I was definitely swinging. We, or should I say they, beat the crap out of those girls and we walked back home feeling victorious.

We animatedly detailed how the fight went down until finally, my mother asked my sister how the fight started. My sister Cherry got so excited telling the story, she let it slip that she'd started the fight and had to run home to get help. As we were all talking, my mother quietly nodded her head encouraging us to continue talking. Slowly, she exited the room and returned holding a belt. Like a cat springing upon its pray, she grabbed Cherry and started beating her with the belt. As each swing met a different part of Cherry's body, the cadence of my mom's words matched syllable-to-strike. We all watched in silence, wondering if we were next. I will never forget her words, "Don't you ever run away from another fight and you had better never run off and leave your sister. Even if you've got to take an ass whooping, you better not run."

I don't remember much more of what she said because the whipping wasn't short. Right after, Cherry laid down and cried herself to sleep. I sat there, too scared to move, while my mother continued preparing dinner as if nothing had happened.

Something happened to me that day. I told myself I would never get that kind of beating, even if I had to fight someone twice my size. It was better to lose a fight than suffer the consequences of my mother after running away from one. I never ran away from a fight since, physical nor political.

CHAPTER 2

I sat on the floor staring at my cards. I tried desperately not to look across the coffee table at the perplexing spectacle before me. I was only in the 4th or 5th grade and although I had experienced many things throughout my short life, I had never seen a man's private parts. I tried to divert my eyes towards something else and for some reason, became ashamed and afraid for having taken a look. I was frozen in time, gazing at my cards with my beating heart racing in my chest. As he shook his leg, trying to draw my attention in his direction, I became increasingly more uncomfortable. Although I heard his voice, I was too afraid to look up from the cards I clutched in my hands.

"You want to try it?" he'd asked as I wondered to myself, "Try what?" But before I could figure out what he meant, he pushed me to the ground.

My sister, Ernestine, had left me and her toddler daughter at home in the care of her boyfriend/husband (I wasn't quite sure which he was at the time) while she made a quick run to the library and store. He had come into the living room of their small, one-bedroom apartment where I'd been sleeping, armed with a deck of cards to ask if I wanted to play a few hands. In our family, we didn't just *play* cards, it was sort of a rite of passage. Everyone in our family played. I can't remember when or how I learned to play just like I can't remember when I learned how to read, write, or count. When we played cards as a family, it was with the sole goal of winning so when he offered, I knew I needed to get better and jumped at the chance to beat him and perfect my skills. At home we played for fun and sometimes for money. My mother had always been the best, I guess you could say she was two steps away from being a professional gambler. Often she would give us money and then win it all back. My mother believed if we made the decision to play, we had to live with the outcome. She would never give us back our money.

The card games covered the gamut of those typical of a Black family including: Spades, Pluck, Bid Whist, Tonk, and Gin Rummy, for starters. So, when he asked if I wanted to play cards until my sister returned, I was excited. We began to play and I was winning which is probably why I hadn't noticed him staring at me. He was in his bathrobe, which had somehow slid open to reveal his naked body. I won't say I was inquisitive as a child, because we knew we were to be seen and not heard. Being one of the youngest, I really couldn't ask questions. So, as a child, I was curiously observant, always watching and listening, trying to understand what was happening around me. I had never seen a naked man. The discomfort caused me to sit with my head lowered, trying not to glance in his direction. When he asked if I wanted to try it, I'd assumed it had something to do with cards until I found myself lying on the floor and him above me smiling and saying, "Now, don't you tell anybody, especially your sister."

Unable to speak, I simply nodded. Afterwards, he instructed me to go to the bathroom and clean myself up. I slowly rose from the floor. Liquids ran down my legs and pain emanated from my vaginal area. As I wiped myself with my own panties, I wondered what I should do next. The more I wiped, the more shame I felt. I figured all of it had been my fault.

I exited the bathroom and was grateful he was no longer in the living room. I got dressed and went outside. As I sat on the steps, my sister's friend stopped by looking for her. I told her she had gone to the store and would be right back. She was surprised and asked who was watching me and the baby. I told her we'd been left with her boyfriend. She looked shocked, and as she brushed past me said, "She left you with him?" I was relieved she stayed until my sister came home. As taught, I never said a word. I had listened and watched, as my sisters had been blamed for their own molestation. I knew I also would be blamed if I told anyone and the fear of getting in trouble created my silence. As I sat alone on the step, my mind raced. I was a thinker and surely I could figure out what just happened, what to do, and more importantly, why any of it had occurred. I thought back on my older sister, Cherry, who had just a few years earlier, been shipped away because of what happened with my grandmother's boyfriend.

* * *

It had only been a few months since we arrived in California. My uncle and his family from Detroit made the rare visit to see my grandmother. Everyone was excited, and they held a celebration in honor of the visit. My grandmother, an excellent cook, prepared all his favorites. My mother bought the liquor and we played and danced. It was one of the rare times when the adults falling into drunkenness was actually fun. After a few hours of partying, my mother noticed my sister Cherry was missing.

My mother inquired about Cherry's whereabouts. When she realized she wasn't in the house, she made everyone search for her. Apparently, they had found her in the back yard, in the dark, in the backseat of the car belonging to Mr. T.J., grandma's younger, married boyfriend. I never really knew what happened or what it all meant but I had overheard them talking later that night. Mr. T.J., was on top of her in the back seat of his car. He'd supposedly given her money and brought her orange juice, spiked with liquor. I remember my mother and grandmother being angry, not at Mr. T.J. but at Cherry. They blamed her, not him. The party went from festive to us being told to go to bed and the situation was never mentioned again. A few days later, when my uncle left for Detroit, Cherry was packed in the car with them. Shortly after their departure, Mr. T.J. was back at grandma's house as if nothing had happened.

I was young and really didn't understand what had occurred but as I sat on that step alone after a man had been on top of me, the pain in my body was overcome by the fear coursing through my veins. I grasped the notion that if something happened, it was my fault and I would be shipped away. Cherry was shipped away and if I told anyone, I too would be sent away. It would be years before I would see Cherry again. She returned around my 6th grade year while we were living in Florida—pregnant.

* * *

As I thought back over my sister's experience, the thought of being blamed and shamed and shipped off did not make "telling" an ideal course of action. Later that night, while battling sleep, I overheard loud voices and noises coming from a bedroom.

I knew those sounds meant an argument and a fight were transpiring and her boyfriend was beating my sister who was now pregnant with her second child. I did what I had always done to avoid the reality of the violence around me. I closed my eyes, used my fingers to plug up my ears, and hummed until it went silent. I laid in the darkness of the living room and wondered why I had begged my mother to let me travel from Mississippi to California to visit my sister. More importantly, I wondered why she let me go. I wanted to go home. The days seemed to drag on and that one-week felt like months as night after night, I would hear the unsettling sounds coming from their bedroom and my sister crying. As I climbed in the car to go back to my mother, I looked in my sister's face. Once again, I longed and begged for her to come with us and leave him. But like before, she refused.

I adored my sister Ernestine. She was the one family member who was loving and caring. Her intelligence and toughness, matched with her willingness to fight, did not overshadow her gentleness, loving spirit, and beautiful smile. From my vantage point, she was perfect. I could never imagine life without her yet while living with our family in California, things happened that tore her apart from the family.

One specific situation forced our move back to Mississippi. My mother needed money to buy us clothes and she decided to play in one of the local card games. She drank and still won each game. As she won, she stuffed the money down her bra. Once she reached her desired amount, she quit. Unfortunately, her fellow players refused to let her quit. She'd won all their money and they wanted a chance to win it back. It escalated into a physical brawl, with my mother grabbing a knife and wielding it until she could run out and get to our apartment in the projects. As she ran into the house, she screamed for us to get down under the bed. With that, we all took a dive under the beds as bullets riddled the building. Cursing the whole time, my mother crawled to the phone to call my big brother. Within minutes, we heard yelling and screaming, along with rounds of gunfire and the screeching of his car tires braking in front of the apartment.

My brother and our cousins from Mississippi had driven down the street, clearing it with gunfire. As he burst into the house making sure everyone was fine, the street was once again filled with bullets flying as police cars and ambulances approached. People were taken to the hospital and questioned. But as quickly as the police came, they left without a single arrest. As my brother and cousins remained, the streets quieted down, and they sat on the stoop drinking, with guns loaded, while my mother prepared dinner, again moving on with no hint of concern for what had happened.

The next day, my mother told us to get up and get dressed for school. Ironically, that meant walking to school beside the children of the people who shot at us the night before. I asked Derick if he was scared. He said, "No." I lied and said, "Me neither." We didn't talk to them and they didn't talk to us.

For about two days after the shooting, the daily routine continued with my brothers and cousins sitting on the stoop armed with guns, drinks, and dinner. Suddenly, we arrived home from school to find my big brother's truck loaded with our clothes and we were told to climb in. My mother left every piece of furniture in the apartment. Everyone loaded up into the two trucks but my favorite sister, Ernestine, and we left for Mississippi that day.

Ernestine was pregnant and still recovering from an argument with my mother. My mother had not been upset with her for getting pregnant, primarily because the father was not Ernestine's possessive and abusive ex-boyfriend. But, when she found out that in spite of her pregnancy, she was returning to him, they got into a big fight. My mother threw a saucer and hit Ernestine in the head. I don't remember much more, except the sight of the blood and everyone wrapping towels around her head, which quickly turned from white to red as the blood gushed out. They worked frantically trying to control the bleeding as they rushed her out the door. Later, she returned with bandages around her shaven head, and as usual, no one ever spoke about it again.

My sister returned to the boyfriend my mother hated. Months later, as our family packed into trucks to flee the violence, a pregnant Ernestine refused to leave with us instead choosing to remain in California with him. We spent the rest of the school year in Mississippi. I missed my with her that summer. People often traveled from Bude to California and as one such family was traveling by car that summer, I had pleaded to go with them and surprisingly, my mother agreed. Little did I know, it would become the longest and most painful week of my life.

My sister endured years of abuse after I left before finally finding the courage to leave him but it was too little, too late. She would never be the same. She had called my grandmother who was still living in California at the time and told her to come and get her and her two kids. But after all those years of physical, verbal and sexual abuse, she had lost the mental capacity to function. She loved her kids and always tried to protect them. But she slipped into mental illness which made her increasingly violent towards everyone else, including my grandmother.

Eventually, in her early thirties, she was placed in a mental institution where she would die in her mid-forties. I had some childhood experiences no child should have. But what Ernestine and my other sisters suffered was much worse. It would not be until I was twenty-five years old and coaching at the University of Tennessee that the dams of silent suffering would break open to reveal the nightmares we had withstood for years.

One day, my sister Gerettia called me crying, telling me she still had nightmares about what had happened to her. No matter how hard she tried to forget, she couldn't. She revealed how my father had started molesting her at the age of eight while we were living in Kansas. It was one of the main reasons my mother drank so heavily and my older sisters would take my brother and me up into the attic. They weren't hiding us from our mother, but our father.

After his shift at the base, he worked at a club and every Thursday or Friday, he would bring home alcohol and get my mother drunk, then prey on my older sisters. As long as I could remember, my oldest sister Alice had been a prostitute, and after finding out about the abuse, I wondered if it was the culprit for her lifestyle. Cherry, who chased after boys and vice versa, was fourteen at the time. My mother, when drunk, would call them a whores. They both said that although they hated what my father was doing to them, at least they made him pay them. I don't think he ever bothered Ernestine. But we would never know because by the time we spoke about what happened to us, she was already in the mental institution.

Derick once told me he remembered my mother screaming at the girls, saying she knew they were, "fucking Kearney" but he never knew what she meant. Now we do. We also understood why she told them that if they thought they were grown, they needed to get out and made them move into the garage. Alice, Ernestine, and Cherry happily moved into the garage, making it look like a cool apartment. It was probably safer out there than in our house.

When my father could no longer isolate my older sisters, he began to molest Gerettia who was only three years older than me. We talked about the time we lived in Florida. She was in the ninth grade. One night, my mother woke from a drunken stupor to catch him molesting her. I told Gerettia that I remembered waking up and hearing her say, "No Daddy! Please! No! Stop!" Then my mom came into the room. She said mama took her to a phone booth that night, where she pretended to call the police. The next morning, when we all woke up, she came in and told my sister to get ready for school. Apparently, my mother never spoke of what happened again, but my sister never forgot what my father had done. Eventually, he would leave to go overseas because that was what he did every time something went wrong.

I witnessed both my sisters' molestations and learned early–nothing happened to the grown men who molested them. So, I knew not to tell. As I took that long car ride back to Mississippi after being molested, I vowed to try, to the best of my ability, to never find myself in a similar situation. From then on, I conditioned myself to stay clear of any position that could lead to a repeat of that instance. I was almost too cautious and shied away from anything that would make me look appealing. After all, we all thought we had done something to make the grown men around us touch us. Looking back, I realize the molestation had a different effect on me than it had on the rest of my siblings. We all developed different ways to live with our experiences. They became more self-destructive and I was more protective of others and myself. How each of us chose to deal with our abuse was all we knew to do. No one ever interceded on our behalf and each of us suffered just as much from the attacks as the silence.

Overall, I believe my sisters suffered more than I did because they took the brunt of the drunken anger and sexual advances. My mother was not much help as she was busy dealing with her own pain and alcoholism. She could not, or simply did not, protect them. The most damaging was the silence and blaming them for their circumstances or the violence against their young bodies. The only thing my mother did right was intervening the night she caught my father on top of my sister. I don't know what she said but he never touched her again. However, for months, until he was shipped overseas, Gerettia had to live in our small, two-bedroom apartment with the man that had violated and hurt her.

We all had to face our molesters, day after day, in silence. It was a miracle I didn't drink or indulge in other self-destructive activities. I grew up witnessing the pain my sisters withstood, which made me more forgiving of their destructive behaviors as they grew into adults. They were considered strong, tough women and yet, I knew they were broken from years of childhood abuse. As adults, they carried those traits into every relationship they had, attracting abusive men and being verbally or physically abusive themselves, almost detached. I learned from them and made it my mission to love them. But I also witnessed the excruciating results of their choices and the choices of my mother. I had to make a different choice. I had no desire to live life in fear, or by struggling, and definitely not in pain. I chose to do the opposite.

My father was gone for more than a year when one day, my mother told us he was returning, and we were moving to Nebraska. Gerettia refused to live with him again and at the age of fifteen, my mother agreed she could return to Mississippi and live alone in my grandmother's house. She lived there for the remainder of high school with relatives checking in on her and my mother and grandmother paying the bills.

That summer, Derick and I accompanied my mom and dad to Nebraska. On the way, I convinced my mother to let us to live with grandma in California for a year, until she got settled. Again, to my surprise, she agreed. At the end of the summer, she put us on a Greyhound bus from Nebraska to California. I had never seen my mother cry and as she stood waving to us as the bus drove off, I saw the tears falling. It had been a bittersweet moment. The combination of watching my mother cry coupled with the excited of living with grandma in California. Little did I know, this time, my seventh-grade year, would change my life forever, and for the better.

CHAPTER 3

He stood at the fence waving frantically, trying to get my attention to come over. The tall, Black man was my hero and I couldn't believe he had come to the school to check on me. I was so thrilled to see him, I took off in a full sprint towards the chain link fence. As I raced towards him, hoping he'd notice how fast I could run, his face suddenly shifted from a smile to a look of terror. He was no longer waving for me to come over, but made a halting gesture, while screaming for me to stop as he frantically pointed above my head and behind me. Confused by the sudden change, I froze and as I did, saw legions of fellow classmates zoom past me. Everything went from joy to horror in a matter of seconds, as the chaotic scene quickly erupted into what the teachers would later label a riot.

As I stood, I realized my recreation leader had been standing behind the fence in the area where the white students gathered during recess each day. As I had raced over to greet him, both Black and Hispanic students assumed I was angrily running towards the white students out of revenge, as they had stolen the Clifton Middle School class presidency from me the day before. The three groups of students rarely associated with one another during recess. But this time, not only were they fraternizing, but fighting together. I looked around in total disbelief as students from all three groups charged either into or away from the chaos that erupted on the playground.

It was the 1970-71 school year and integration had just begun at our school, which had been all-white only a year or two prior. I was in one of the first groups of students of color within the system and a lot was happening. It was the period following the death of Dr. Martin Luther King Jr., the tail-end of the Civil Rights Movement, the various race riots throughout the U.S., the beginning of Black Panthers in Northern California, and the Bloods and the Crips in Southern California. Movements and uprisings were spreading throughout the country.

For most Blacks around me, our fears had turned to frustration, yet we had found a growing sense of pride in being Black. The non-violent movements of the South gave way to the violent movements of the West and for some reason, as a seventh grader, I witnessed our own uprising smack dab in the middle of the playground with the Black and Hispanic students confronting the white students.

Few words were spoken and within no time, the playground became a battleground as police, teachers, and administrators tried to regain control. Eventually, order would be restored while demands were blasted over loud speakers and bullhorns urged everyone to return to their homerooms.

I barely made it to the fence to speak with our recreation leader who had only come to warn me that he had heard several students talking about fighting. But he was too late and ironically, his presence at the fence ignited the spark. I stood silently at the fence, looking back onto the playground wondering how everything had gone awry, when a teacher aggressively grabbed me, pulling me back towards the classrooms. Just a day earlier, I was the most known and noted student on campus and now I was literally being dragged by a teacher I didn't know.

I was not the most popular student on campus although I got along with classmates of all races and ethnicities. I was an unassuming, shy student who drew very little attention to myself. As a result of moving so much, I had learned to be quiet until I could assess my new surroundings before interacting. I had just returned to California, so I was the most unlikely candidate to run for any student body office, much less class president of a newly-integrated middle school. My English teacher, who said she enjoyed reading my papers, convinced me to run for office. She was a white woman who believed a minority student needed to run and I would be a great representation for my class and the entire student body.

My writing ability developed from my thirst for reading as I was an avid reader. I had grown especially fond of poetry and books that provided insight into my life and those of others. I loved reading about life and life's circumstances. So, I read books on those topics by some of the greatest African American thinkers and writers, as well as newspapers and I listened to any conversations pertaining to the Civil Rights Movement. I was already a closeted thinker and with all the material I was digesting, I began to write before going to bed at night.

Winning wasn't going to be easy or likely, but I decided to run for office anyway. If I was going to win, I had to garner 100% of the Hispanic and Black votes, as well as a fair share of white votes. I wrote my own campaign speech with approval from my teacher. But I didn't realize I would have to recite it before the entire school. Although I loved writing, the thought of speaking in front of a crowded room of fellow students and teachers terrified me. As the assembly grew and the auditorium filled, I sat off stage, terrified and on the verge of tears. For the first time, I regretted agreeing to run for office. As I sat, engulfed in fear, my name was called. I approached the podium and everything seemed to fade away. I heard the strength in my own voice as I spoke without reading. It wasn't until the end that I realized not just the Black and Hispanic students were standing and cheering, but a very large portion of the white students as well.

When we reached the time to vote, I had the majority of the votes out of more than six candidates, meaning I was about to become the first minority student president of Clifton Middle School. Or so I thought. They said I didn't win by a large enough margin, so they had a run-off with another round of speeches from the top three candidates. For the second time, I got the most votes. Again, I was told the margin of victory was not large enough and by now the minority students had become angry and started yelling at the white students.

They finally got everyone to settle down and hosted a third round of speeches, except this time, it was just a white male student and me. I lost by a narrower margin than all my previous wins because some of the white student delegates pressured and harassed other students to switch their votes. Although the margin of victory for the other candidate was smaller this time, he was declared the winner.

Once the winner was announced, the pushing started and whispers of racism turned to screams and shouts. I sat onstage in shock, not knowing what to do or what to think. I never thought I would win, so the thought of winning two times and yet still losing was unthinkable. I congratulated the victor and walked away, somewhat happy with my efforts, but confused about the process.

Now, the day after the election, the confrontation on the playground happened and even as we were escorted back to our homerooms, I was thoroughly confused. We waited in the classroom wondering what would happen next. Students were mad at one another but no one dared speak. Two administrators entered our classroom and whispered to our teacher, who informed me in front of the class, I was to report to the principal's office immediately. The administrators escorted me to my judgment without saying a word. As we got closer to the office, fear rose within me. With each step, I fought to hold back my emotions, not knowing why, for the first time in my life, I was being taken to the principal's office.

Once inside, I was angrily told I was the cause of the fights and was being expelled from school, without further notice and for an indefinite amount of time. The reason—inciting a riot on campus. I tried to explain, as I was being escorted off campus, but no one listened. I squatted down on the curb across the street from my school, wanting to cry and wondering how I would tell grandma. She had always been proud of my smarts and the fact that I'd never gotten into trouble. Now with the thought of being expelled from school hitting me, I couldn't hold back the tears. I wasn't a troublemaker. In fact, I got along with everyone and my speech had been inclusive of all students.

With our unpredictable home life, I looked forward to going to school. I found it to be a safe and happy place. Frankly, I needed school. But as I sat on the curb, none of that mattered more than the thought of disappointing my beloved grandmother. How would I tell her I was no longer allowed to attend because I was considered a troublemaker?

I stayed outside as long as I could, but I knew I had to be in the house before the streetlights came on. I walked in, hearing grandma hum as she moved about the kitchen preparing dinner. I stood at the kitchen's entrance, observing my hard-working, loving grandmother who I had watched and helped scrub floors, cook meals, and care for her white employers. On those trips to assist her with cleaning, I became motivated to work hard so one day, she would not have to be on her hands and knees scrubbing other people's toilets and having to say, "Yes sir" and "No sir" to white children. I would roam through the different homes she cleaned and notice they had rows of books. For some reason, I saw those books as a necessity to owning one of those homes. That observation started me on a journey to reading. I consumed books of all kinds. But it was books about Black life by Black writers like Langston Hughes, Richard Wright and others that touched my soul. I read fun books, thought-provoking books, historical books, and magazines. Then, one day I found books of poetry which touched me the most. I read every moment I could find and went on a relentless quest for knowledge.

I was petrified to tell grandma I had been kicked out of school for starting a riot. I never saw her stand up to any of her white employers and there I was causing trouble with the whites at my school. I was a great student and I never got into trouble or caused worry for my grandmother or my mother. As she cooked, Derick and I told her exactly what happened. I waited for the big explosion, but it never came. My grandmother continued humming softly, moving about the kitchen and preparing our dinner. I couldn't tell if she had been listening because all she said was to go wash up for dinner. We had dinner that evening and I didn't bother to pick up a book or do my homework. Instead, I laid down and cried myself to sleep.

The next morning, I could hear my grandmother and Derick stirring around in the kitchen, getting ready for work and school. I didn't know what to do. I slowly walked in and said good morning. My grandmother turned to see me still in my nightgown and said, "You had better get ready for school or you'll be late." I didn't know what to do. Did she not hear me when I said I wasn't allowed at school anymore?

Again, I tried to explain to her in the most respectful way that I was not allowed to go back to school. This time, in a stern voice, she told me to get ready for school. As Derick and I headed for the door, prepared for our usual trek to school, she told us to get in the car. Wow, was grandma going to actually drive us to school?

We walked outside to the big, black Oldsmobile with the batwings on the back. My grandmother was short, so she had to look through the steering wheel, not over it. It felt like it was taking hours to get to school, not only because she drove slowly, but because I was confused as to why she was taking me there.

She asked me to take her to speak with the person in charge and as we walked to the principal's office, I had a huge knot in the pit of my stomach. I was afraid. I watched my grandmother walk towards the door with her freshly ironed maid's uniform, her white nursing shoes, wearing her Sunday wig and her pocketbook pressed close to her body. Her head was up higher than I had ever seen before. I sat in the waiting area for hours, well probably only a few minutes, before they returned to the room laughing and grandma looked at me and simply said, "Go on back to school." Shocked, I didn't move. Then my principal said, "Didn't you hear your grandmother? Now go on back to class."

I was stunned beyond belief. My grandmother had stood up to the school on my behalf. I later found out, not only had *she* stood up for me, but many of the students, Black, white and Hispanic, as well as the teachers, had spoken up for me.

I always knew my grandmother had a quiet inner peace and strength, but I never imagined I would ever see her stand up to whites on behalf of anyone. I looked at my grandmother and saw the stern look on her face and the pride, as she held that pocketbook tightly to her breast, and thought as I walked away, "*One day I am going to make her so proud of me.*"

Things went from great to bad, to even better than I could have ever planned. A week after losing the election, being accused of starting a riot, being expelled from school, and being re-admitted to school, I was summoned out of class once again to the principal's office. After meeting with my grandmother, the principal had become my new friend and offered me the office of student body vice president, to which I declined.

As I walked into the office, several administrators were sitting there, and my heart dropped. All I could think of was, *"What have I done now?"* The principal told me the white male student, who had been elected president, had been expelled from school for smoking pot in the boys' bathroom and they were going to appointment me class president. My surprise soon turned to reality and I thanked them for thinking of me but told them I had no desire to be class president.

In the midst of all of the confusion, after everything ended, I knew I didn't care about being class president. Being treated fairly and winning were more important. I didn't want to be given something I had already earned. I could never lead with a clear heart knowing what had transpired to keep me out. More than anything, it didn't feel like I had failed. I had won. I knew I would be the best person for the job and their words were enough validation for me. Not long after the offer to take the class presidency, I received a note from a teacher at our school, one I had never met. It was not the election or the recognition that would impact my journey for the rest of my life, but that note.

Right before Christmas break, I received what is still the best Christmas gift I have ever gotten. Although it was 1971 and I would move constantly throughout my lifetime, this was the one constant I always carried with me. I still have the actual letter today and it read as follows:

Dec 10, 1971
Dear Beverly,

Except to come into my classroom, I don't believe you know me, but I want very much to write this note to you telling you how very much I admire you.

First of all, having been defeated myself for some offices; I know how very disappointed you are. I can remember feeling that I would never try for anything again - but you know, I did - and once in a while I actually won! Your talk before the student body was one of the finest I have ever heard a young person give and you so aptly said the things many of us want badly for Clifton. For this reason, you have real concern for people. You are going to be a very important person on whatever campus you attend. Please keep on with your strong ideas. You ran a good fight and were so gracious in losing - I want you to know you have my deepest admiration.

Sincerely,
Mrs. Knagg

Words could never express what her letter meant to me at the time, or what it would continue to mean throughout my journey. No one had ever told me I was going to be important and I clutched that thought as truth and it became a part of me. I began to feel important and somewhere in this experience, I found my voice. Important people were not victims and thus, when the man who had molested me years earlier approached me again, I not only cursed him out, but threatened to tell my big brother. He never bothered me again and I was never a victim of anything or anyone again, because in the eyes of someone with great importance—a teacher—I was important.

I had no idea how much one letter would influence my life. But in a way, it predicted the outcome long before I processed the impact. The letter and its content had a greater lasting result on me than the emotional effects of losing the election, the fights that broke out, my expulsion from school, and all that went into me getting back into school. I didn't even know I had strong ideas. I didn't know I had a real concern for people and I definitely didn't think I would ever be important. That letter became my go-to motivator. Whenever I doubted myself or became fearful, I would pull it out and read it.

To show you how powerful failure can be, I was once again pulled out of homeroom and escorted to the principal's office. There, he told me I would be receiving a citizenship award from the City Council of Monrovia, California. This time, I raced home after school where again I found my grandmother in her colorful muumu, humming softly and preparing dinner. As I told her the great news, she looked up and gave me a loving smile before turning back to the stove to continue her humming and cooking. I had made her proud and to me, that was all that mattered. It wasn't the letter, the offer, or the award. It was my grandmother's smile that meant the most. I went to my room to open a book so I could one day give her the most important gift of all, a big white house with tons of books inside.

* * *

Living in California and helping my grandmother clean homes led me to discover my love for reading and learning. My experiences enabled me to find my voice and confidence. But not everything I learned was positive. I also picked up a bad habit of stealing. It all started innocently. I'd go to the local library to read books and soon I would become so engrossed in the content, I would borrow them and return them once I finished reading them.

I never had a library card because I knew my grandmother wasn't going to go downtown with me to sign up. After a few times of stealing and returning, I decided I would start to collect books for my own library. So, I began taking books without the intention of returning them. The bigger the size of the book, the harder it was to sneak out, resulting in a greater challenge. My only rule was that whatever book I stole, I had to read. Thus, after reading several books I didn't understand or like, I slowed down on stealing books.

I had never stolen anything in my life other than those books, until our middle school trip to Disneyland. Grandma, who was quite cheap, gave me $5.00 to eat with the entire day. After one snack, I was broke. That's when I stole my first item from one of the gift shops. All day, I stole and resold items to my classmates at a reduced price. I then took the ill-gotten funds and purchased gifts for everyone in my family including grandma. I will never forget the look of joy on everyone's faces, especially my grandmother, when they got those gifts. Grandma wasn't used to people doing something for her because she had always given to everyone in our family. She even commented on how well I had used the $5.00 she'd given me. As I laid in bed that night, all I thought about was how happy the gifts had made everyone.

At the end of the year, Derick and I boarded the Greyhound bus headed from California back to Nebraska to live with my mother again. By now, I had become a pretty adept thief. I was only in the eighth grade, yet I was stealing, not for myself, for my family. I stole clothes, clocks, perfume, and just about anything and everything my petite body could carry. I had gotten so confident with my newly-formed skill, I started taking orders. Sometimes I would ask them to pay me for the item. But most of the time, I just gave it to them. Everyone was amazed at what I could steal and their compliments motivated me to keep doing it and doing it bigger. I became so engrossed in the challenge, I never thought about getting caught. Until one day when I got caught.

After spending a year in Nebraska with my mother, we went to Mississippi to my sister's high school graduation. My mom and dad had given us money to go shopping in Natchez. The day it happened, my mom was at home drunk and daddy was out partying or cheating or doing whatever he did. Gerettia, my cousin Fannie, and I drove to Natchez from Bude which was about thirty miles away. We went to a Woolworth's and I of course asked Gerettia and Fannie if they wanted anything. Gerettia wanted a jar of hair grease. Now, I could have gotten the small jar but instead, I went for the extra-large jar of Ultra Sheen to impress her. I had been in California and Nebraska for a while and forgotten how intensely they watched Black people in the deep South because you weren't really welcome in the stores anyway.

As I proudly walked towards the store's exit, a hand pressed appeared on my shoulder from behind. I froze at the firm grip and heard the words, "Hold on, what do you have in that purse?"

I was one step from freedom. I stared at the door trying to decide if I should run or stay and try to talk my way out of it. Either way, I was in big trouble. My sister and Fannie had already exited but came running back in to try to help me. They looked more afraid than I did because they both knew getting caught stealing from a white store in Mississippi was dangerous, especially for Black people.

We all pleaded with the store clerk and offered to pay for the items I had stolen. He appeared to have given in when this older white lady who'd been shopping in the store came over and asked, "What did the little nigger do?" That is when I realized I was definitely my mother's child. I had wondered years earlier why my mother had spoken so harshly to my father after he'd caught her with another man. I wondered why she didn't shut up and plead for mercy and forgiveness. Now I understood how hard it was to *just* shut up.

Before I realized it, I snapped and said, "Mind your own damn business!" Immediately, I knew I had made a mistake. But there was no way I could take it back. I was no longer in California. I was in Mississippi and being Black and proud in Mississippi was dangerous. Just like I wondered what my mother was thinking that day, as I was being dragged into the back of the store, I thought to myself, what was *I* thinking?

There was no pleading my case. The police arrived and I watched as the white lady talked to them. As the white police officers threw me into the back of the police car, my sister yelled that she was going to find a phone to call my mother. I began to cry, not out of fear of the white officers, but the fear of what my mother was going to do to me.

I was escorted from the cell to the front desk where I saw my father standing there in his full military uniform and hearing, for the first time, my mother saying, "Yes sir" and "No sir" to the white officers. My father knew the only hope of saving me was to show that he was fighting for our country and the only way my mother could save me was to bow down. I didn't understand it while we were in the station, but as we walked to the car, I feared the worse was not over, but about to happen.

I sat in the back seat waiting for either a cursing out or the first licks to strike. Instead, my mother's voice shocked me. It was soft and weak as she said, "They could have killed you and we may never have found your body and even if we did, no one would care. This is Mississippi. They could have hung you from a tree."

I sat quietly for the entire ride home allowing her words to sink in. I placed my hands in my pockets touching the money I could have easily used to pay for all the items but hadn't. As was the norm in our family, once we were safely home, we never spoke another word about what had happened. But there were no words to explain the look of terror on my mother's face that day. I had never heard her humble herself. She was a fighter. Yet that day, she and my father literally begged for my life. I left there knowing I would never steal anything again in my life and with the insight that I could have been beaten to death, tossed away and there would have been nothing anyone could have done about it. From that day forward, if a store clerk gave me too much change, I returned it.

As we departed Mississippi, heading for Florida, I told myself everything would be better. I managed to get over the trauma and embarrassment of the police station and focus on a new location. It was 1972 and I was entering high school in a warm state and moving into a real house with my own bedroom. My mother had told us my father was going to retire from the Air Force after his last stint overseas. In preparation for his retirement, they had already purchased a brand-new home. If finally having a real house to live in wasn't enough, she also told us this would be our final move. I was overjoyed. I planned to play sports and earn a scholarship like Gerettia had just done. She ran track while living alone in Mississippi and had earned a full scholarship to Alcorn University. I had no idea about the names and types of colleges. But I knew I needed to go so I could afford to buy my grandmother that house I had promised her.

For some reason, I assumed our last move would be our best move and maybe if I had known what was ahead of us, none of us would have been so excited about our final move. It ended up being more of a final move than any of us could have imagined.

CHAPTER 4

Deeply engrossed in a book, I sat in the living room, feet propped up, snack in hand while my sister's newborn baby slept beside me. I was enjoying a rare occasion, quiet time and the rare victory in an argument with my older sister. Right as I was getting into the heart of my book, the telephone rang from the kitchen. I got up somewhat annoyed. My first thought was it had better not be "that lady" calling again to harass my mother.

I put down my book, glanced at the baby, and walked over to the phone ready to explode. I had long decided the next time my dad's new girlfriend called, and I answered the phone, I would let her have it. I said hello and waited to hear her voice on the other end of the line. Instead, it was my sister Gerettia. For a second I was confused because instead of saying "Hello," in response, it sounded as though she said, "Bev, mama's dead."

Over and over she kept saying it, but that couldn't be true. I hung up the telephone without saying much. I tried to re-open my book, but her voice kept ringing in my head, "Mama's dead!" My heart sank. I walked over to the front door and called for Derick who was at a party next door. When he ran into the house I said to him rather calmly, "Gerettia just called and said Mama's dead."

He must not have believed it either, because without saying a word he turned and walked back out the house, returning to our neighbor's party. As the baby began to stir, it drew my attention away from my sister's statement of "Mama's dead. Mama's dead." I shed no tears as I cared for the baby and waited patiently for them to come home wondering what was taking them so long. I shut out all thoughts of "Mama's dead," knowing it was not true and when my sister didn't call back, I knew it had to have been a mistake.

She's just messing with me because for the first time in my life I won an argument with her. Although she was only three years older, Gerettia had always been more than a big sister. She was more like a mother figure to Derick and me. So, whatever she said had always been the law, but not this time. She and I had agreed for her to take our mother to our old neighborhood in west Tampa to help out one of her friends who was blind, and I would pick her up. My mother had lost her license and was no longer allowed to drive in the state of Florida because she had too many car accidents and DUIs. When the lady called for us to come pick her up, Gerettia and I actually got into an argument about who would go. Although I had previously agreed to go, she relented to my pressure and agreed to pick her up.

As I sat watching the baby, I looked around at the house we had all been eager to move into. We had arrived in Florida the summer of my ninth-grade year and moved into a brand-new house for the first time in our lives. My mother loved her new ranch-style house with the yellow and gold lush shag carpet she had picked out. Every Saturday morning I remember having to rake that carpet with the outside rake so every strand stood at attention. For the first time in our lives, we each had our own rooms and more than one bathroom for a house full of people. My mother looked forward to growing old with my dad in that house. By this point, I was a twelfth grader and everything seemed to be falling apart and my mother's dream home had slowly evolved into a nightmare.

Our first year back in Florida had been amazing. With Gerettia away in college and my dad overseas in the military, it had only been my mom, Derick, and me in a four-bedroom, two bath house. Within her first year of college, Gerettia got pregnant and had to return home. Both Derick and I had started playing sports and we loved our new school, neighborhood, and home. But the greatest gift of all was that after years of drinking, my mother had several small strokes along with a spinal condition, which required surgery, all resulting in her having to stop drinking. She'd always had the perfect petite hourglass figure but for the surgery, they wanted her to gain weight and placed her on steroids. The steroids caused her to gain a lot of weight fast. When they told her the surgery was dangerous, she made the decision to take her chance in life without having it. She sat us down and for the first time, explained her decision to us, telling us she would never drink again and she would be fine.

As the date for my father's return home neared, my mother tried to lose the extra weight but couldn't. I am sure my father was a bit shocked to see her weight gain along with seeing Gerettia back home with a newborn baby. Everything seemed okay at first, but as I finished the end of my junior year in high school, everything began to fall apart. We heard my mother begging my dad not to go out each night. He would leave the house for long periods of time until finally, he didn't come back. My mother was devastated. Unbeknownst to us, after he left the house and didn't return, my mother hired a private detective to find him. I asked my sister how my mother could afford a private investigator and she told me, the same way she can afford our life insurance policy, getting the cars fixed, and other things she needed to get done. She slept with the investigator. I always knew my mother had several ways of getting money when she needed but usually that consisted of getting salary advances while working at the drycleaners, or gambling, or pawning our stereo or television, and now I was finding out she traded her goods for services. It must have worked because within days, she had an address and telephone number of the other woman. That is when things got serious and crazy.

My mother would call them all times of day and night and then the lady started calling her and they would curse and scream at each other over my father. One day, my mother told Gerettia to drive her to run errands so we all got in the car without a clue of where we were going. She directed her street by street, turn by turn until we arrived at the old apartment building in what looked like a factory district. We all got out of the car and followed behind my mother without a clue as to whose apartment we were approaching. As we came upon one particular apartment, my mother looked at a piece of paper she held in her hand to verify the apartment number and then proceeded to bang relentlessly on the door screaming for my father to come out.

As the door was cracked open ever so slightly, my mother kicked the door open as she reached into her purse and pulled out a gun. We all stood behind her in shock. She ran through the house waving her gun demanding my father and his new girlfriend come out. Finally, the three small children who had opened the door told her they were home alone and that their mother and our father were not there. They told her they hadn't seen them all night. My mother continued roaming through the house, even looking into their refrigerator before turning to leave. As we got into the car in silence, we passed a grocery store where my mother instructed us to stop. I couldn't believe after brandishing a gun she was actually going to stop and get groceries. But as usual, we did what we were told and as we moved through the store, she picked up lunch items, bread and other snacks. We got back in the car expecting to go home, she instead instructed my sister to return to the apartment despite our protest to do otherwise. Upon returning to the apartment, she took the two bags of groceries, went back upstairs and left them for the three small kids and walked back to the car as if nothing unusual had just happened. Once we left the apartment, none of us mentioned it. We had become accustomed to crazy and the silence of crazy. Almost pretending that crazy didn't just happen. To tell the truth, I was stuck on the fact she owned a gun. To this day, I wonder what would have happened if my father and that lady would have actually been home.

From that point on, things spiraled completely out of control with both sides declaring war on the other. One day my dad came over while my mother was at work. We hadn't seen him in a while and he didn't say much, just roamed around the house collecting his things. Once he had taken what he needed, we expected him to leave but no, he hung around. Finally, I said, "Daddy, you might want to take off. Mama is on her way and you shouldn't be here when she gets home." But he didn't move towards his loaded car. He sat smiling as usual. When my mom came home, for a brief moment she must have thought he had come back home to her, but her good mood changed as he re-entered their bedroom and took out a few more items just to show her he didn't want her anymore. As he headed for the door, she pleaded for him to stay and he appeared to revel in her misery as he smiled and walked even slower towards his car. Within seconds, my mother's mood went from humble to a violent outbreak and she jumped on him. He quickly threw her to the ground, holding her neck to restrain her as Gerettia and I watched through the living room window. Shortly thereafter, we heard her choking, screaming that he was killing her and then she appeared to have passed out.

As we rushed for the door and into the front yard, Gerettia dove at my father knocking him off mama. As they tumbled in the front yard, they both ended up facing off in the boxing position. As my mother laid there apparently unconscious in the middle of the yard, the two of them squared off. I was stunned that I was standing in the front yard of our suburban home watching my sister square off with my dad at five o'clock in the evening, just as people were returning home from work. Before I knew it, my sister took a swing at him, which he defended and took a swing at her and she ducked. She swung and caught him with an uppercut. That hit shocked him into fight mode. With the customary smile no longer on his face and my mother lying unconscious on the ground, I knew I had to jump in. With cars moving by slowly to see what was happening, my father, sister, and I were all in the front yard in 100-degree Florida temperatures squared off for a fight. As arms swung, I took a swipe at my father to distract him from hitting my sister and as he turned to punch my lights out, he must have realized he was fist fighting his own kids and girls at that. He stopped, put his hands down, walked slowly towards his car and sat there.

With neighbors now coming out of their homes to watch, Gerettia and I decided we needed to get our unconscious mother out of the front yard and into the house. My mother had gained a substantial amount of weight and it was dead weight because she was passed out. Gerettia had the strength and size to carry her end but I weighed less than 120 pounds and was struggling, which turned a five-minute move from yard to house into a twenty-minute spectacle. Exhausted but successful, we finally got her laid out on the living room carpet when my supposedly unconscious mother jumped up and ran back outside to attack my father who was still sitting out front in his car. When he saw her racing towards his car, he zoomed off and that would be the last time he would ever see her.

Things were really bad and although my mother wasn't drinking anymore, she now possessed the anger of a woman scorned. Night after night, the calls between the two women escalated into pure evil and hatred and I can't help but to think my father loved every minute of it, especially seeing my mother suffer. He no longer wanted her and it was apparent to everyone but my mother. After what felt like weeks of calls, there came one call between them that shook my mother to her core. I had never seen my mother scared but she seemed beyond scared, more like terrified. In the midst of their last argument, the other woman told my mother that within weeks, not only would my mother be dead, but she, the other woman, would be living in her house and sleeping in her bed. As we listened to my mother telling my grandmother about the call, we were all in shock knowing this was getting out of control but we were helpless to stop it. To our surprise, my mother's conversation shifted to black magic and voodoo. She was concerned the lady had put a spell of some sort on her and she was actually scared. She became worried and fearful. Grandma must have reassured her that she would take care of it because when my mother hung up the phone, she looked relieved. She told Gerettia that grandma was going to contact the voodoo lady in Mississippi to send something to her.

Everyday my mother came home, she checked the mail for the package from Mississippi until it finally came. She followed the instructions my grandmother had given her sprinkling things around the house and in the yard. None of us knew what was going on at this point, just that we were all worried because we had never seen my mother so afraid. Finally, Gerettia asked my mother why she needed voodoo stuff from Mississippi. My mother told her of the conversation with the other woman and about the spell. A fist fight, a knife fight, a gun fight and my mother was ready and willing. But a voodoo black magic fight terrified her. The woman implied that my mother would be dead soon which scared my mother to no end. None of us paid much attention to the voodoo story but we were concerned that my mother was concerned. Now the inconceivable had happened, just as my mother had feared. She'd died in her sleep not even a month after the call to my grandmother about the voodoo.

As Gerettia walked back into our home after discovering my mother's cold, dead body, my mind raced immediately to "that lady." We had never seen or met the other woman but just as she had predicted, my mother was dead. Gerettia explained to Derick and me how she had called out to mama that it was time go and there was no answer. So she walked over to the bed where mama had laid down and hit her on the butt and said, "Mama let's go," and she didn't move. It was only then that she touched my mother's skin, realizing it was cold, and she was literally frozen in the fetal position on the bed indicating she had been dead for hours. As she spoke, my mind raced between disbelief, gratitude, and anger. I refused to believe my mother was dead, I was grateful I had not been the one to discover her body, and finally, I was angry at the woman who had predicted my mother's death and with my father for allowing it all to happen.

My sister told me she had called an ambulance before calling me. Then she had to calm my mother's friend down when the blind lady realized my mother had not been asleep but dead. My sister went on to tell me how the medical staff had her leave the room because they were going to have to actually break my mother's bones to get her stretched out to place her in the ambulance. I was listening, but it simply wasn't registering. I didn't cry. To this day, I don't know how I'd won that argument with Gerettia but I am so grateful I did. God knows I would not have been prepared to handle things as calmly and effectively as my sister did that night. Even as she spoke, I somehow managed to convince myself it wasn't true. Because I didn't see her in that position, it meant she was still alive.

In our hearts, mama's death was "that lady" and my dad's fault. We all held them responsible. It was October 11, 1975, my senior year, and we were all struggling to deal with my forty-five-year-old mother's sudden death. Gerettia took charge as she'd always done because she was the one who was strong like my mother and grandmother and she had always been the one they trusted with their business. She called my grandmother in California to tell her Mama was dead. My grandmother and mother were the strongest people I knew, even stronger than any man I had ever met and I could hear my grandmother saying, "What? NO! NO! NOT MY BABY! OH MY GOD! NOT MY BABY!"

The next day my grandmother went into action. There was no time for mourning. She, along with Gerettia, made arrangements with my dad for the funeral services. Grandma had burial plots for her and her two children already paid for in Mississippi, so it was decided that she would have a small funeral in Florida and then she would be flown to Mississippi for her final resting place.

My father did everything right during the funeral arrangements and was supportive of my sister and grandmother. Gerettia was the one who literally dressed my mother and prepared her for her burial and as always, she told me to put on her my mother's signature red lipstick.

For my family, it was business as usual, thanks to Gerettia. My mother died over the weekend and on Monday, my brother and I were back at school. I went to classes and to basketball practice and told almost no one. At the end of the day, and without tears since it still didn't feel real, I stated matter-of-factly to my coaches and teachers that I would be out for the remainder of week because my mother had died. When we got to Mississippi, it was the first time all seven of my mother's kids were in the same place at the same time and unfortunately, we were not there to celebrate, but for her burial.

Although it was a funeral service, everyone, including me, was in a good mood except my grandmother who kept herself busy. Even my dad's family, who we barely knew, had come down from Virginia for the funeral. It felt almost like a family reunion but without my mother. People were stopping by and dropping off food. It almost felt like a celebration as people told story after story about my mother's crazy antics and kind heart. I felt happy for some reason. I think it's because it hadn't settled in that she was actually dead.

On the day of the funeral, as everyone got dressed, I started to feel ill. I decided I didn't want to go to the service and went first to my father to tell him. I figured he wouldn't care if I went or not, but he told me I needed to go and while smiling, said, "You'll be all right."

I walked away thinking, *What the hell? Can't he see I am not all right.* Next, I went to my sister followed by my grandmother. I went to each family member pleading, but no one would hear me. They told me I would regret not saying goodbye, but what they didn't understand, was that's the precise reason I didn't want to go. If I didn't see her in a coffin, it would mean she wasn't actually dead.

When the limousine came to take our family to Sweet Home Baptist Church at the bottom of the hill of our house, I refused to get in. I wasn't going no matter what anyone said and the next thing I knew, I was being lifted up and forced into the limo. I sat numb as the tears streamed down my face, repeating over and over almost begging not to be forced to go.

Once we arrived at the church, I refused to get out of the car and I screamed and fought until they finally picked me up again and carried me inside. I told my sister I didn't want to see the body and she promised me I wouldn't have to. So, I sat with my head on my father's sister's lap trying not to listen and definitely refusing to look at anything. Then it came time for the family to view the body and say our final goodbyes. I refused to get up and as they dragged me from the pew, I went crazy screaming, crying, and shaking, until my father's sister who was a nurse, took me outside to sit in the car.

Once we were inside the car, it got so bad she finally reached into her purse and gave me a pill to calm me down and I immediately began to drift out of consciousness. Before I could pass out completely, she had me sniff something that jolted me back awake. Thus began a cycle of shaking, crying, passing out, and being revived. The next thing I remember is being in an emergency room being given a shot of some type of heavy sedative, and from that point on, I don't remember much else.

Gerettia later told me that as she drove us home, I was in the back seat with my father and she caught him feeling on my unconscious body. She pulled over and told him to drive while she sat in the back with me. I finally recovered from all the medication thinking I had only been asleep for a day. I was told I had been out of it for almost a week. I wondered what was going to happen to us and that's when I realized my grandmother had come down to Florida. I thought she was going to stay but she and Gerettia made arrangements to pay all the bills each month and Gerettia would take care of us. My dad even came over and he was so nice while my grandmother was there. But then she left to return to California.

Days after my grandmother's departure, my dad returned to the house. Because he had been so nice to us, we were actually glad to see him until we noticed a woman entering the door behind him. I was sitting on the floor as Gerettia sat on the sofa combing my hair for school. The lady was small, dark-skinned, and fairly young. She wasn't pretty, not ugly, just average-looking. You could tell she didn't like us and was pleased with herself as she stood boldly and comfortably in my mother's living room. I thought of my mother's death and her words to my mother and immediately labeled her in my head as cold-hearted and dangerous. Gerettia looked up and said what we were all thinking, "What she doing here?" He didn't even sit down. He just looked at us and said he was moving back in. In fact he said "they" were moving in, meaning he, the lady, and her three small sons. He explained he had no intention of paying rent in two places and that's when we all tried to explain that my grandmother was going to pay the rent. He didn't care. That lady wanted the house and that was it. He told Gerettia she had to be out by the end of the week and that neither Derick nor I would be allowed to leave with her.

Although my dad was not Gerettia's biological father, I never thought he would be so cold as to throw her out of our house with her young son. He had raised Gerettia since she was three years old and he was treating her like a stranger and there was nothing we could do. Not even two weeks after my mom's death, he kicked my sister out, made Derick and I stay, and moved "that lady" and her three children into my mother's house. It was just as she had predicted. Within a month, my mother was dead, the lady had not only taken over her house but was sharing my mother's bed with my mother's husband. I don't know if voodoo really works or whether it was right or wrong to blame voodoo and that lady for my mother's death, but I did and now I was literally being forced to live with her. Derick adjusted well. Needless to say, I did not. I was angry, hurt, and scared. I was angry at my dad for kicking my sister out of the house and for allowing the other woman to move in. I was hurting because I missed my mother and sister. I was also scared to eat anything the woman cooked because I still wasn't sure about the voodoo thing that may or may not have resulted in my mother's death.

I never got an opportunity to cry with my brothers and sisters after my mother's death. We didn't have the luxury to heal and mourn because life changed in an instant and we were in survival mode. There was no time for self-pity. Derick and I were forced to live in a home where it was evident we weren't welcomed. Bitter, scared and scarred, school became home for me.

* * *

Throughout everything taking place, the thing that gave me peace and happiness was school and sports. Upon our return to Florida, I looked forward to attending high school at the all-Black school in Tampa. However, as a result of Brown vs. The Board of Education and the Civil Rights Movement, the school systems not only in Florida, but across the country, were to be integrated. Black students were bussed over thirty minutes to the racially charged town of Brandon, Florida to attend Brandon High School. Around the same time, public schools were also being forced by law to have equal opportunities for girls in education and sports under Title IX. Title XI stated, "No person in the United States shall, on the basis of sex, be excluded from participation in, be denied the benefits of, or be subjected to discrimination under any education program or activity receiving Federal financial assistance." As a result, Brandon not only had to create diversity through integration but also, their previously all white male sports programs had to include girl's athletic teams. I always wanted to play sports after growing up watching Gerettia and our cousin, Fannie, play sports. I had visions of earning an athletic scholarship to attend college. I wanted to be like them and this would be my first chance. Sports would not only be an escape for me from home life, it would serve as an outlet for my competitive spirit. I needed to get a scholarship to attend college in order to take care of my grandmother, especially now that my mother was no longer alive.

The first sport a group of us Black girls decided to play was volleyball but as practices began, it became clear none of us knew anything about the sport. One by one, we quit. We had also never played basketball but we all loved the game. I loved it more than anyone and I worked hard to get better at it. I also ran track but didn't really like it, so I ran just to have something to do and because we all loved Ms. Carter, the only Black coach of any sport at the school. All the sports in my first two years had female coaches but as I had entered into my senior year, every female coach had been replaced by white male coaches.

The newly-hired white male coach for our girls' basketball team instantly started picking on all the Black players in practice, trying to force them to quit. We went from having almost half the spots on the team to maybe two or three. The only reason I survived the cuts was because of something I had learned from my mother prior to her death. I knew the coach wanted to cut me, but I made sure, as I had learned from my mother while working at the drycleaners each summer, to make sure he and the team needed me more than he could afford to cut me.

My mother unknowingly taught this to me the summer of my tenth-grade year before she stopped drinking. She had the unwritten rule that when you turned fifteen you needed to work, even if only for the summer. So that summer, she got me a job pressing clothes alongside her and my sister Gerettia. For the next two summers, I worked that job until she died. Working at a dry cleaner's in the 100-degree temperatures of Florida was hard enough, but the heat from the large presses made it almost unbearable. I was so small that I had to get up on my tiptoes and literally jump up to pull the lid down on the pants presser, burning my leg time and time again. It was actually illegal for me to work there because I was underage, but that didn't stop my mother from getting me a job. They simply paid me in cash each week. My mother never took the money we earned.

It was an early Friday morning on the job and we were all excited because as hard as the work was, payday made it worth it. On this particular Friday, my mother went to lunch early and alone but when she returned, I could tell by the look on her face she had been drinking. At some point, I heard a commotion and stopped what I was doing. I heard my mother's voice getting louder in the distance. She cursed out the owner of the dry cleaner and before I knew it, I heard her say, "Kiss my ass. I quit!" Then she stormed out. I looked over at Gerettia who just kept working. Confused, I wasn't sure what to do. Follow my mom and walk out or follow my sister and keep working? I didn't like the job anyway, so I took off after my mother. I will never forget the look on her face when I caught up to her at the bus stop. She looked at me and said, "You'd better take your little ass back to work." As I walked back in I was so embarrassed. Gerettia just looked at me and laughed.

Then something amazing happened. That day, at the end of our shift, as we lined up to get paid, the boss came over and gave Gerettia my mother's pay check and told her to tell my mother he would see her on Monday. I hadn't realized that my mother quit whenever she wanted to, and they always took her back. I asked my sister about it and she explained that mama was so good at what she did, they couldn't replace her. In return, they had to put up with her behavior at times. My mother was a hard worker and she pressed all the expensive and hard to clean items and ninety-five percent of the time, she was an ideal employee. But they realized they had to put up with the five percent of her they hated.

So as the coach got harder on the Black athletes, I spoke up about the unfair treatment and I knew speaking up made him want to get rid of me. The more I spoke up, the harder I worked. The harder he was on me, the harder I worked. My competitiveness drove me to become better and what I lacked in skills, I more than made up for in hustle and athletic ability. I knew from working alongside my mother that if I was going to speak out, I had better be worth having around. I had grown up trying to live up to the excellence by which my mother had in pressing clothes or my grandmother had in cleaning houses and therefore, I took the same approach in school and sports. I had even begun to have articles written about me and my picture in the local papers. The successes made me work even harder. Eventually, my family started to take an interest in me and would come watch me play. My mother would listen to me talk about the game and had promised that during my senior season, she would come to watch me. She never made it to a game. She died in October, before my season started.

My mother used to warn my older sisters, all of whom had a smart mouth, "Don't let your mouth write a check your ass can't cash." The meaning of which was if you aren't willing to pay the price for your words, sit down and shut up. My mother never shut up. She was always willing to back up her words. I still wish I could shut up. I couldn't stand by in basketball allowing my coach to speak to us unfairly and I paid a price for my outspokenness not only with the basketball coach but at home as well.

By the end of my senior year in basketball, I led the team in almost every category and yet I was the only one on the team at our annual basketball banquet not to receive an award. Even the players who sat on the bench and never played got awards. I sat at the banquet smiling on the outside but angry and heart-broken on the inside. He had paid me back in the most hurtful and humiliating way possible. I wanted to run away and cry but thankfully, my family had taught me that crying wasn't an option.

At home I faired no differently. As basketball season ended, the banquet wasn't the worst thing my mouth would get me into. I was living in the house with my brother, my dad, and his new family when I turned eighteen on February 25, 1976, my senior year of high school. Graduation was set for June and I had visions of freedom and college. Unfortunately, the moment I turned eighteen, things went from bad to worse. The lady and I never talked, but she would leave notes telling me what to do. I wanted to ignore her and the notes, but I was my mother's daughter and always responded with a note of my own. One day she left a note on the refrigerator about washing the dishes in the sink telling me, "If you mess them up, clean up" and I in turn left her a note saying, "And if you wash them up, put them up." It was apparent she didn't like me and I, in turn, didn't like her. That's when it all hit the fan. As I walked into the house once again without speaking, she turned to me and said, "You're lucky to still be living here. We intended to put you out when you turned eighteen but decided to let you stay until you graduate." Just as I had thought, my mother at times should have shut up when she spoke up, this was probably one of those times I should have kept my mouth shut. But of course, I didn't. I turned to her and said the stupidest thing I could have said at the time, "If you are so bad, put me out." Yep, I was a dumb ass and for some reason, hadn't realized just how much my father didn't care about any of us.

I thought she would accept my challenge to fight. Even though I hated fighting, I was eager to punch her lights outs, but that's not what happened. She looked almost pleased with my response as she said with confidence, "You're out of here as of this moment." I looked at my dad as if he would defend me. She smiled and said, "You got to go." As I packed what little I could gather, my heart dropped because I never thought my father would allow her to put me out. I hated the big white car with the red interior he had purchased for me my junior year, but now it was all I had. It looked like a police car. I think it was a Montego. It always ran hot so I had to keep a jug of water in the car to constantly refill the radiator.

As I exited our house for the last time, I knew I had only one person left in the city I could go stay with, my sister Cherry. I arrived at her apartment in the hood in west Tampa. Even on a school night, her apartment was filled with all types of people drinking and doing drugs. I had no choice. I had to go to her and explain that I had been put out and had nowhere to stay. I still had two months left to finish high school and I was in the middle of track season. She welcomed me in and I tried to make it work for a few weeks. At times, I slept on the floor and men were always coming in and out of the house. It was not clean and there were more roaches than there were grains in a bag of rice. They were everywhere and in Tampa, they had roaches that not only crawled but flew on everything you owned looking for food. I called my grandmother in California and told her what happened. She told me she would send me money and to try to stay there until I could finish school and she and my sister Gerettia would come and get me.

One night I had gotten in late after track practice and work and went to take a bath when a man walked in and used the bathroom while I was bathing. I realized the doors had no locks and more and more people were hanging out at Cherry's apartment. The familiar feeling of being unsafe set in. I wasn't sleeping and staying up all night as a result of the noise left me exhausted.

One day, with about a month left in school, I was so tired I couldn't make the twenty or so mile drive home. I saw some apartments and pulled over to take a nap and woke up the next morning. After that, I regularly slept in my car and took a shower in the girl's locker room at school. I knew if I could just hold on until June, everything would be okay. I would get a scholarship soon to play basketball. I was running track but because I didn't like it, I mainly ran relays to have something to do because I had nowhere to go. I never expected to get a scholarship in track, so I never put my heart into it.

I was determined to make it. I only had a month and I was certain I was going to get a scholarship and be off to college. Every night I slept and cried in my car, promising myself I would never live this way again. I had a great basketball season before being put out of the house and I was confident I would get all types of basketball offers. I kept checking in with the girls' basketball coach to see if any colleges had called on my behalf and he said no.   I later found out he had made sure I didn't get any offers. He didn't like me and refused to pass on my information to any colleges. I even checked with Derick to see if anyone had called the house for me, but he said no, not that he knew of. I later found out I had gotten a couple of calls and letters for basketball, but they told them I didn't live there.

For over a month, I drove the thirty miles or so back and forth to school each day from Tampa to Brandon, Florida, never missing a track practice, and keeping my grades up until I could graduate. As track season ended and graduation drew near, I began to panic because I still had not received a scholarship offer. As both the track season and my high school years came to an end, I had not received one scholarship to college. I began to realize I might actually have to move back to California with my grandmother and get a job either cleaning homes or pressing clothes. The thought depressed me but staying in Florida was not an option. I had no money and nowhere to live, so choices were few. The week before graduation, I was called into the track coach's office. I had no idea what I had done. When I walked in, there stood the coach from a rival high school, King High School in the inner city of Tampa. Their coach had trained some of the best athletes in the state in track and field. Mrs. Falsone told me she had just been appointed the new women's track coach for the first women's track and field team at Hillsborough Community College in Tampa. She informed me she had one scholarship left and that she was offering it to me. I was so grateful. I might not have cried in front of everyone, but once I got back to my car, I sat in it and cried my heart out. I desperately wanted, no needed, to go to college and now I was being given an opportunity. I was so appreciative of the scholarship, I totally forgot how I didn't like running track and never cared that I would be attending a junior college. I was simply happy to have somewhere to go and someone who wanted me. As I sat in my car, I promised myself I would not let Mrs. Falsone down. But mostly, I couldn't wait to tell grandma I was going to college and I had a scholarship.

That scholarship literally saved my life. Years after my running career ended and I was a coach, I asked Mrs. Falsone why she chose to give me a scholarship when I was an average runner? I never expected to get the answer she gave me. I had no idea. She told me she and the boy's coach, Jeff DeCola, at Brandon High School were great friends. One day she happened to speak with him about her new job at the junior college and told him that she had one remaining scholarship to give out but couldn't decide who to award it to. He told her of a young Black girl on the girls' team who had lost her mother earlier in the year and he thought for sure I was living in my car because he would see me coming out of the locker room each morning. He told her even though he thought I was homeless, he had never seen me miss a day of school or a day of practice. She told me what really touched her heart was when he told her that if she signed me, "I promise you Joan, she will never disappoint you." Mrs. Falsone said that's what convinced her to give me the last scholarship. She also told me that in the twenty plus years she had known me, I had never disappointed her. Mrs. Falsone was a lifesaver. Had it not been for that track scholarship, I am not sure how life would have unfolded. I remain grateful to her for always believing me in me throughout the years.

When my grandmother and sister came to Tampa for my high school graduation in 1976, we all stayed at my sister's apartment. Cherry made my elderly grandmother sleep on the very floor upstairs in the hallway that I had been sleeping on, so I cuddled up on that floor next to my grandmother and slept the best night's sleep I had slept in months. I slept well knowing I was going to college and soon, my grandmother would never have to clean another person's house or sleep on anyone's floors.

The day of my graduation was happy and sad. I had given my brother a graduation invitation to give to my father and somewhere in my heart I thought, in spite of all that had happened, I was still his daughter and surely, he wouldn't miss my graduation. But he never came.

That summer, I not only found a job that paid well, but I moved into an apartment along with my best friend from high school. I couldn't wait to start college in the fall. It might have been a junior college, but it was college. I had a scholarship, an apartment, a check, and a future even if I had to run track to get it. In the fall of 1976, I entered my first year of college at Hillsborough Community College in Tampa, Florida. As I sat surveying the campus, I knew I had to make it. I was determined to win.

CHAPTER 5

I was alone in my one room efficiency trying desperately to finish the first of several papers due in my final year of college at Auburn University. After graduating from Junior College, I had received a full scholarship to Auburn University to again run track.

While deep in thought, the phone rang and I answered to hear Gerettia on the other end. She was still living in California with my grandmother since being evicted from our home in Florida. A lot had transpired during the past four years and finally there was light at the end of the tunnel. I was now in my last year of college and on my way to a better life for my grandmother and my family. She was calling not to discuss travel plans for my upcoming graduation that May, but travel plans for my grandmother to return to Mississippi. My grandmother had not been feeling well. She had severe headaches and was becoming increasingly forgetful. My heart dropped. I had never known my grandmother to ever be sick, ever forget anything, or ever even miss work as a result of any illness. She always had high blood pressure but that was it. I ask Gerettia if she thought it had something to do with her pressure.

Gerettia had no clue what was happening but she told me grandma felt it was because someone had put a roots or voodoo spell on her. I was floored thinking to myself, *"Here we go again with that darn voodoo stuff."* After dealing with my mother's death and voodoo, I was not going to fall for the voodoo trick again. I all but laughed at the notion. She told me I could laugh if I wanted to, but my grandmother had just purchased an airplane ticket to Jackson, Mississippi to go see the voodoo lady and her family doctor, both of whom she had used for years. I knew right then things were serious because my grandmother had never flown in her life. If she had an airline ticket to anywhere, it was serious. After asking what I could do to help, Gerettia told me she needed me to leave school and meet Grandma at the airport the next morning and take her to the family doctor in Meadville, Mississippi. Gerettia would be on a plane the following day to meet with us to go see the voodoo lady. My mind refused to accept thoughts of losing my grandmother. I wouldn't allow myself to think of it, but I couldn't shake the idea.

As we had been taught, there was no time to dwell on what was happening. I needed to take action. My mother had drilled into our heads and hearts that in cases of emergency, take action and no matter what happened, get over it and keep it moving. As I packed to leave that morning, I had accomplished the "take action" part but I failed the latter half because emotionally, I was a wreck, fearing the worse. The next morning, I drove from Auburn, Alabama to Jackson, Mississippi, praying all the way that my grandmother was all right.

I examined her smiling face as she saw me waiting at the gate. Upon meeting her, I noticed that while she looked exactly the same, her speech pattern was off. As we drove to her house in Bude, Mississippi where we had all been born, she kept asking the same questions over and over and the longer we spoke, the more I wanted to cry. I loved my grandmother more than I loved anyone in my life. I wanted so much to make her proud of me and to provide for her, but she seemed almost childlike and kept grabbing her head. We made several stops, one of which was to her doctor and another was to fill the prescription he had written for her, so by the time we reached her house, it was dark outside. Even in the darkness of the night, I could see it was not the house I remembered. It was in a total state of disrepair. The once stable home looked abandoned and dilapidated. As we stepped carefully towards the front door, I held her hand to prevent having her fall through the broken planks on the front porch. We had only one night there but it would be the longest night of my life.

My grandma had two habits each night. She always placed a glass of water by her bed and a pot, which she used to urinate during the night. I went to the bathroom to bathe her, but both the tub and toilet were literally falling through the floor. As I looked into her eyes, I saw the hurt and I immediately went into action, promising her that as soon as I graduated, I would build her a brand-new home. She smiled and as we went to bed that night, I had a renewed determination to make life great for her.

I didn't sleep much because every time she got up to use the pot by the bed, I had to make sure she didn't wander off. The next morning, we took a wash off with a bath towel and I had to help her get dressed. When we got ready leave, I went to empty the pee pot my grandmother had been using all night and to my surprise it was empty. I was sure I had heard her using it, but it was empty. I thought to myself, *Oh well, less work,* but as I grabbed her purse from beside the bed it was heavy and leaking. Yep, she had used the bathroom that night but not in the pot, in her purse. Something was definitely wrong and seriously wrong. As I cleaned out the purse I looked at grandma realizing she had no clue what had happened.

That afternoon, we picked Gerettia up from the airport and I told her of the night's events, letting her know something was terribly wrong and grandma needed to see a real doctor. It was decided she would make sure grandma got a full exam by good doctors when they returned to California. We picked up grandma's friend who directed us to the voodoo lady's home. Down winding two lane roads, we drove farther into wooded areas transitioning from paved roads to dirt roads and finally onto a trail which lead us to an opening. And there it was, surrounded by cars and people, the voodoo house.

As I pulled up to the house I kept thinking to myself that I was about to graduate from college so how in the world had I ended up on the back roads of Mississippi going to see a voodoo lady about removing a spell. As we prepared to get out of the car, I wondered if it was the same voodoo lady grandma had conferred with concerning my mother. If it was, whatever she'd sent my mother didn't work so why were we relying on her again? I intended to ask her about my mother. I may not have had an actual belief or disbelief in voodoo but I knew something happened to my mother.

As we exited the car, we saw several people waiting outside, but my grandmother's friend bypassed them as if she and grandma had special privileges. I was glad we didn't have to wait in line. I wanted out of there because my courage to tell the voodoo lady off had quickly turned to fear. When we walked into the house, it was dark, dimly lit with candles, and had all sorts of weird images hanging across the walls. It felt like something you'd see in a scary movie except it was real. Soon we were greeted by a rather large, dark-skinned lady with a necklace of herbs. I actually giggled but when the lady stared at me, nothing was funny anymore. I looked around and told my sister I would meet them in the car. When they finally came out, Gerettia felt it had been a waste of time because the lady provided my grandmother no new information and simply gave her a jar of something to sprinkle in various places in her house and on her person.

After dropping my grandmother's friend off, we headed to the airport in silence. As I walked them to the gate, Gerettia assured me she would get grandma a full exam to determine exactly what was wrong with her. We didn't know what was wrong but we both knew for sure it had nothing to do with voodoo. As they rose to board the plane, I held my grandma in a hug so long it became uncomfortable. I told her I loved her and not to worry because I would take care of her for the rest of her life. We hugged once more but this time, as I released her, tears fell from my eyes. She smiled at me as they boarded the plane, which made me smile through my tears.

That night, as I drove back to Auburn to finish my last few months of college, I had no idea that moment would be the last time I would ever hug my grandma. Somehow I felt she knew it, which was why she had smiled so lovingly at me as she boarded the plane.

The doctors in California ran several tests and identified the cause for her severe headaches and memory loss due to a grapefruit sized tumor that had lodged itself in her brain. Surgery was needed immediately but due to her high blood pressure, it was risky. Once they got her blood pressure under control, they operated to remove the tumor. She survived the surgery but fell into a coma while in the recovery room. Gerettia recalled her moaning, "Lord take me, take me now. I am so tired." Eventually, they placed her on life support. I think grandma was plain old worn out. She had been through so much in her lifetime. Things that none of us would ever know. She was always strong, but I wonder if like me, she was strong to the outside world but cried alone at night. After several days on life support, it was decided to turn the machines off and she passed away on November 15, 1980 just as I imagined my mother had died quietly and peacefully in her sleep.

I had been taught to suffer in silence and not to show any weaknesses, but losing my grandmother was different. My whole world changed the moment she died. It had been hard to live without my mother but now the backbone and true family matriarch was gone as well. I was in my final year of college at Auburn, which had been inspired by her. I picked a major based on taking care of her and now I would be graduating with a degree in which I no longer cared or had any interest. I'd fought to get to that point and now I was lost as far as what to do next.

Going to college had always been a life-long dream and even though getting through Hillsborough Community College was a challenge for me, somehow, I had made it. Throughout the past four years of college, I had felt alone and on my own with only my desire to help grandma as my driving force to keep going. Mrs. Falsone and her husband, Mr. Falsone, had become like second parents while I ran for her at Hillsborough. I was unprepared for college, so much so that my first year was a disaster. I did everything I shouldn't have done. I partied, I tried drinking (hated it), I tried to smoke weed (hated it), I skipped classes to hang out, I didn't do homework. I had my first real relationship, well two of them. One was with a fellow female student and another with a male student. Neither worked out. I did everything but get pregnant, thank God. But the party ended that summer as reality set in. In one year I would graduate with a need to get into a four-year school. I had to buckle down and get focused. I had no money and nowhere to live.

At the end of my first year in junior college and true to that lady's word, when Derick turned eighteen, he too was asked to leave the house. With nowhere to go, he moved into the apartment I shared with a roommate. He'd asked my father to help him pay to go to junior college, but he told him he wasn't smart enough to go to college and should enlist in the military. Countering my father's guidance, I told Derick he was smart enough and that I would help him. Subsequently, he got into college and over the next several years while in college, I supplemented his Pell Grant with the extra money I received from a full scholarship at Auburn University.

Had it not been for my grandmother and Mrs. Falsone, I would never have made it. I was on a mission to get a college degree and I pressured myself my last year of junior college, but I pressured Mrs. Falsone even more. She told me years later she would study every workout in anticipation of my questions. Mr. and Mrs. Falsone were, I think, of Polish decent and they literally took me under their wings. They were the kindest people I had ever met, and they never demonstrated any signs of prejudice. She treated each of us as if we were someone special. I loved that about her, along with her passion to see each of us succeed. There were very few junior college women's track programs in the state of Florida. Therefore, Mrs. Falsone sat down and wrote every school in the states of Florida, Georgia, and Alabama begging them to let us compete against them. She knew we needed to run against the best to get scholarship offers to major colleges and it worked. I was awarded a two-year scholarship to Auburn University in Auburn, Alabama in 1979.

Coach Bill Katz was the women's coach at Auburn and he was the funniest, fastest talking person I had ever met. He was Jewish with black curly hair, a heavy New York accent, tough, but with a great sense of humor. Out of all the coaching role models I ever experienced, he was the one from which I learned how to be a focused winner. He was a true salesman and it worked because I, along with several athletes from all over the United States, signed with Auburn that year. We became the first female track athletes to receive full scholarships to attend the university. I went on the become the first Black athlete to be crowned Auburn's female athlete of the year and I was, if not the first, one of the first Blacks to graduate from the school of social work.

Coach Katz was the total opposite of Mrs. Falsone. He was fire and yelled, screamed, cursed, and was demanding. It didn't bother me because the people in our family acted just like him so I loved him even when he was mad and somehow, he pulled the best out of us. He was unapologetically driven to win and so was I. Auburn was a small country town and I don't think they were prepared for Coach Katz. He talked fast and cursed more. Eventually, Auburn parted ways with Coach Katz and we were given a coach the complete opposite of him. He was timid, small, quiet and didn't exude confidence.

I was now driven to be great. I realized that even though I didn't love running track, I hated losing more. I went to the men's coach, Mel Rosen and begged him to allow me to train with him and the men's team. Coach Rosen was considered one of the best men's sprint and hurdle coaches in the country and I wanted to be the best. I got to work with him for maybe a month that fall and then he told me I had to go workout with the women's team. I later found out he felt women were not as serious as men and he had no desire to ever coach any woman, including me. Heartbroken, I went over to train with the new women's coach and needless to say, it didn't go well. He couldn't handle my strong personality and I couldn't understand his weak personality.

That fall, I trained harder than I had ever trained before and got to the indoor nationals. In the preliminary round of the 300-meter run, I broke the United States record while a freshman at Nebraska, a future Olympic legend by the name of Merlene Ottey, broke the World Record. The first call I'd made was to grandma telling her how I had broken a national record. She didn't sound excited but worried and ask me how much it would cost to fix it. Grandma didn't care about track or awards. She cared about me getting an education. I had promised her I was doing great in school and I would take care of her and told her not to worry. Now she would never see me graduate from college.

My grandmother was to be buried in Mississippi next to my mother and unlike my mother's funeral, grandma's funeral was a cross between a sad movie and a comedy show. Everyone had benefitted from her generosity and therefore, thought that she was rich and that they should all profit from her death. Gerettia took charge of all the arrangements, which, immediately pissed off all my other sisters, and before long, there were fist fights, cursing outs, and overall dissension. It was an all-out war with my sisters, Cherry and Alice, both accusing Gerettia of stealing grandma's money. Every fight that occurred in our family was started by Cherry and this was no different. Here we were at grandma's funeral and my family was actually having a fist fight over money. It was crazy. All of this anger over money and everyone forgot about the loss of our grandmother. Finally, so angry they yelled, "F—k Brady! I hate her! She ain't never done shit for me." It got so bad they angrily announced they weren't even going to attend the "damn funeral."

The next day when the car arrived to take the family to the church, to our surprise, there stood both Cherry and Alice dressed and ready to go. When we got to the church, it was packed. Everyone was worried about me fainting and falling out like I did at my mother's funeral four years earlier, but I didn't have time to react. Before the funeral services were fully underway, both my sisters, Cherry and Alice, starting screaming grandma's name (Brady) and crying. Gerettia and I looked at each other in shock and I think had it not been at a funeral, we would have burst out laughing. We buried my mother my senior year in high school and now in my senior year of college, we were burying my grandma. The two most influential women in all our lives were now gone.

School and college had always been a safe place for me. It's where I often felt the most secure. Now as my graduation approached and without my grandmother by my side, I felt adrift for the first time in my life. I was lost with very little money, no job, no home to go back to, and no clue on what to do next.

On the day of my graduation, not only did my brothers and sisters come, but to our surprise, my father actually came. My family was so proud of me. I was one of a handful of Blacks among a sea of white graduates. I stood out, not for being dark-skinned, but for how loud my family cheered and catcalled as I walked across the stage. True to my family's history, just as I sat back in my seat, they were calling for me to sneak out because they didn't want to sit through the other hundreds of graduates who had to walk across the stage.

I had never noticed how few Blacks went to Auburn University in 1981 but after noticing how few were graduating, I comprehended how significant it was that I had graduated. I had become our family's first college graduate and it was something to be proud of, at least in that moment. After the graduation, my dad proudly handed me an envelope. I thanked him for coming because he had not attended my high school graduation. I never expected to see him at my college graduation but when I opened the envelope and saw it contained only $200, I laughed. In five years of never giving me one dime, he thought giving me $200 was something special. As I packed my bags that evening, I could not tell if my heart hurt my mother and grandmother, if it was because I was leaving the security of college, or if I was terrified of the unknown that waited for me once I drove off that campus for the last time.

CHAPTER 6

Exhausted, physically and mentally, I sat alone in the middle of the floor silently crying. It had been a long summer since my graduation from college. Since then, I had moved from Auburn back to Tampa where I discovered all the money I had put away over my last year had been used for "emergencies" by my younger brother. I was broke and living with him and three other guys. I got two jobs right away. One job as a long-distance telephone operator at Bell and the other as a part-time bookkeeper for Orkin pest control. I literally hated both jobs and at this time, Gerettia, who was still living in California, suggested I move back to the west coast. I sold my car and gave the money to my brother and boarded Greyhound to California. I was working three jobs, as a publication coordinator, as a part-time secretary, and as an aerobics instructor at a local gym. After working for over a month, I figured I would be able to afford an apartment or a car but not both. The thought of having to continue to work three jobs and then decide whether I wanted to live alone without a car or live with my sister with a car made my present circumstances unbearable.

As I sat on the floor, my heart felt as if it would explode in my chest and I felt defeated by life. I went into survival mode after the death of my mother and my grandmother, so I had not had time to mourn the loss of either. Now as I sat on that floor, I called out for my mother and longed with every fiber of my being for my grandmother. *Why had they left us?* I begged, not prayed, for their help. As I rocked back and forth, tears streaming down my cheeks, I didn't know who to call for help so I spoke to them. Gerettia had been generous in allowing me to live with her and use her car. I didn't have the heart to tell her how lost I felt. She, like the rest of my family, endured our challenges without complaining or breaking. I couldn't let her see me broken. I had given myself permission to cry but only alone in silence. It had been the only way I knew how to release the fear and anger gripping me.

Out of sheer desperation, I opened my address book and searched for someone to call. My book was full of numbers, yet there was not one name I trusted. As I closed the book, Mrs. Falsone's name came to mind. I opened the book once again and found her number. As I dialed, I prayed to my mother to please send someone who could help me. As always, Mrs. Falsone answered the phone in her chipper voice, "Well hello kiddo, how's it going?" I'm not sure if she even finished her sentence before I literally erupted in a sobbing mess of dialog about my present circumstance. Mrs. Falsone patiently listened as I went on and on until finally, I ran out of words and tears. Her response to almost an hour of venting was simple.

"Ahh, don't worry about it. You are a smart girl so just go back to school and get your master's degree to buy time until you can figure out what you want to do with your life." I thought to myself, *I have poured my heart out to you and this is your advice.*

I tried to explain the timing and how impossible it would be to secure a spot in August when most schools were set to start classes the following week. No matter how much I objected, she responded with optimism. In the end, she literally demanded I call the operator and get the number to colleges to call first thing in the morning. She suggested I start with Florida State University because both she and her husband had graduated from there and she believed they might have an opening for a graduate assistant. She was convincing because by the time I hung up, she had me thinking it was actually possible to get into graduate school and get a scholarship in only a matter of days.

I slept well that night armed with several phone numbers to colleges and a renewed determination to enroll in school in a week. The next morning, just as Mrs. Falsone had instructed, I made my first cold call to Florida State University. I took a deep breath knowing I had no other options. I cautiously dialed the first number and to my surprise, the head coach answered the phone. We spoke at length about the position and my background and although the position had been filled, instead of issuing a firm and final "No," he suggested I call The University of Tennessee. Again, I reached the head coach at Tennessee, Terry Crawford, and again I didn't meet their needs but she referred me to another school and after about six different referrals by six different coaches at six different schools, I was finally connected to Coach Sam Bell at The University of Indiana in Bloomington, Indiana.

Coach Bell, along with several other major universities, said they'd love to have me but would not be able to get me into school until January. It made sense to them but they didn't understand I could not survive until January. I needed urgent and immediate help. Finally, he suggested I call Coach Stolley at Indiana State University. Just as I had done in previous calls, I referenced the last coach during the call. I told Coach Stolley that Coach Bell had recommended I call him. We spoke in detail and he said if he could get me in school, he would take me right away and promised to call me back the next day. After six hours on the phone, I had a possibility. Needless to say, I stayed awake all night in anticipation of his call the next morning.

True to his word, he called me early the next morning to tell me he had spoken to a friend in the physical education department and if I could submit all of the paperwork and be there by the following Monday, they would admit me. I had no idea where Terre Haute, Indiana was and I didn't care. I had four days to get my paperwork in and be there for a meeting with the department. Although I had no background in physical education or physiology of exercise and anatomy, I could have majored in "nothing" and been happy. I accepted the job on the spot and went to work getting everything in place. By that Friday, everything was submitted and on that Saturday, my sister dropped me off at the Greyhound Bus Station to go back to college.

I knew nothing about coaching, Indiana State, Coach Skip Stolley, or what a master's degree required. I only knew somehow, someway, I would make it work. I was told I would coach both the men and women's sprints and as the bus plowed down the road, I was at peace. Although I had never coached before, failing was not an option and whatever I needed to do, I would find a way to make it work. If I could learn how to press clothes in the tenth grade, I could surely figure out how to coach at twenty-two. Besides, it's not like I had other options. This was a sink or swim decision and I had long ago learned that if drowning is not an option, you swim.

The beginning of my coaching career didn't stem from a passion for sports and coaching but out of desperate circumstances and the need to survive.

SPEAK IT

"My beliefs created my truth and through the process of believing my truth, I began to live through it. As I experienced truth, I spoke it and speaking my truth created the anchors for achieving. I anticipated many life experiences and now, I was better equipped to handle the circumstances. Because of that, I became very action-oriented."

CHAPTER 8

The last thing I ever expected to do after graduating from Auburn University was find myself seated in another classroom. As I reviewed the syllabus for one of my classes at Indiana State, it dawned on me, I had no idea about the class or the major. Being a student had always been effortless for me so surely, I would find a way to master the course requirements for the program. I listened as my new professor, apparently reveling in his reputation as one of the toughest graduate level professors in his department, literally bragged about failing students. I listened attentively as he spoke, hoping he would give me a clue as to what the class was even about. He mentioned our need to have taken undergraduate level courses such as Kinesiology, Physiology, and Anatomy among several others. I never took any of the classes he mentioned. I had been a social work/psychology/speech major in undergrad now in graduate school, I was faced with courses such as kinesiology, physiology and a bunch of other "ology's" I didn't have a clue about. As he continued to brag, he finally concluded by proudly proclaiming that it was a rarity for any student to earn a B in his class and A's were darn near impossible.

He asked us to raise our hands if we had not taken several of the required undergraduate courses he'd rattled off and to my surprise, I was one of only three people to raise their hands to verify we had not, in fact, taken the required courses. He told the three of us we needed to drop his class immediately. No one moved, no one spoke. *There is no way I am dropping this class or any class, for that matter.* I had been awarded a two-year graduate scholarship and taking too many extra courses would require an additional year. Nope, I was staying.

The next class session, I walked into the room and took my seat looking around to see if the other two students had returned. They had not. As soon as the professor walked in, he glanced my way, probably surprised to see me sitting there. He walked from behind the podium, strolled casually around the room, until he finally stopped at my desk. Leaning into my face as though he intended to whisper, he proclaimed loudly, "Ms. Kearney, did I not tell you to drop this course?" I answered, "Yes, sir." He then asked, "Then Ms. Kearney, why are you still here?" I told him I couldn't afford to drop the course and was willing to take my chances. He tried to impress upon me his truth—I would surely fail. I, in turn, impressed upon him my truth—I had no other options. I was staying. Frustrated, he walked away, hands behind his back, shaking his head as if I had sentenced myself to death by failure.

As the semester wore on, everyone started to struggle. We were told to create study groups but of course, I was not invited to join a group and when I inquired about participating, they all claimed to be full. I was the only person of color in the class but that was not the reason they rejected me. It was because if the teacher thought I was too dumb for the class, then inevitably, I would be the weakest link in any study group. There was only one other student who lacked a group. He was a tall, lanky white guy with thick glasses, a briefcase, wrinkled clothes, and the reddest pimples I had ever seen, covering his entire face. I approached him and asked if he'd like to study together and he shyly replied, yes. We ended up becoming great study partners and although he wasn't the most organized or smartest student, his briefcase more than made up for his shortcomings. It did not contain papers and books, instead it was filled with an abundance of snacks. The entire semester, we studied hard together but more importantly, we ate well each session.

At the end of the semester, as we entered the classroom for the last time. Our professor stood in his usual position at the podium, a stern expression on his face. He held up the final grade sheet, again reminding us that he rarely gave out B's and it had been well over three years since he had awarded anyone in his class the coveted "A" level grade. I closed my eyes and prayed for a C. He walked around as he spoke before stopping once again in front of my desk. I thought, *Here it comes, he's going to announce with pleasure to the entire class just how right he was and that I had indeed failed his class.* My heart pounded in my chest as he leaned in closer. I braced myself for the dreaded "I told you so" speech. Instead, his voice softened as he turned and walked away from my desk announcing, "One student has exhibited the excellence, fortitude, and hard work demanded to succeed in my classroom. Although this student was one point shy of the requirements to receive an A, I am, for the first time in the history of my class, awarding one point for effort, moving this student from a B+ to an A. I couldn't believe my ears as he turned around to face me and said, "Congratulations Ms. Kearney, you have the rare honor of earning an A in my class."

As the class stared at me in total disbelief, I exhaled, more relieved than excited. I didn't make an A because I was smarter than everyone else. I made an A because I knew I wasn't as prepared as everyone else, thus I worked harder. I'd worked harder than I had ever worked before. I even devised a study program consisting of studying class material the first thing each morning, in between classes, and again each night. The thought of failing never crossed my mind. What the teacher said during the first class never crossed my mind. I had no time to focus on who or why others in the class didn't want to study with me. I had to stay focused on succeeding. Along with figuring out the graduate program, I also had to learn how to coach.

I began graduate school and coaching at the same time and I equally knew very little about either. Although I was succeeding in the classroom, I grappled with the demands of coaching. I had a few great coaches and role models in the past, but none prepared me for Coach Skip Stolley. He was a neatly dressed, short, blond-haired, matter-of-fact kind of guy whose presence commanded respect. What he lacked in people skills, he more than made up in organization. He demanded I be organized and prepared each day of each week of each month. He instructed me to give him a written copy of my weekly workouts for all the male and female sprinters and then to explain to him the focus of each workout. He talked about training cycles, micro cycles, and macro cycles and he might as well have been speaking a foreign language because I had no clue what most of that meant at the time. He challenged me more as a coach than my professors challenged me in the classroom. But no matter how hard I tried, I found it difficult to keep up with his demands. I couldn't study for his questions because I had no clue where to find the answers to questions I barely understood. I had to find solutions and although I didn't know much about religion, I had started praying for help.

Shortly after I began praying, Coach Stolley unwittingly hired the answer to my prayers. Bernie Dare was brought on shortly after I was hired to coach the team's throwers and jumpers. He was a bit eccentric. He was a tall white guy with wild hair and thick glasses, bearing more resemblance to a mad scientist than a coach. Yet, I discovered he was brilliant and at that time, I needed brilliance. We became friends right away and although his behaviors were a little odd, he was the perfect teacher. He had a bad habit of belching and farting right in the middle of us running together or carrying a casual conversation. This combined with his tendency to ramble on in conversations made me have to focus more on his words than his actions. He might have been a bit annoying to most people, but he was a lifesaver for me. I listened to everything he had to say and read everything he wrote, even if I didn't understand what the heck he was talking about or what I was reading about. He was a better teacher than any of my college professors. I had never met anyone like him. He was open and shared his knowledge and presented all the information in ways that made the complex seem simple and I thrived on simple.

He even saved me from walking in the snowy, rainy weather of Terre Haute by selling me his beat-up, patched up, brown Oldsmobile for $200. I gave him the first installment of $20 (because I was so broke, $200 was impossible to pay at once). As he handed me the car keys, he proudly proclaimed that although it wasn't much to look at, it ran like new. He was right. I drove that car for two years all across the country and never had a problem with it. I would never forget his kindness and promised him I would hire him if I was ever a boss somewhere.

I might not have known how to coach when I started at Indiana State, but within a year, I was a coach and I mastered the art of *what you don't know, fake it until you learn it.* The team was comprised of about fifteen or so male and female athletes from the toughest parts of the country such as Gary, Chicago, New York, and New Orleans. They were talented, under developed, and competitively tough, just like me. I was only twenty-two when I started coaching, which was practically the same age as the athletes. Most of them even lived in the same dorm as I did. I quickly learned to separate being friends in the dorm and being a demanding coach on the field. On the field I was taskmaster and coach but in the dorm at night, we would hang out. I didn't realize how rare it was for a female to coach male athletes because I knew nothing about coaches or coaching. From coaching both genders, I learned to never make distinctions between coaching a male and a female athlete. I coached to win and therefore, I equally demanded they all work hard, be disciplined, tough, and run to win. The athletes trusted me from the beginning because I cared about them both on and off the track. By the end of our first year together, not only did I manage to finish the year as an honor student, meet the demands of the head coach, but all the athletes I coached had personal best performances. Some even qualified for the first time to compete at the National Championships.

By the second year, I was more seasoned and came into the year excited. I knew at the end of the year I would have to have a job, so I needed not only to focus on winning on the track and completing my degree but I needed to figure out how to make a living. As autumn turned to winter and December break came upon us, I panicked. I was on track to graduate by June of 1983 with a master's degree in Adaptive Physical Education. Except I didn't know what to do with my degree and I had no job offers and no option of staying. As I packed to leave for my final Christmas break as a student, I sat in my dorm room and again prayed for help and guidance on what to do next. Not even two days after that prayer, I received an unexpected phone call from our head coach giving me a number to call. He wanted me to speak with someone by the name of Gene Jones from Toledo University in Ohio. I had no idea who he was or how he knew me, but I called. Coach Jones was nice and from his voice and conversation, I determined he was Black. Apparently, I had come highly recommended and he was calling to offer me a job as his assistant coach at the University of Toledo. I was ecstatic. Although I had never thought about coaching as a career, it was a job and I needed a job.

My excitement quickly became a dilemma as Coach Jones explained the job's starting date was not at the end of the season in June, but in the beginning of January. Moving wasn't my concern. My family and I moved so often growing up that moving was second nature. However, for the first time, I was conflicted about a move. Of course, I needed a job. But I knew my athletes needed me and I wanted to finish grad school. I loved my team but in the end, I needed the job. I accepted the position from Coach Jones, thanked Coach Stolley and the staff, made arrangements with the graduate school in Indiana to finish my degree at Toledo, said my goodbyes to the team and left Indiana for good. Toledo became my new home.

I knew nothing about Ohio or Toledo and similar to Indiana, I really didn't care. It was a job and I needed a job badly. Coach Jones told me the starting salary was $8,000 a year. I was actually happy. I had no idea just how little $8,000 a year was until I started looking for an apartment in Toledo. I ended up only being able to afford an efficiency apartment where the bed pulled down from the wall but I loved everything about it. It was my home and I was grateful to have a place to live and a job. I promised myself that I would not let Coach Jones down.

Just like Indiana, Toledo was snowy, icy and cold as heck. I hated the cold and I hated the snow, but I discovered I actually loved coaching. I had never thought about coaching as a profession but now it was all I thought about. Coaching gave me a chance to help others reach their goals on the track and in the classroom. I had always felt the coaches at Auburn University had very little belief in female athletes and in me. I felt cheated as a student and an athlete because they never motivated us to be the best. While competing at Auburn University, only coach Katz pushed us and after he was released, no one urged us to be the best again. Because I never got to know just how good I could have been, I was determined to see that every athlete was given the attention they needed to succeed.

Coach Jones was also the perfect head coach for me to thrive under. He pretty much left me alone to do what I wanted to do, how I wanted to do it. He trusted me and the more he trusted me, the harder I worked. He not only allowed me to coach both the male and female sprinters, he gave me the responsibility of recruiting high school athletes. I had always been shy and a bit reserved but recruiting literally forced me out of my shell. I had to call and make home visits to people I had never met before. I approached recruiting the same way I had learned to coach, I recruited to win. The better the athletes we recruited, the better our team would be. On the track and in recruiting, we competed against the bigger schools like Ohio State, Purdue, Michigan, and Michigan State and slowly we began to win a few of the battles although they always won the war. The more the other universities beat us, the more determined I was to defeat them. Coaching fit me like a glove and I had finally found that something in life that excited me—WINNING!

I adored coaching and I loved Toledo but by the end of my first full year, I would make a mistake that would change my outlook on being at Toledo and coaching. I had been at Toledo for a year and a half and the women's team had never had an athlete qualify for the Collegiate National Championships and our goal was to be the first to do so. We got really close to the qualifying marker in the 4x400 relay, but someone knocked the baton out of our hands just steps before crossing the finishing line and we were disqualified from the race. The race had been so exciting Coach Jones gave us permission to go to the last chance qualifying meet in which teams who had failed to meet the standards were provided with one more race to try to qualify. He did his research and found the closest and most competitive meet for us to attend. He simply told me the time the meet started and that it was being held at Penn.

The following Friday, my assistant coach and I loaded up six female athletes to make the trip to Penn. We drove late into the night to get there and all along the way, my assistant coach, a young Black female from New Jersey, kept pleading with me to allow the team to have dinner and spend the night at her mother's home in New Jersey. I knew her offer was our best option as we had very little money and no hotel reservations. Still, there was no way she could have known it was absolutely out of the question for me to stay at someone's home overnight. Not only was I not going to place myself in that situation, I was responsible for the safety of each of those athletes. I could never explain to her my fears, developed after being molested by my sister's boyfriend while staying overnight. Staying in someone else's home was a non-starter. Although my fears were unwarranted in the situation, the memory and fear associated with staying overnight had nonetheless lodged itself deep within my mind.

Once within the city limits of Philadelphia and without a saying a word, I pulled the van into a shady, cheap rundown hotel off the highway. As we piled into the one or two cheap rooms, my assistant's cold glare was noticeable and understandable. I could not blame her. We were staying in a two-bit hotel, eating cheap food, and her mom probably had a big beautiful house with a feast prepared for us. The room was so dirty, I sat upright in a chair all night preferring that to sleeping on the nasty bed or even worse, the dirty floor. Needless to say, I didn't get any rest that night.

The next morning, although my assistant was still a bit upset with me, the girls didn't seem to mind as everyone cheerfully loaded the van to get to the track meet. After a cheap breakfast, we headed for the Penn Relays stadium in Philadelphia, determined to make the qualifying standard for the National Championship. As we approached the stadium, expecting to see the hustle and bustle of a big track and field meet, we instead found silence and locked gates. We tried every entrance and finally we bumped into a grounds keeper who informed us that there was no meet scheduled on the track. I was shocked, dumbfounded and just flat out confused. We all silently retreated back to the school van and without hesitation, I looked for a pay phone. It was 1984 and cell phones were not available yet. This wasn't a small mistake. It was a major mistake and I needed help. I found the nearest telephone and called Coach Jones.

I told him we were in Philadelphia and there was no track meet scheduled for the track and all I heard him say was, "What are you doing in Philadelphia?" He went on to inform me that the meet was not in Philadelphia, the meet was in State College, Pennsylvania at Pennsylvania State University. My mind raced back to our conversation about the last chance meet and I remember him saying he had booked us to run in a big meet at Penn. That's all he said, "Penn" and Penn to me meant the famed Penn Relays Stadium in Philadelphia. He didn't give me any more information, nor did I ask any questions. Coach gave me the time of the race at Penn State and I thought it couldn't be that far away and we could try to make it. But as my assistant pulled out the atlas map, we quickly realized it was about a four to five hour drive and there was no way we would arrive in time.

The team stared at me through the van's windows while I paced the pavement. I couldn't have lied about the situation even if I wanted to because I couldn't come up with a good enough excuse for the mistake and the only option, other than telling the truth, was to blame it all on Coach Jones. Needless to say, I chose to tell them the truth. I explained the mistake to them and they were gracious in their understanding. While I apologized repeatedly, they told me they should not have needed a last chance meet and promised to make the standards early the following season. As we headed back towards Toledo, they talked excitedly about the upcoming year. They were forgiving and even though I should have felt better, I didn't. I laughed and sang with them on the drive back, but my heart was heavy. I had let them down.

In my head, I tried to blame Coach Jones for the mistake, but I knew deep down inside it was my fault. Once everyone was dropped off and for the rest of that weekend, I tried to justify or figure out how I had made such a terrible mistake. The answer was clear. I had not bothered to get all the information needed. Instead, I made assumptions and those assumptions were not based on facts. They were wrong. I had been wrong. The mistake had not only cost the young ladies I coached an opportunity, but I had wasted the university's money.

As I arose early the following Monday morning along with my fears, I had to face the music for my mistake. I didn't want to lie or blame anyone other than myself, but I also didn't want to admit the truth of my stupidity. As I walked into my cubical sized office, the first person I ran into was the women's athletic director. She was an amazing woman who I had admired during my year and a half stay. She asked how we'd done at the meet and I told her we did not qualify. It wasn't a lie but it wasn't the entire truth. I waited for the next question, assuming she'd ask for details and knowing it would be at that point, I would have to confess but the question never came. Instead she patted me on the back and said we would get it next year. She then asked me to follow her to her office saying she needed to talk to me. As she closed the door behind me, she expressed how impressed the administration was with my efforts. I was being promoted. I would still be the assistant coach for the men's team but I would now be co-head coach with Coach Jones for the women's team. Along with the promotion, I would be given a raise to $12,000 a year. She told me the promotion to co-head coach would probably rank me as the youngest head coach in NCAA Division I Collegiate history at age twenty-four. I should have been overjoyed but I wasn't. I didn't deserve to be rewarded after making such a major mistake. I did my best to sound excited. Why shouldn't I be? I was given a raise, a promotion, and a compliment.

When I left her office, I didn't head for my own office. I headed home. Although I had gotten away with it, I still felt awful and stupid. Totally unworthy of such an honor. I had come to depend on prayer and even committed myself to reading the entire Bible from cover to cover. I didn't know much about God and had decided if I was going to pray for help, I had darn better learn who and why I was praying. Somewhere along the way, I became reassured that God knew me and loved me. I had joined a church at the suggestion of one of my athletes and had been re-baptized as we were all baptized as children but never attended church service. All I knew about God for sure was that when I prayed, I usually got what I had prayed for. I went home, sat on my sofa/bed and prayed. For what, I didn't know, I just prayed. Suddenly, it hit me. I no longer wanted to be at Toledo and I couldn't explain to myself why not. So, I prayed for guidance and in a way, that prayer signaled the beginning of the end for me at Toledo.

I am not quite sure how it all came about but I was called about a job opening at The University of Tennessee in Knoxville for a women's assistant sprints and hurdles coach. I was not only told about the position, but was encouraged to apply for it. Before applying, I informed both Coach Jones and my athletic director and they discouraged me. I especially didn't want to disappoint Coach Jones after he had given me such a great opportunity at Toledo and he chose not to tell anyone in the administration about my mistake at Penn. He could have cost me the promotion but instead, he supported me all the way. They explained, and they were probably right, that I was too young, not experienced enough to coach at such a noted program as The University of Tennessee, and taking a job as an assistant, when I was now the women's head coach, would be a step in the wrong direction. They were not aware how much my mind was already made up. I was ready to leave and the call from Tennessee was an answer to my prayer. I listened to them fully knowing I would apply regardless of their dissent. I couldn't explain it to them and although they were right, Tennessee was probably going to hire someone older and with more experience but I had to at least try.

I applied for the job and was shocked to learn I was selected as a final candidate and was scheduled for an on-campus interview. Terry Crawford had recently left Tennessee and moved on to the University of Texas and ironically, the coach replacing her at Tennessee was from Penn State, the very place I was supposed to go to for the last chance meet a month earlier. I had never met him, but in the back of my mind, I wondered if he knew about me driving to the University of Pennsylvania and not to Penn State. Once I met him, everything happened quickly. I was beyond eager to be on the campus, so much so, I forgot about everything except my intention to get the job. The new head coach gave no indication I was being seriously considered for the role, so I made it my mission in the one day I had on campus to convince him and the administration that they needed to hire me.

While there, I met with the new head coach, Gary Schwartz, the women's senior athletic director, Joan Cronan, and several others. Although I was only twenty-four, I had the confidence of a twenty-year coaching veteran. He had already decided the person he intended to hire, and that person didn't look like me. He told me it wasn't personal but he wanted to hire one of the former athletes from the men's team from Penn State. Coach Schwartz was a middle-aged, white, male coach intending to hire an even younger, white male to coach a team whose main point scorers were Black and at a university who was at the forefront of the women in athletics movement of Title IX. The athletic director insisted he hire me, a Black female, but he insisted on hiring his guy. As I drove home to Toledo from the interview, I once again prayed. I desperately wanted the position at Tennessee.

After returning home, I waited day after day for a call and after several days of waiting, concluded I didn't get the job. Regardless, I had to get myself together because Toledo had done nothing but provide me with great opportunities. Just as I started shifting my thinking to remaining at Toledo, the phone rang and on the other end was Tennessee offering me the job.

I spoke with my administrator at Toledo and she offered me more money to stay but she had no idea, I wouldn't stay, regardless of what she offered. I considered the fact that the Tennessee head coach really didn't want to hire me and by staying at Toledo, I would be my own boss, but it was to no avail. I had accepted the position and more importantly, had already mentally left Toledo.

As I loaded my car to depart, I didn't head to Tennessee. I drove in the direction of fulfilling a promise I had made to myself. After the mistake of not knowing enough information, I had decided I would never not do my homework and learn what I needed to know. I needed to learn more about coaching the sprints at a higher level and I knew nothing about coaching the hurdles. I looked up the results of the best hurdlers in the country and the top three teams in the country and called the coaches from those universities to set up a time to talk with them about coaching. During my second season at Toledo, I had purchased a brand-new car. It was a small, sporty Nissan Pulsar. I could afford either an AM/FM cassette player or air conditioning and I had chosen music. I drove from state to state in the heat of the summer learning something from each coach I met. I traveled for an entire month, eating, sleeping, and working from that small car without air conditioning and it was more than worth it. As I finally made my way to The University of Tennessee in the fall of 1984, I had learned more in one month than I had in my three years of coaching.

As I entered the campus in July of 1985, I was ready, or at least that's what I thought. I had learned from and been embraced by some of the most successful and powerful coaches in the country. I was not only equipped with information but their phone numbers with promises to provide help if I called with a need. I was determined to never again allow my own personal issues and hang-ups to impede another's success.

When I look back on my decision to coach at Tennessee, I should have paid more attention to a few clear facts. The new head coach was transparent about not wanting to hire me. He had been forced to do so by the women's athletic director who felt Tennessee needed diversity. My enthusiasm overrode any fears and I didn't heed the warning. In the long run, that would cost me.

CHAPTER 9

I hadn't gotten on campus good before I made my first mistake at Tennessee. While recruiting at Toledo, I had signed a 6'2" sprinter by the name of Lana Rice from Oakland, California. The previous summer I had driven from Ohio to California to recruit her. I met her grandmother and immediately fell in love with her. She reminded me of my own grandmother. I can't tell you if I signed Lana because of her talent or because of her grandmother. Either way, it didn't matter because before leaving their house, I not only had her signature on the scholarship papers, I had made a promise to her grandmother that no matter what happened on the track, I would ensure Lana would graduate from college. In Lana's freshman year at Toledo, not only did she struggle in the classroom and on the track, but she and I didn't get along at all. It was a total disaster and when I left that summer, the easiest thing to do would have been to leave her in Ohio. But I knew that without me riding her, she would surely fail. I had two options, to keep my promise to her grandmother and take her with me to Tennessee or to break my promise and leave her in Toledo.

My first decision was a mistake on paper but the right thing to do in my heart. I vowed to take her with me to Tennessee. Now, all I had to do was convince the new head coach and now my new boss to give her a full scholarship. I tried to convince him to give her a scholarship, but he refused. I then begged and pleaded without success. Running out of options, I finally flat out lied about how dedicated, talented, and great she was. I insisted so hard for so long I think he finally just relented to my pressure and signed her merely to shut me up. This might have been the first time I was unhappy about winning anything because I knew she would not be able to handle the competitive demands of Tennessee. Not because she lacked the talent, she wasn't dedicated or passionate about running. Over the next three years, each time she competed and failed, I sensed him glaring at me afterwards. I was wrong for bringing her to a team of that caliber, but he would never understand my agreement with a beautiful, elderly Black woman in Oakland. I had no choice. I had to bite the bullet on a bad decision. I believe if he could have fired me for that one decision alone, he would have, and I wouldn't have blamed him.

The good thing was, although Lana never scored a point for the team, she eventually graduated around 1987 or so. I hadn't seen her since then until 2017 when we happened to bump into each other at a speech I gave in Oakland for an amazing group of women called Black Women Organized For Political Action (B.W.O.P.A). We hugged and I was amazed at the beautiful and intelligent gentle woman whose smile lit up the room. We talked and laughed together and although I had never regretted my decision to take her to Tennessee, I now knew why God had led me to keep her on track. She was not a successful athlete but had gone on to earn a master's degree and was enrolled in divinity school working towards a doctorate degree. The decision to keep Lana was solely based on a promise and having grown up where people made and broke promises with ease, I had been disappointed too often to ever want to fail anyone else by not being true to my word. This philosophy would be both a blessing and a challenge for me for the rest of my career and life.

Even though I had made the worse decision upon my arrival at Tennessee with Lana, I had also made the best decision of my life by doing my homework in preparation for my coaching debut at a higher level. I was prepared and excited to meet the team. I knew how great the team had been, having read about their history and top National team finishes as well as always having several Olympic level athletes on the team. When the former coach, Terry Crawford, left to take over at The University of Texas, she not only took her entire staff but she transferred most of the talent from Tennessee's team to Texas. The team was a shell of its former self. All that remained were a few good athletes and one of the most talented incoming freshmen class in the nation. I had always had a great relationship with my athletes but when introduced as their new sprint and hurdle coach, they looked more than disappointed. They were angry. They trusted the old staff and had been left without the option to transfer as freshmen. Thus, they were stuck for at least one year with me, a no-name coach who looked more like a teammate than the person in charge. I had prepared myself with as much knowledge as I could, but I had failed to prepare mentally to handle the rejections and disappointments that the young team of jilted athletes felt after being left behind. It would be more than an uphill battle to gain their confidence, let alone their respect. I quickly realized Tennessee was going to be much tougher than expected.

The women's athletic department held its annual all-staff meeting each year at a country club. I looked forward to the event because I knew some of the most powerful and successful women coaches in the country were on Tennessee's staff. The administration had called for more diversity on the staff and within the women's department but it didn't register how badly it was needed until we all gathered for the annual retreat. I recognized I had been hired to fill a racial void and a gender demand and as the staff gathered to leave for the retreat, I saw that although most of the staff was female, I was the only Black staff member. It never dawned on me to ask about diversity because there had always been a large portion of the athletes who were Black, so I'd assumed the department would reflect that diversity. It did not.

As we drove deeper into the rural areas of Knoxville and approached the club, it was clear I would not only be the only Black member of the athletic department, I would likely be the only Black person at the golf club. I still felt safe because as a member of the staff, I was sure no one would bother me. Boy was I wrong.

I was the only Black person present not serving food or cleaning something. I dwelled in my room when the staff wasn't meeting. For two days, I managed to stay within the safety of the group. The men's and women's programs and athletic departments were totally separate so the meeting was only attended by the women's sports. Tennessee was at the forefront of the title IX battle for equality and it was well represented with powerful, driven, strong, and knowledgeable, yet down to earth, women. The two people who impacted me the most were the legendary women's basketball coach, Pat Head-Summit, and the athletic director, Joan Cronan. I sat back each meeting to listen and learn from the best in the United States. I took more notes during our two-day retreat than I had taken the entire summer traveling to meet with track coaches across the country. I had been given the honor of representing greatness and I took pride in being a part of the "Lady Volunteer" family. As I scanned the room during the last sessions, I vowed to not only be a great representative for the university, but for women and minorities. I could not help but feel as though I was part of something bigger than just winning. I was now winning with a purpose.

By the end of the retreat, I had gotten comfortable with everyone and actually forgot about being at an all-white golf resort. On the last night, we met for dinner at the club restaurant. As the dining area filled with mainly white, male golfers, I was reminded that I was definitely in rural Tennessee. As the evening wore on, several of the male diners became intoxicated. One of them began to joke around with our staff. At first, he was funny, but as time wore on, he turned his focus to me. The more comfortable and drunk he got, the more disrespectful he became, and his jokes gradually evolved into insults. Finally, everyone at the table became uncomfortable and tried to get him to move on but he wouldn't. After several more minutes of light insults, someone told him his jokes were a bit racist. He seemed shocked and offended and then said the most stupid, most racist thing I had ever heard. His defense was, "I didn't mean no harm. I'm just joking around. I love Niggras. I grew up with Niggras. Hell, I was raised by a Niggra nanny." *Did he just say that? Are you kidding me!*

As I sat, thoughts of my mother crossed my mind and I understood how helpless and scared she must have felt entering that police station in Mississippi to pick me up after I was caught stealing. Her words echoed in my head and I could still hear the pain in her voice as she told me how they could have killed me for talking back. How my parents could have found me hanging from a tree or never found me at all and not one of them would hold any guilt in their hearts for doing it. In that moment, I felt her fear. I was hurt and angry but too afraid to speak up. Finally, I couldn't take it any longer and did the only thing I had the power to do. I walked out of the restaurant and stood on the deck. I looked into the darkened skies searching for my mother in Heaven. I cried out to her to come and rescue me just as she had done in Mississippi. The worst feeling I have ever felt is not of fear, but of helplessness. I stood outside on the patio, helpless and alone.

As I cried, the athletic director walked out and stood in front of me. I waited, expecting her to give me a hug and say something nice to make me feel better. She instead said, "This is just the way things are. If you're going to work at places like Tennessee, Bev, you had better get a tougher, thicker skin and you better get it fast or you are not going to survive." At the time, I considered her words heartless and insensitive. But as she went on to explain the difficulties women in sports faced and how extra difficult it must be for Black women, I understood. It may not have been the words of compassion I thought I needed to hear, but it was what I needed to learn, not only to survive but to succeed.

That night, alone in my hotel room, I reflected on everything that had happened since my arrival at Tennessee. I had to be stronger and most of all, never cry in public again. It projected weakness and I was anything but weak, even my tears made me stronger. If I ever needed to cry again, it would be in private.

* * *

As fall training got underway, I was a bit overwhelmed considering the sheer quantity of freshmen and potential challenges with the upperclassmen. One day, the head coach asked if I would retrieve one of our late returning athletes from the bus station. The student had competed for her native country, Jamaica, at that summer's "1984 Olympic Games" which was held in Los Angeles. I was more than willing. Not only was I meeting an Olympian but I would be her coach. Ilrey Oliver was tall, slender, and dark-skinned with a big, bright smile. We got along from the moment she arrived, and as I dropped her off at her apartment, I knew it would be a great season with her as a member of our team.

After two or three weeks of rest, Ilrey was due to join the team, which had already started their fall conditioning program, but she never showed up. When she was absent on day three, I figured something was wrong. I called but she did not answer the phone. I sent messages by her teammates but still no answer. Finally, after a week of not showing up for practice, I pressured her roommate to tell me why she wasn't attending practice. Ilrey had told her she assumed I was the team manager and when she found out later that I was the actual coach, she told them she would not be coached by a female, especially me. I couldn't believe it and I actually laughed. I had been discriminated against because of the color of my skin but now I was being told I wasn't good enough to coach her because I was a woman. I sent the message via her roommate that if she didn't show up for practice the following day, I would rescind her scholarship. I didn't have the power to take back her scholarship and even if I could I wouldn't, but I had to find a way to scare her. It worked because she showed up, visibly angry, but she showed up. After practice, we had a long talk and I asked her to give me a chance. I promised her that I would not let her or her teammates down and I would help them reach every goal they had and more. She agreed and from that point on, Ilrey and I bonded. Within my three years at Tennessee, Ilrey and I connected both on the track and off. She not only kept her word and gave me a chance at coaching her, but I kept my word to her as she broke national and world records.

Ilrey proved to be one of the easiest challenges. The freshman class was another story. They were understandably hurt and resented the fact that the coaches they had signed to compete for were gone. They felt lied to, betrayed, and stuck at Tennessee with coaches they neither knew nor wanted. They were respectfully cautious of me as a person and as a coach. The great relationships I had shared with my athletes in the past no longer existed and I knew I would have to work hard and have successes to earn their trust and respect.

For the first time, it was not the head coach who questioned everything I did, it was the athletes and even some of their parents. They were always respectful but their constant questions and apparent lack of faith in me only made me push myself harder. I didn't take it as an insult, I regarded it as a challenge. Some of the athletes were driven but none were as driven to be great as the freshman hurdler, LaVonna Martin, from Dayton, Ohio. She pushed me every day with her questions, her knowledge, and her passion.

I used the study habits I had developed in grad school and applied them to coaching. I researched and read everything I could get my hands on about the 100-meter and 400-meter hurdles. I watched film of the athletes from Team USA until I met my next great mentor and friend, an age group coach from Denver, Colorado by the name of Tony Wells. He might have coached youth track and field but he studied international athletes. It was Coach Wells who provided me with articles and film of the best athletes, not only in the United States, but the world. I watched the films almost every night and if there was a seminar or clinic, I went. I even called a couple of coaches again just to make sure I was on the right track. I was not going to let what I didn't know cause someone else to fail.

During my time as a student athlete at Auburn, there were no organized study halls or tutors available for female athletes and most of my former teammates never graduated. As I entered coaching, my vow was not to allow any student to forget why they were in college. I had drilled into my own head that the key to success was to be found in books and education. Not graduating was never an option. Neither was graduating in a major you didn't like. After talking at length with Ilrey about her major and why she was off track on getting her degree, I realized she had been mislabeled. They had assumed because of the language and dialect of her native country, Jamaica, she was not smart. They felt she needed prep college courses to prepare her for her required courses but she did not. After working with her to re-organize her classes and major, I took a deeper look into the needs of the team based on academics. I surmised that without structure, they would find it difficult to keep up with the demands of their courses. Armed with this new information, I spoke with the head coach about creating study sessions three nights a week. I monitored the study hall in a classroom and after a while, Coach Summit approached me about sending several of her students. Eventually, the department saw the benefits and needs of hosting study hall and I was grateful to no longer be solely responsible for its management.

At the end of my second year, we were a Top 3 team and setting school, conference, and national records as well as putting on world-leading performances in some of our events. Coach Summit called me into her office but this time it was to request my help understanding and addressing the unique challenges Black athletes faced. Coach Pat Head Summit, one of the best coaches in the country, in any sport of any gender, wanted assistance from me! She needed to get up and down the court faster and asked if I would work with a few of her young ladies on technique. I'd admired Coach Summit from the moment I met her. It was not only her disarming sense of humor that had made me comfortable around her, but her unrelenting drive for greatness and perfection attracted me the most. She was unapologetic about her goal to always be number one. Her efforts and conversations, in a way, gave me permission to be driven, to desire to be the best. I adopted her ability to strategize in preparation for competition, her attention to detail, and her high demand for hard work and discipline. But her humility in seeking help taught me the most about being successful.

Always seek help from those who know what you need to know but don't, became my motto.

On the track it was a different story. The head coach and I were two very different people. He was laid back and I was extremely ambitious. Over time, our opposing styles began to clash. We were always nice and respectful to each other, but I could tell I annoyed him. I pushed to do whatever I felt needed to be done to win and he would push back. It all came to a head when we, as a staff, made one of the biggest mistakes we could have made. Our top athlete, slated to win that year's NCAA indoor national title in the 60-meter hurdles and possibly break the national record, decided she wanted to run at the USA Indoor Championships which were being held in New York. The problem was that the USA Championships were being held in New York on a Friday but the SEC Conference Championship was being held in Baton Rouge on Saturday and Sunday of the same weekend. She and her parents believed she could do both but I did not. The debate continued all the way up to the week of the meet and on Wednesday evening, they were still trying to convince us to allow them to compete in both meets. I spoke to the head coach one final time and he said he agreed with me and I went to bed with the final decision having been no, it was impossible. The double meet participation itself would be hard, but the travel between New York and Baton Rouge in a day only to race again would be a mental and physical suicide mission. I had fallen asleep when the phone rang that night. On the other end was the head coach calling in the middle of the night to tell me he had again spoken to the athlete and her parents and he now agreed with them to do the double. I was told to pack because the athlete and I would leave the next day. For a minute, I suspected I was dreaming or at least, wish I had been. As predicted, it was a total disaster. Not only did she not do well at the USA Indoor Nationals but the SEC

Championships were an even bigger disappointment.

I had one week until the NCAA Indoor Collegiate Championships. Training her would be difficult because not only was she tired, physically and mentally, but losing both races had shaken her confidence. She and I worked hard to get her recovered from that double and although she was the number one hurdler in the nation at the NCAA Indoor Championships, she fell over the last hurdle in the final. As she fell, I perceived it as my own failure. I was devastated. I had told myself I would never make a decision or not know something that caused any harm to any of their dreams. I hated failing myself but I hated failing others even more. I wondered what I could have done differently.

Devastated, I went behind the bleachers, because I knew better than to cry in public, and found a corner and allowed the tears to fall freely. After a few minutes, someone placed a hand on my shoulder. I turned to find Coach Bibbs, the men's head coach at Michigan State University. Coach Bibbs was an elderly Black coach who had mentored me since I had met he and the women's coach, Karen Dennis, during my time at Toledo. They had been the only two coaches who talked to me while I was there and slowly we had developed a great relationship. Both were mentors that celebrated and congratulated my successes and advised and encouraged me throughout my defeats. It was only fitting that Mr. Bibbs would be the first person to find me. He said he knew I would take it hard and had decided to check up on me. He was right, and I was glad to see him. He took my hand and looked into my teary eyes and then gave me the best advice I could have ever hoped to hear.

"Now honey, you listen to me. You're doing a great job and you are a great coach. These young ladies need you. Athletes like that Vonnie girl are rare because they are winners, but now they ain't gonna win all the time. Sometimes they are gonna lose! But I guarantee you athletes like that will always win way more than they will ever lose, but they gonna lose sometimes."

After he spoke, he leaned over and gave me a big wet kiss on the cheek. Coach Bibbs sometimes forgot to put his teeth in which made his kisses extra special because they were wet and filled with love. Over the course of my career, he would always give me one of those special wet kisses on my cheek laughing, as he'd announce me as the only other woman with whom his wife would allow him to share one of his wet kisses.

After we parted ways, a new energy came over me. The warrior rose within me and I marched back into the stadium ready to finish like a champion. My upbringing taught me that no matter what happens or how bad things get, you keep it moving. I wiped away my tears and went to work. As the meet wound down and as teams lined up for the final event of the Championship, the women's 4x400 relay, I was ready, and we were ready.

The best team on the track was from the University of Texas and we decided we were going to beat them in an epic battle on the final event, the mile relay. I told the team to go silent, no talking, no eye contact, no laughing, no nothing. I even told them to sit in a corner while the other teams warmed up and we waited until thirty minutes prior to the race to do our warm-up. Vonnie, having just had one of the worst meets of her athletic career, completed warm-up with tears still in her eyes. Ilrey, who had set the school and national record while winning the 600m, sat quietly without even warming up. When one of the Texas athletes, Juliet Cuthbert, also from Jamaica, asked her why she wasn't talking, she replied, "We are going to kick y'all asses today and if you get the stick in front of me, I'm going to run you down and if I get it ahead of you, I am going to bury you." They both stopped talking. Juliet was the anchor for Texas and Ilrey was ours. Juliet was faster but Ilrey was stronger. They were equally tough.

The energy inside the stadium increased as everyone lined the track to watch what was sure to be an epic display of talent between two powerhouse relay teams. As the gun went off, the two lead off legs battled handing the batons they carried to the second legs of the four-person relay and we managed to maintain contact with the pack of six teams. As Vonnie got the baton on the third leg, we were closer to the back of the pack than to the front. She may have been hurting inside, but she ran through the pain she carried in her heart and put us back among the leaders. Texas had pulled away from the pack just as they were handing off for the anchor legs. Cuthbert took off and widened the gap even farther on the field, pulling away from everyone, including Ilrey. Ilrey, taking her time on the small 180m track began to make her move, gradually overtaking the other teams leaving only Texas ahead of her. As both Juliet and Ilrey raced towards the final turn into the homestretch of the race, Juliet became fatigued while Ilrey ramped up into second gear. Neither would back down and both drove towards the finish line with Ilrey overtaking Juliet, not only winning the race, but also setting a new school, collegiate, and world best in the relay. Vonnie and I could not change what happened to her in the hurdles, but winning that race went a long way in the healing and recovery, more than tears could have ever helped. Vonnie not only went on to win several national championships in the 100-meter hurdles and the USA Outdoor National Championships, she would eventually win the Olympic Bronze Medal in the 1992 Olympics.

The events of that day taught me a basic truth. Although everyone loses from time to time, the great ones don't get consumed by their losses. They find the strength to push through to achieve greater victories. No matter what happens, stay in the fight until the fight was over. That's the sign of a true champion and the athletes from

Tennessee demonstrated they were in fact champions. LaVonna Martin, Ilrey Oliver, Robin Benjamin, and the freshman, Carla McLaughlin, took a stand and made a statement about who they were individually and who we were as a team by not only winning the championship relay but by placing amongst the top three teams in the nation.

When I entered my third season at Tennessee, I was exhausted. Although I was developing into a top-notch coach, maintaining my mental sanity was a challenge. When something needed to be done, I was the one who'd jump in and take care of it. Like when Adidas wasn't sending the team equipment we needed, I took care of it. I helped restructure our agreement with the company and that's how I discovered the head coach was getting paid by Adidas and had a personal equipment allowance while the assistants got nothing. I helped the manager when they needed it with uniforms and laundry. I ran study halls, I recruited, I did whatever needed to be done to help keep the team running at the highest of levels. My intent was to help but I think I was so strong-willed, driven, motivated, and capable, it probably drove my head coach crazy. I tried to determine where to draw the line. I was still young and an assistant coach, but I was put in a position to do head coaching duties, especially when it came to discipline and structure. When the athletes realized the head coach would overrule my decisions, it became even more difficult to keep everyone on track, especially myself.

When my hair began to fall out, I had to accept the truth. I needed help. The more responsibility I was given and the more successful I was at completing tasks, the harder things got. The tougher things got, the harder I had to work. Until finally, things got so bad I wasn't sleeping or eating. Even though I needed help, I didn't know where to turn. After giving it serious though, I went to the only coach I thought I could trust, an elderly white male coach from Auburn University, Coach Mel Rosen. When I called him, he was so nice, it made it comfortable to tell him what was happening and how much I found myself struggling to balance being an assistant.

He seemed to listen intently as I told him of the pain, hurt, and confusion that existed within me. I told him how most of the responsibility for the day-to-day activity of running the program had fallen on my shoulders and that the head coach appeared uncomfortable dealing with the strong personalities on the team, especially the Black athletes. I explained that whenever I made a decision, the athletes or parents would go over my head and the head coach would reverse the decision. I told him how underappreciated and unwanted I felt and how uncomfortable things had become. I didn't know what to do to make things better.

Finally, I was done talking. I waited for his advice as to how to move forward without upsetting my boss, but also without letting the program needs go undone. All he said was give him a day or so and he would get back to me. I was confused. I had poured my heart out and all I got was silence and a promise to call back later. I hung up the phone exhausted and disappointed. It didn't take a return phone call to find out what he really thought and what he had done to help me.

The very next day, as I walked into the weight room, which was located downstairs in a dimly lit basement of the athletic building, I ran into the men's head coach, Stan Huntsman. He was a short, older white man who looked more like a weight lifter than a distance coach, but he was a legend in the sport and I admired him. He had always been nice and helpful to me and he and the head coach were great friends. He stopped me and without warning, cautioned me saying, "Bev, you're doing a good job here, but you need to be careful what you say. Gary is a good friend and he gave you a great opportunity to be here."

My heart dropped to my feet as he went on to say how he had gotten a call from Coach Rosen expressing to him my displeasure and unhappiness. I couldn't believe it. I had trusted Coach Rosen. He went on to say, "If I ever hear about you not being loyal to Tennessee's program, or Gary, I will personally make sure you not only lose this job, but that you have trouble getting jobs in the future." I tried to explain why I had called Coach Rosen but it didn't really matter so I kept my conversation brief and moved on. When I saw Coach Huntsman again, he acted as though our conversation never happened. To him it wasn't personal but for me, everything about it was personal. Once again, I was in a position that hurt more than helped. The last thing I was trying to do was be disloyal and yet that's how the information was relayed and that's how it was perceived.

The very next morning, I called Coach Rosen and asked why he had felt the need to call Coach Huntsman. He said he didn't know what to tell me and assumed Coach Huntsman would be in a better position to offer advice and guidance. I made up my mind right then that I would never trust personal information with anyone. I wasn't mad at Coach Huntsman. He was only trying to protect his friend and the program but I was angry at myself for trusting Coach Rosen. I figured if Coach Huntsman knew then surely Gary knew what I had said and it only served to make the situation more uncomfortable.

I grew up with two of the toughest women I would ever know, my mother and grandmother. I watched as my grandmother got up each day, tired and worn out at times, put on a maid uniform and went out and scrubbed and cleaned other people's toilets and floors until well into her seventies. I watched my mother vomit violently after having gone on a weekend drinking binge. But even with the worse hangovers, she'd get up every Monday morning and go to work in a hot laundry, pressing clothes. They taught me that regardless of how hard things had gotten on my job, I had to go to work and do my best. I had to cut my hair into a short Anita Baker type of style due to the breakage. I was barely sleeping and I was not happy. I worked hard all day and sat alone in my apartment at night worrying and crying. Yet, every morning I'd wake up, lace up my shoes and go to work just as my mother and grandmother had done their entire lives.

One positive that happened off the track and outside of recruiting was finding out my brother had completed his tour of duty in the Air Force and had decided to move to Knoxville. While I was in college, I had always helped him financially with school and after I graduated and could no longer assist him, he had to make a choice. Joining the military allowed him to earn VA benefits to attend college. He was now enrolled at the University of Tennessee in the business program and doing well. Being in the military matured him in expected ways. He had learned discipline, leadership, and it provided him with the stability he needed to figure out what he wanted to do with his life. Because he was doing well at Tennessee and was so proud of his big sister, I didn't have the heart to tell him how miserable I had become. Just knowing he was there somehow gave me comfort.

By that point, my routine was to go to work, do my best, come home, and either cry or pray or both. I prayed over the course of several months. I prayed silently and then began to speak with God out loud. I had to impress upon Him how much I needed guidance and help. I was lost and desperately trying to find myself. I had not grown up in a religious family and although we were all baptized at Sweet Home Baptist church in Bude, Mississippi, we rarely, if ever, attended church. Throughout my journey, somewhere, I found God and approached religion as I had done with anything else I needed to learn. I studied all aspects of God. I figured if I was going to pray and trust God I needed to know God. Finally, the answer I sought each night came to me, and with it came immediate relief. The answer was that either I had to find another job coaching or find another career. Either way, it would be my last season at Tennessee.

By making a choice, I had removed the option of staying and therefore, as my third year came to an end, I scheduled an appointment to speak with the athletic director. I walked into her office and asked for assistance. I explained that things were no longer working out and although I loved and appreciated being at Tennessee, it was time for me to move on. My only request of her was to provide me with a recommendation if she knew of any open coaching positions. Prior to our meeting, she must have gauged my unhappiness or figured I would come to her since the head coach and I weren't on the same page. Either way, she didn't seem surprised. She asked if there was any way I would stay and I told her no. It was in the best interest of the program that I move on. She assured me if I stayed, there would be changes but I didn't want to infringe upon the head coach's leadership any longer. There was nothing that could be done to fix it. Before I left her office, we hugged and I thanked her for the opportunity and reiterated how much I loved being a member of the Lady Vol athletic family. She promised she would help me in any way possible.

Within a month of our conversation, there was a job opening for a head women's coach at Auburn University, the University I had competed successfully for as an athlete and against as a coach. The prospect of leading my old school to victory was exciting and I intended to talk to Coach Rosen again because I knew he was heading the search committee. I waited until the final meet of the season, the ~~1986~~ 1987 USA National Outdoor Track and Field Championships. Before I could schedule a time for us to talk, I saw him in the lobby of the hotel. It was kismet. Every fiber of my being believed God had planned our encounter. I approached him and began to talk about the job opening at Auburn. He sat silently as I spoke to him about how great of an asset I would be to the program and how much I loved the university. After my sales pitch, I popped the question, asking him to please put in a good word for me with the school. I asked if he would give me a recommendation for the Head Women's Track coaching position at the University. He looked at me thoughtfully as he gently and calmly explained, "If I were you, I wouldn't bother to apply to Auburn." He went on to explain that Auburn wasn't ready to hire someone like me. He didn't even have to explain because I knew what he meant. Auburn would never hire a Black coach or a woman. I was speechless for a moment before re-gathering myself and thanking him for his honesty. I walked away upset and hurt. I thought the position was the perfect job for me only to be told I wasn't good enough because of the color of my skin and my gender. To add insult to injury, I later found out Auburn hired a white, male, high school track coach who had no college coaching experience. It was clear. I loved Auburn but Auburn didn't love someone who looked like me.

Some twenty-five years later, in 2004, I was honored to become the first African-American and only the second female in history to be honored with Auburn's Lifetime Achievement Award. At the ceremony, it was Coach Rosen who delivered a speech on my behalf and in his speech, he said one of the biggest mistakes he had ever made at Auburn was not hiring me in 1987.

Not long after being turned down for the Auburn job, someone told me the University of Georgia had an opening for a women's track head coach. This time, I decided not to go out on my own to get the position. I went back to ask for help from the athletic director, Joan Cronan. She again asked me to reconsider leaving and when she realized my mind was made up, she stayed true to her promise to support me. She not only told me she would call Georgia on my behalf, she also told me the University of Florida was in the process of hiring a new women's head track coach as well. Within a week of our conversation, I received calls from both universities.

The telephone interviews went well and both Georgia and Florida seemed impressed with my experience. I waited to see if I would make the final cut for an in-person, on-campus interview. The first callback came from Ann Marie Lawyer, the women's athletic director at the University of Florida, letting me know I had been selected as one of the three finalists to be interviewed for their position. In the back of my mind, Coach Rosen's words that "they would never hire someone like me" played out. But I could not change being Black and female and neither attribute should be an obstacle. At the age of twenty-nine, I was a coach, a darn good one at that, and I intended to provide it during the in-person interview.

Shortly after receiving the call from Florida confirming my candidacy, I received a call from the University of Georgia. The women's athletic director informed me that although they were quite impressed by my telephone interview, she and the women's director from Florida were friends and they had decided not to pursue the same candidates so I would not proceed in their interview process. She actually wished me well. I didn't think it was possible to feel good about rejection, but I felt happy as I hung up the phone. Excited, I turned my focus on my only option, Florida. I researched as much as I could prior to my interview but mainly, I prayed. For the first time in months, I slept peacefully. The next day, I told the head coach and the athletic director at Tennessee about my scheduled interview at the University of Florida.

The more I saw of the University of Florida's campus during my interview, the more I loved it. For some reason, it gave me a sense of comfort and I was determined to make it my permanent home. Towards the end of the process, I was seated before the hiring committee for one final interview. Up until that point, I had not faced any racial or gender-based questions and thought maybe it was not an issue at the school. The committee began by informing me of the difficulty of the academic demands at the university and for that reason, they believed the school would be better served as a distance powerhouse than a sprint program. They were implying that the Black inner-city kids, sprinters and hurdlers, would not be able to handle the academics of Florida. Then I was hit with the following question, "Coach Kearney, do you think you will be able to recruit and sign white athletes?"

Without hesitation, I responded, "That depends." Looking puzzled, they asked, "That depends on what Coach?"

"If they can help us win a National Championship, I will. If they can't, I won't recruit them. But if they can, I will get them signed." I figured my reply sealed the deal. In my mind, talented, motivated, and driven student athletes always outweighed race, events, and religion, but nothing outweighed academics. I went on to explain that if any future student athlete had a sincere desire to graduate and be among the best, I would have no problem convincing them that Florida was the place to be.

After returning to Knoxville, I waited and waited for a response. The hours turned into days and the days turned into a week, and still no answer. As I waited for the call, doubt crept into my head and the reality of being at Tennessee another year was an unbearable thought. Not only had I emotionally checked out, I think the head coach had checked out on me. Georgia had already filled their position, and Florida was the only alternative left.

Just as I was sinking into the bottomless pit of self-doubt, the phone rang. It was Ann Marie Lawyer of Florida. I tried to act causal as I said hello, but my heart was beating so loud I swore for sure she heard it over the phone. My mind drifted in and out of her conversation, waiting to hear the final outcome as she talked about the long process and apologized for the length of time it had taken them to reach their decision. The longer she spoke, the more my mind wandered and I barely heard her offer me the job as the new head women's track coach at the University of Florida.

I was overjoyed and accepted the position on the spot. She went on talking but I had long stopped listening. I was too busy doing a silent happy dance. She explained that their main hesitation in hiring me had been my age and lack of experience. I would be the youngest head coach in the history of the University of Florida's athletic program and with that she offered me a starting salary of $28,000 a year. I could not have cared less about the size of the salary and would have taken the position even if she offered $20,000 a year. I desperately needed the opportunity. As she continued to speak, her point became more pronounced. She was impressing upon me that they were in fact, taking a big risk in hiring someone so young. Knowing they had taken a chance on me only made me more determined to succeed once I got there.

In August 1987 at the age of twenty-nine, I became the youngest head coach and only the second Black head coach, behind Lacey O'Neal, in any men or women's sport in the history of the University of Florida.

As elated as I was about leaving Tennessee, the track staff at Tennessee was even as happier. The administration was sad to see me go and up to that point, the only athlete I had told I was leaving was Ilrey who was now like family. While she had been extremely happy for me, the other athletes had mixed emotions. Some were probably pleased at my departure, others may not have cared one way or the other, and some were visibly sad. Then there was one athlete filled with anger. The next year would be the Olympic year and she was upset I was leaving her during the time she felt she would need me most. She took my departure as a betrayal, later telling me her thoughts were, "Is she fucking serious? Does she realize that the Olympic year is coming up? Why would she do this to me?" Although I truly understood her perspective, what she could never grasp was my lack of choice. It was simple. She had to remain at Tennessee as it was her senior year and I had to leave.

Ilrey, on the other hand, who had just graduated, debated whether to follow me to Florida to train for the Olympics or to stay in Tennessee and work towards her Master of Education. In the end, she remained in Tennessee and eventually decided to give up running. Ilrey was talented but never loved track. She ran because she adored the University of Tennessee, Lady Vols, her teammates, and me, as both a friend and a coach. She visited Gainesville often and eventually ended up with two master's degrees, became a professor at Knoxville College, and married a police officer.

Tennessee took me through the deepest, darkest, and most tumultuous moments of my career. But unbeknownst to me, those challenges prepared me for what was to come next. I would not have been able to face the tribulations of Florida or achieve any success, had it not been for the lessons I learned while at Tennessee. Primarily, learning how to have thick skin.

CHAPTER 10

Not long after arriving on the University of Florida's campus, they held their annual coaches meeting and unlike Tennessee, it consisted of both men's and women's head coaches. The only assistant coaches in attendance were from the football program. As I surveyed the room, sure enough I was by far the youngest coach in the room and aside from a Black football assistant coach, I was the only Black coach in the room. There were several Black administrators in attendance, which was quite unusual and probably why I felt comfortable in my new environment.

I sat through several hours of the meeting, quietly listening and learning but mainly, in disbelief that I had a seat at the table amongst such great coaches. As I surveyed the room, I noticed the football coach kept biting his nails and I recall wondering if it was merely a bad habit or if the pressure of coaching at Florida was that bad. As I continued listening, Florida's expectation of greatness and winning was at the forefront of every word spoken. The other sports and their coaches were quite accomplished and I knew I was meant to be in that room.

As the meeting began to wind down, the athletic director asked if anyone had any questions. Everyone, including me, wanted to get out of there, but before I knew it, my hand went flying up. I hadn't said much the entire time, and now I had a question. When called on, I asked which sport team had the highest grade point average. Everyone looked puzzled as to why, of all the questions, that was mine. Who cared? I cared. During my interview, they stressed how difficult it would for me to recruit sprinters, basically Black students, into the program because of the academic demands. I had not forgotten it, and as the director of academics informed me that the top teams were usually golf, tennis, and gymnastics, a bigger thought crossed my mind.

In the past, I had big dreams and kept them to myself. But for some reason and before I could stop myself, I blurted out, "We are going to win that award." I rarely let people know what I was thinking, and it was too late to take it back. I had declared to the entire athletic department and in front of every head coach, that within the next couple of years, women's track and field would win the award for having the highest team GPA in the department. It was so quiet you could hear a pin drop. No one knew what to say.

Historically, sports that were predominately Black hadn't fared well academically but I intended to change that. People had underestimated me all my life and I was determined not to underestimate any of my student athletes. Giggles and whispers gradually moved throughout the room as they realized I was dead serious. That's when I overheard one of the football assistant coaches whisper rather loudly, "She might want to worry about keeping her job because if she don't win, she won't have one." I know I should have just shut up. I had apparently said too much already, but nooo, not me. I instinctively responded, rather confidently, "If they aren't eligible, you can't win, and I intend on winning on the track and in the classroom."

The room remained quiet until the athletic director broke the silence by declaring the meeting was officially over. I walked out of the room and thought to myself, *Why didn't you just keep your thoughts to yourself.* I couldn't take it back, so I added to my list: recruit top athletes, win conference championships, win the national championship, and now, win top team academic award. This time, the pressure on me was not being applied from the outside. I was heaping extra demands on myself.

Soon after the meeting, I was pulled aside by the only Black administrator I had ever met at any of the institutions at which I had attended or worked. His name was Keith Tribble. He was a tall, handsome bear of a man whose personality was even larger than his physical presence. I stood before him, anticipating the scolding and lecture he was about to lay on me for my comments in the staff meeting. To my surprise, he put his large arm around me, displayed the biggest most disarming smile I had ever seen and said, "That's why I insisted they hire you." He would later explain to me the true process of my hiring and how he had been scouting coaches for months for the position and at one of the track meets, he noticed me coaching my team. He told me how impressed he had been by my intensity and focus and that my athletes seemed to match that intensity and they were fierce competitors. He said he knew that's the type of person Florida needed to create a winning program.

He explained that I was one of three candidates who had been interviewed for the position. The women's side wanted to hire a white, female candidate by the name of Dorothy Doolittle and the men's side of athletics wanted to promote the white, male assistant men's coach by the name of John Webb. Neither side would agree to hire the other's choice thus they found themselves literally at an impasse. They only had two viable options. They could start the candidate search all over again or they could choose to compromise by hiring the third candidate interviewed—me. I don't know what Keith told them, but thankfully they chose to comprise by hiring me.

From the time I was hired at Florida, track coaches across the country, primarily white male coaches, whispered and gossiped that the only reason I had been hired was to fill a double minority void. Basically, they felt the reason they had not been given the job was because of their race and gender. They were white and male and I was Black and female. To be honest, they were partly right. I had been a compromise hire but none of that mattered much to me. If for once in my life, the color of my skin and being a female worked to my benefit, I was thankful. Far too often, race and gender had been held against me and rarely worked for me. It didn't matter to me why or how I had gotten the job. What would matter the most is what I intended to do with the opportunity. I couldn't afford to fail. I was in a historical position and my success or failure would not only be a reflection of me, it would influence how predominantly white institutions viewed people of color and women. All the talk, the doubt, and underestimation of my ability only served as a greater motivator to succeed.

The first year at Florida felt like a rollercoaster. We had very little talent, no organization, and we were not a team contender at the conference or national levels. We were in one of the toughest conferences, the Southeastern Conference or SEC, with not only some of the best coaches in the country, but also some of the toughest competitors in the nation.

My first task was to recruit more talent in all event areas, especially in the sprints and hurdles. I recruited so hard and well that within my first two years, it garnered the attention of some of the most powerful track coaches in the country, but not in a good way. At one of the high school summer meets, where all the college coaches recruited, most of them no longer talked to me. I was accused of cheating in the recruiting process. They not only stopped speaking to me, they actually reported me to the NCAA and conference offices for breaking recruiting rules. I had never broken a rule and in fact, I had read the NCAA guidelines, learning as much as I could. What I wasn't sure of, I'd always ask questions about for clarification. After that summer, as long as I was losing, I was embraced. But once I started succeeding, I was viewed as a threat.

If that wasn't bad enough, Track Florida, one of the most powerful age group track programs in the country, was located in Florida and I believe the club was funded and sponsored by Macintosh computers so it had a lot of money and a lot of clout in the state among high school track and field student athletes. One of the top recruits from the state of Florida who'd recently signed a scholarship letter to come to Florida, told me she was not going to run summer age group track. When I inquired as to why she'd decided against it, she told me about a letter she had received from Track Florida informing all female high school athletes in the state of Florida that if they signed with the University of Florida women's track program, the club would not support them for summer track meets. Again, they accused me of negative recruiting because no one could figure out how we were signing the best athletes in the country. My methods were not a secret. It was called hard work. When they attacked me, I was more prepared because as Tennessee had taught me, I had toughened up and developed thicker skin. I had no intention of taking the abuse, running away, or even crying. I decided to tell my administration and let them handle it. I asked for the letter and submitted it into the head of the athletic department. Once he read it, all he said was, "You don't have to worry about this. I will take care of it." I am not sure what action they took but I never had another problem with the track club.

During my first year, I had been told to keep the old staff except for one member. He was a young, enthusiastic Black male sprint/hurdle coach who had been at the University on a graduate assistant scholarship but had failed to take any classes. He failed to enroll in school once again, therefore, I was instructed to release him. So, not only did I have to maintain staff I didn't know, they also demanded me to fire someone that happened to be the only Black person on staff. When I talked to him, he was perturbed with me and I couldn't blame him. However, I offered some advice. Not having his degree would cause him to be placed in the lowest paid positions for the rest of his career and he needed to finish his education. Over the years, that young man ended up being like a little brother to me and not only did he eventually get his degree, some years later, he became the head coach of both the men's and women's track and field and cross-country programs at the University of Florida. Mike Holloway became one of the most successful coaches in the history of the University of Florida and in the nation. He overcame his obstacles and achieved greatness. But at the time of his firing, neither of us were happy about the circumstance. It was the first time I ever had to fire anyone and although I would go on to fire many people throughout my career, it never got any easier.

My first year coaching at Florida was akin to someone removing the lid off of a pressure cooker and the hot steam hit hard. The former coach was a distance coach. Since he was no longer there, I was not only coaching the sprints and hurdles, I had to take over the distance program until I could find a replacement. Knowing nothing about coaching the distance events, I contacted my eccentric buddy, Bernie Dare, who had recently left Indiana State. Fortunately, he gave me a crash course in the distance events.

For a short time, I enjoyed coaching the distance team until we traveled to Madison, Wisconsin, in the dead of the winter to compete in a major cross-country meet. I was freezing and could barely function. I glanced around at the other distance coaches from the other schools and they were moving around in light running gear all over the course. Me, I was balled up in a corner wishing they would run faster so we could get back to the Sunshine State. Right then, I knew I needed to hire a distance coach more suitable for the conditions and needs of the team.

As the cross-country season ended, I'd developed a solid bond with the team. But then, things went crazy. It wasn't the funny crazy either. It was the "lock 'em up" kind of crazy. One day, a young man from the men's team burst into my office. He was visibly shaken, and before I could ask any questions, he opened the door wider allowing one of my cross-country team members to enter the room behind him. I didn't have to ask what was wrong because as soon as she started talking, I knew.

With the weirdest look on her face, she proclaimed, "Coach Bev is God. I am God." If that wasn't enough, she then proclaimed that her boyfriend was God. I barely had time to look up and ask a few questions before I saw him bolting for the exit door leaving the two of us alone in the office. I causally picked up the phone and dialed the women's athletic director's office while still engaging my young athlete in conversation. I did my best to explain my reason for the call without letting the athlete know I was calling for help because I was scared shitless. I don't know if the young man had gone to her office as well or if she was able to deduce from my coded conversation that I was in trouble but she asked, "Do you need help?"

"Yes, of course. Thank you and hurry." In no time, people arrived to take the student to see a medical professional. She was subsequently admitted to the hospital until her parents arrived to take her home.

Next, I learned about eating disorders. I had no idea people intentionally ate too little to control their weight and there was a name for it, anorexia nervosa. It is when an individual severely restricts the amount of food they eat or they stop eating in order to limit their daily caloric intake. There was also bulimia nervosa, which is when a person eats or binge eats and either induces vomiting after eating or misuses laxatives, diet aids, diuretics, and enemas to control the effects of food consumption. All my life I knew people who ate too much and were overweight but never too small and ate too little. The distance team was riddled with eating disorders. They were starving themselves to death thinking it would make them better. As a result, I had to actually suspend about five or six athletes from the team until they got healthy. Within the first five months of my head coaching career, I had to fire someone, have someone committed to a psychiatric ward, remove athletes from the team for eating disorders, learn how to coach new events, and bond with a whole new team, staff, and administration. I might have grown up in craziness, but this took crazy to a different level.

With the problems the team faced and the pressure I put on myself to ensure we were all successful, I uncovered that the staff I had inherited did not meet the demands of the program. After releasing them, I tried several different people until I ran across the best assistant I would ever hire. I didn't find her, she found me. LaTanya Wynn was a young Black woman who called me every single day about the graduate assistant coach position. Her persistence won me over. If I could write a manual for what a great assistant for any position in life would be, I would use her attributes as the model. She was loyal, enthusiastic, confident, tough, outspoken, funny, hardworking and independent. LaTanya was a jumper who competed for and graduated from the University of Virginia. She was the perfect fit. Her motto was, "What's my name? Wynn! Because all I do is WIN!" She, like me, didn't care what others thought. She was focused on winning and together we went about the business of creating a powerhouse program.

It is easy to brag about my best hire but my worst hire, by far, was a best friend. He wasn't the worst hire because he was a bad person or a bad coach. He was the worst because of bodily functions. Bernie Dare's somewhat eccentric behavior didn't fit in at Florida. When I first started my career at Indiana State, I'd promised him that if I ever got a head coaching job, I would hire him. Being true to my word cost me again and I should have realized what was bound to happen considering he was working for the forestry department somewhere in a mid-western state at the time. Whereas LaTanya was a lifesaver, Bernie was sinking the ship. Let's be clear, he knew his stuff. He helped me figure out how to train athletes, but he had no connection to them. I got complaints from the administration, track meet officials, other coaches, and the athletes. They all mentioned the same thing, his bodily functions and his short shorts. He had an unbearable habit of farting and belching loudly and it drove people crazy. That, along with his short shorts which highlighted his man parts, was the reason I had to fire him. Yep, when all was said and done, I had to let him go because of shorts and farting. We remained friends after his departure and he has always been available when I need him. He is a great person with a big heart and an amazing mind but he wasn't a college coach. He was perfect in every way, except when it came to actually coaching, he didn't connect well with people.

I had finally put together a great staff, but more importantly, we had amassed the most diverse and talented team in the country. As challenging as my team had been at Tennessee, my Florida team was the most coachable and enjoyable team I would ever have. They were intelligent and tough. They never backed down from anyone or any challenge. Within the first three seasons, they not only won the academic team of the year award at the University of Florida, they set the conference record for the most SEC All-Academic student athletes from one team. Our team had moved from the bottom of the top 20 teams in the nation to one of the top 3 teams.

Right as we were working our way to becoming National Champions, tragedy stuck in such an unimaginable way it not only shook the University of Florida at its core, it sent shock waves throughout the entire collegiate system. They simply labeled it, "The Gainesville Murders" and they called him the Gainesville Ripper. The story was so outrageous, Hollywood created the movie, "Scream," based on the murders.

It was August of 1990. As the freshman students moved into their dormitories and apartments, a man later identified as Danny Rolling, went on a killing spree in Gainesville. As news of the murders spread throughout campus, everything went on lockdown. The athletic department was so frightened, the coaches gathered team members in their homes. Parent, students, and the faculty were all afraid. The entire university shut down for about a week. As many as twenty athletes stayed in my two-bedroom condo for several days. Having them in my condo was how I discovered they lacked certain basic skills like boiling an egg. One night, I was awakened by an explosion. I jumped up and ran downstairs to find about six of the young ladies staring at the boiled eggs they had placed in the microwave. They wanted to make sure the eggs were cooked all the way through. We all doubled over laughing which broke the tension.

During that tragedy, we banded together and even after they caught the guy, we continued to look out for one other. The staff and I developed a policy—everyone's responsible for each other's wellbeing and safety. If someone went to a party or went home for the weekend, they had to notify either a staff member or teammate once they made it home safely. The team bonded so much during that time, those bonds became lifetime bonds, and they are still looking out for each other.

On the other hand, the coaching world was so competitive that other university coaches used the murders against Florida, telling recruits it wasn't a safe place to attend school. Yet despite the negativity, we still signed more great athletes. Seeing the tactics of other coaches showed me what not to do. I decided to never negatively recruit against another school. I would not police other programs and I turned a blind eye to whatever they were doing. My focus was defeating them on the field of play. Trying to win by hurting others was a cheap win and I intended to beat my competitors fair and square. Time had taught me the only way to shut down critics, was by winning. I wanted to win on the field of competition, not by actions taken in administrative offices.

CHAPTER 11

It was a dark, chilly evening as LaTanya and I were returning from a brief recruiting trip to a small town somewhere between Baton Rouge and Shreveport, Louisiana. We had decided to leave a day early for the SEC Indoor Conference Championships, which were being held in Baton Rouge, that weekend. After flying into Baton Rouge, we rented a car for the drive to see the recruit. After a successful visit, we headed back to Baton Rouge to meet the team. As we drove down a sparsely lit two-lane highway, in the distance we spotted glowing flames that lit up the night's sky. Slowly, we realized we were staring at the white hoods of the Ku Klux Klan. We were in the middle of nowhere, stopped in the middle of the road, staring at a Klan march heading our way.

I immediately turned off the lights. There were only two options, the first being a suicide run where we would gun it and try to drive around them. The other option was to hide. We had just passed a broken-down gas station with a lot of old cars surrounding it. I turned around with the lights off and hid amongst the cars. As the Klan march approached, we ducked and prayed. After what seemed like a lifetime, they passed, and we pulled out and finished our drive, not in silence and fear but by "trash talking." We got real brave once we hit the main interstate. LaTanya even rolled down her window and screamed into the night, "Where ya at? Have you seen the Klan? Where ya at?" We laughed about our encounter and how brave we were once out of danger but as we drove, the conversation turned to, "What if's." That's when it got real. They could have killed us. She thanked me for saving our lives by instinctively knowing what to do and taking quick action. But neither of us could believe it was 1991 and the Klan was still marching.

When we re-joined the team, we never mentioned our undesired encounter with the KKK. We only knew we now had a greater purpose in winning. I had already beaten LSU at the Conference Championships to become the first Black head coach in any sport to ever win an SEC conference title outright, but I had never won in Baton Rouge. It was historically impossible to win in Baton Rouge and I would soon find out why.

On the final day of competition, it was clear that we were on our way to pulling a major upset of LSU at LSU. Until somewhere in the middle of the meet, things started happening and several of the meet officials started focusing on our team, disqualifying us for various unwarranted reasons. Our high jumper, Maria Galloni, was forced to jump out of turn, jumping back to back at progressive heights. After protesting, we were told either she jumped now, or be disqualified. Needless to say, she failed to win the event. Emotionally it was starting to wear on the team and staff. I had prepared them for the physical battle of competition, but this was mental warfare and we were not prepared. It got progressively worse as the LSU fan base started harassing and yelling at our athletes in every event.

As one of our strongest races, the 400-meters, entered the final turn, one of our athletes, Tasha Downing, sustained an injury, falling to the track right in front of the rowdy fans who actually cheered at her fall. I stood outside the ropes and waited for the race to end before sprinting onto the track to check on her. It was instinctive to run to her, although as a coach, I should not have been on the track. I was already angry and being rational was not an option. The meet official told me to leave the track and I told him I would, as soon as the medical support arrived. My athlete was hurting and crying and I was not leaving her alone among the barrage of screams coming from the stands.

By now, the LSU fans seated in the stands screamed at me with one rather large, older, hairy white male screaming the loudest. "Kick her ass off the track and kick her ass out of our stadium." Remembering the Klan, and already angry because of how we were being treated, I screamed back at him, "You bring your fat ass down here and kick me off. I'll beat your ass." By now, several other LSU fans had chimed in and it was them, and me, screaming back and forth.

As the final event, the 4x400 relay, rolled around, we were still in a position to win the meet. We had the better relay team and it should have been an easy victory. As my lead off leg lined up for the final event, the crowd pounced on her, screaming all types of things at her and even though she was from the Bronx and tough, this was different. I saw her starting to sweat, meaning she was nervous and as they got into their starting blocks, which indicated quiet in the stadium, someone screamed something, and she moved, causing the team to be disqualified. The meet was over. We lost by a few points and my assistant LaTanya and the team lost control. It was almost thirty minutes of preventing fights and quieting screaming arguments that were popping up everywhere. It got crazy and it didn't stop there. The whole night, the team traded stories of being harassed. I had cursed out several of the meet officials who had made, what we perceived to be, intentional miscalls against our team. By the time I returned to work the following Monday, I had not only been reported to my institution, but I was also reported to the conference and national offices as well. I got a letter in my file and a wink because my administration knew it was a natural part of coaching.

The team and I carried our anger through the outdoor season and as a result, we had the worst season you could imagine. To add to our demise, I had accepted a position on the NCAA rules committee, which required me to work at the championships. At this particular championship, I was actually the chairperson, a position that required I attend more meetings away from my team. We, as a team, had remained consumed by the loss of the conference meet at LSU. That coupled with my distraction of being on the committee, lead to us having the worse Indoor National meet performance since I had arrived at Florida. It never got any better, even with a team of talented athletes, we struggled and continued the downward spiral during the outdoor season.

Needless to say, 1991 ended up being one of the longest seasons of my career but it was also the most beneficial. I learned one of the most integral and significant lessons of my career. Don't carry negative emotions including fear, anger, or hatred in your head. It destroys everything it makes contact with and it destroyed our opportunity to rise above our circumstances. I learned that you should never take anything in the field of competition personal. It's never personal and we, mainly I, took it personally when we felt cheated out of a championship. We harped not on what went well, but everything that went badly and on feelings of unfairness. I should have known it's the nature of the game that each team should and will do whatever they believe is in their best interest to win. Somehow, I had lost sight of the bigger picture. I should have looked beyond the loss and continued to focus on winning the next encounter, but I didn't. I should have known better. I had grown up in an unstable environment where at any moment, things could change. My mind had remained focused on what had already happened as opposed to what was happening.

I had developed the habit of self-evaluation at the end of each season. I would evaluate not only myself, but my staff and each athlete to identify ways to improve. I intended to get better each year and the only way to do so was to seek the truth of what was good and what needed improving. I had learned a powerful lesson from our defeat in the 1991 season that would set the stage for all my future successes. I had to have unrelenting focus on the goal and not only expect for something to go wrong, but to accept it and move on as part of the journey to succeeding. I developed a mindset of what I called *natural fallout*. It's the mishaps and setbacks that occur within competition that have to be allowed for. You could be injured, sick, have disqualifications, or have a bad day, but they should not impact your overall purpose. They are merely part of the process. That refreshed perspective took away the notion of perfection and allowed for mistakes without distracting from the focus of winning.

* * *

The next season was my fifth year at Florida. It was the Olympic year, 1992, and we'd re-grouped from the prior year's disaster and were all on a mission. I had a dynamic team and had hired a new assistant, JJ Clark. With JJ and LaTanya on board, I was primed to succeed. Not only did I know it was our year, the team knew it as well.

The first decision I made was to resign from the NCAA Rules Committee to better tunnel all my energy and attention to my team at the championship meets. Also, I created a system of evaluating and assessing all of our competitors. I wanted to know how each team functioned, their strengths, weaknesses, and how each of their top athletes raced in their events. As a team, we rededicated ourselves to our goal of winning. That fall, we worked harder than we had worked in the past with everyone pushing each other to be great. We made a pact not to be distracted because the bigger the goals, the greater the obstacles and distractions. As we entered the 1992 season of competition, it would prove itself to be one of my most challenging years when it came to focus. Not because of failure, but because of our successes.

Our first championship was the SEC Indoor Conference Championships, which were held on our campus. We had amassed a powerhouse team lead by a Jamaican superstar by the name of Michelle Freeman. On the first day of competition, Michelle opened up the meet by setting a world record in the 55-meter hurdles. We went on to have a great first day and set ourselves up to win all of the final events the following day.

In the middle of the night, my phone rang. Startled, I grabbed it only to hear Michelle's voice on the other end of the line, "Hey Coach."

I angrily looked at the clock realizing it was one o'clock in the morning. She asked shyly, "Coach, I was wondering is it true that I really broke the world record?"

"Yes, you did."

"But what if I can't do it again tomorrow?"

I was so focused on the goals we all set that I responded rather aggressively for her to get off the phone and get some rest because breaking a world record in the semi-finals does not give us points. I told her she needed to win the final and garner the team ten points towards our total team score.

The next day she not only won the 55-meter hurdles, missing her own world record, she became the first athlete in SEC history or maybe the only athlete, to ever win the 55-meter hurdles, walk back to the starting line after her race, and win the 55-meter dash, and later win the 200-meter dash as well. We didn't just win the meet, we dominated as her teammates quickly followed up her victory with victories of their own.

We had decided to fight our battles on the track and our next biggest challenge came right after the conference victory at the NCAA Indoor National Championships. We entered the 1992 Championships as favorites for the first time in the University's history. Florida had never won a national championship in the history of men's or women's track and field. Neither had a Black coach from any institution ever won a national championship in the sport of track and field. The only African-American coach to have ever won a Division I title up to that point was John Thompson of Georgetown University in men's basketball. The meet not only evoked the pressures of winning that we had placed on ourselves, but it would mean a historical victory for both the University of Florida and for African-American coaches.

The first main event was the 55-meter hurdles and one of our top three athletes, Monifa Taylor, had been knocked out of the finals when another athlete fell into her lane, knocking her down. This was one of those unforeseen obstacles I had now mentally prepared our team to overcome. Now, with only two runners in the race, the margin for error had decreased dramatically. With Dionne Rose and Michelle Freeman in the final race, we had to finish with both of our athletes in the top four to have a chance to win the meet.

Michelle bolted from the blocks leaving the field behind by almost an entire five meters at hurdle number two of the five hurdle race. Dionne Rose, a fellow Jamaican and Florida athlete, was in hot pursuit of her along with athletes from Miami and LSU, chasing close behind.

It appeared to be a clear victory for us until Michelle crashed into the fourth hurdle, stumbling slightly but still in the lead. She barely cleared the fifth and final hurdle before literally stumbling and diving for the finish line, still aiming to win. Right as she fell across the line, the athlete from the University of Miami and Dionne, both leaning forward hard for the finish line, appeared to have passed her. As we all stared at the overhead score board for the results, I was relieved to see that although we didn't win the race, we still managed to finish second and third, resulting in the total number of points needed to be victorious.

As Michelle lay on the ground, we saw Dionne go over to her, help her up, and say something to her. We assumed she had been consoling her countrywoman and teammate until Michelle later revealed the contents of Dionne's whisper.

"Homegirl, I was right behind you. I saw you falling and I felt bad for ya but I still had to go for the win." They both took the concept, no distractions and no obstacles will stand in the way of victory, to another level.

At the conclusion of the women's triple jump, Leah Kirkland's victory gave us enough points, along with points in the 800-meters, 400-meters, 55-meters, and high jump competitions, to hold a fourteen-point lead going into the final event. We were guaranteed the team title as the mile relay team gathered. Before stepping onto the track, I gave them the option of running easy or going for it. They made it perfectly clear, they were going for the win stating they had started the meet with a champion mindset and intended to finish it that way. The mile relay team of Michelle, Kimberly Mitchell, Anita Howard, and Nekita Beasley extended the scoring lead to twenty-four after winning the event. Not only solidifying a historical win for the University of Florida, for me, the first African-American coach to win, and for the NCAA setting the record for the largest margin for a team victory between 1ˢᵗ and 2ⁿᵈ places in NCAA history.

With achievement came more obstacles. We had to release one of our top athletes because she refused to leave an abusive relationship. As a result, the team had gotten into an altercation with her boyfriend, a member of the men's team. The boyfriend had thrown her from a moving car and beaten her several times. Finally, when given an option to go to counseling in an effort to leave the relationship or leave the team, she wanted both to stay on the team and in the relationship. Ultimately, I made the decision to release her from the responsibility of the team and she chose to stay in the relationship. I allowed her to keep her scholarship despite the fact that she was no longer on the team so that she could complete her degree. Other challenges such as unforeseen jealousy erupted on the team, but we fought not to let our challenges and successes destroy our goals for the outdoor season and Olympic dreams of our athletes, team, and staff. Luckily, the team got together and decided to stay unified on the track, even if they didn't talk off the track.

I had begun to flourish at Florida and dismantled doubts from naysayers who had wrongly predicted I would never make it. I had finally found what I had been looking for, a place to call home. Florida felt more like home than any place I'd ever lived and there was nothing I didn't love about The University of Florida. Even the hot, muggy air seemed fresher than anything I had ever inhaled. I longed to stay there for the rest of my life but not by living in a condo. It was the only part that didn't feel like home. As we prepared for the outdoor championship portion of the season, my promise to my grandmother to one day buy a big family house, kept coming to mind so I went looking for a house.

I knew I'd found the perfect house because it felt like home from the moment my feet crossed the threshold. After talking it over with the realtor, I needed a larger income than my present $33,000 salary to be able to qualify for the loan. For the first time in my career, money mattered. I needed, and had earned, a raise. Over the years, I had developed the habit of never asking for anything I had not earned. I would find a way to succeed with what I had. This was different. This was not about winning and losing. This was about the little girl in me who had always felt homeless. I had lived most of my young adult life either homeless, or feeling like I was on the verge of being homeless. I needed to make $46,000 to buy my dream house, a place that my entire family could always call home. Excited about the purchase, I skipped happily into Ann Marie's office and asked for a raise. She agreed I had earned it and said she would look into it at the end of my season. To give her additional clarity, I told her I didn't need *a* raise, I needed a raise to $46,000 and that's when the conversation got uncomfortable. She might have been proud of my work with the team but $46,000 was out of the question. She thought maybe she could get me $38,000 or so. I, in turn, told her $38,000 was not enough. I even told her about the house and my family, but still the answer was, "Impossible." She told me I was asking her to pay me more than she got paid. I told her she should get both of us a raise as long as I got $46,000 because anything below that didn't matter. I needed the money and I needed it before they sold the house I was confident was meant for me.

I pleaded my case and finally, I think to shut me up, she told me the only way I could get a raise that high was if I was offered a job somewhere else and they would match the offer. *Okay, all I have to do is to find another institution to make me an offer.* Knowing who I can always turn to, I prayed for an offer. I had no idea how to go about getting an offer, but I needed one. I had no intention of leaving Florida, it was only meant to get my house. As the team prepared to for the

1992 outdoor conference championships, I received a message from Florida's former assistant athletic director, Keith Tribble, who had moved on to the University of Nevada, Las Vegas along with another former Florida athletic director, Jim Weaver. Keith reached out to let me know he and Jim were going to seek permission from Florida to speak to me about their job opening for a track coach. I was so excited and when asked what would it take to get me to leave, I said $47,000 a year. "No problem, we'll pay it," was all I needed to hear. I left for the conference championships in Starkville, Mississippi, with a huge grin.

We won the Outdoor Conference Championships and were listed along with LSU for team favorites for the NCAA Outdoor Championships, which were being held at the University of Texas in Austin. Before we got on the road, rumors were already floating around the track world that the staff at Texas would be replaced at the end of the year. I had never liked rumors of people losing their jobs and the only reason I listened was that the person telling me was also saying Texas intended to hire me. I was not interested in Texas and UNLV had already given me leverage to get my raise at Florida. I was happy.

As we prepared to leave for the meet in Texas, the athletic director had been informed that UNLV and now Texas were interested in hiring me. She wanted me to give her a guarantee that I was not leaving. I told her I intended to stay at Florida but I needed a raise. Surprisingly, she still balked at the amount. I don't think they considered UNLV a serious contender. I had to entertain the other offer from Texas, if they were in fact interested in hiring me. And they were. Shortly after the rumors began and right before we left, someone from Texas called requesting for an informal meeting during the championship. I agreed, not because I wanted to leave Florida, I needed the leverage.

Needless to say, things got a bit dicey and before long, my team heard rumors that I would be leaving for Texas at the end of the year. I pulled them aside at the airport before departing Gainesville and reminded them to remain focused. I also assured them I was not leaving. Their relief was short lived, for as we departed the plane in Texas, a newspaper blasted the headline, "UNLV and Texas vie for Florida's Beverly Kearney."

Next, I got hit with three distractions that could have totally derailed our championship hopes. The first was the circus surrounding the job offerings from both Texas and UNLV. After talking with Keith Tribble from UNLV, I had a brief meeting with the famed Texas women's basketball coach, Jody Conradt, who had just been appointed the new women's athletic director. She let me know she had one candidate on her list to hire and it was me.

The next distraction was the hotel we had pre-booked. It was a wet mess, literally. The carpets in all of the rooms were soaked and the rooms themselves were so small, our high jumper, Maria, had to stand in the shower to close the bathroom door. I called the athletic director and told her the rooms were prepaid but impossible to stay in and without hesitation, she told us to find a new hotel, transfer, and not to worry about the cost.

The final challenge was a personal one. I had been slated to not only speak at the coach's clinic, an event held during the meet, but the major television network covering the Championships, NBC or ABC, decided to focus their attention on the team and myself. Meaning, I would be followed by cameras throughout the entire meet.

As if those weren't enough distractions, my athletic director came to the meet, nervous about the possibility of me leaving after getting calls from both UNLV and Texas. The night before the meet started, I prayed for guidance to keep us focused and unified on our goal.

Even with all of those diversions occurring around us, we started the meet with a bang. Within the first two days of competition, we scored in the javelin, high jump, and the 10,000-meter, which never happens. Then, on the day before the finals, and in the preliminary race of the 100-meter hurdles, the beginning of the unthinkable happened, Dionne Rose, one of the top four hurdlers in the country, fell over the last hurdle and didn't make the final. She laid on the track crying and none of the officials could get her to move. Michelle walked over, grabbed her up from the track, and told her to show some dignity by kicking ass in the long jump. Dionne, with an ever-present smile, jumped to her feet and walked over to the long jump pit, put on her jump shoes, and jumped farther than she had in any competition, finishing second by inches. With the cameras following me around, coupled with me being mic'd the entire meet, we found it difficult to focus. My athletes were tense as a result of all the media coverage and rumors of me leaving. Slowly, we started to lose focus.

In the midst of the downward spiral, I told them to be themselves and win or lose, we will fight to the end. On the final day, we re-grouped and they started talking trash and winning. They were having fun. Anita Howard, running the 400-meter for the first time, was terrified as she entered the stadium for the finals of her race. However, Dionne screamed her name and cheered so loudly, the entire field of athletes looked up at her as she screamed back to them with a big smile, "What are y'all looking at? I'll jump over these barriers and kick all of y'all asses in the 400." Dionne could barely run a 200, and the thought had not only Anita laughing, but the entire field of athletes. All Anita needed to ease her fears was a good laugh. She won the race, adding ten more points to our team total. Considering how hard we had worked, we could not have predicted what occurred next. We had the lead going into the women's 200-meter. We had counted on the other schools breaking up the two LSU girls, giving us the lead heading into the final event, the mile relays. As I glanced down at the track, three athletes from other schools had scratched from the final and were no longer in the race, allowing LSU to pull ahead of us with a margin we couldn't overcome.

As the team prepared to head onto the track for the final event, I pulled them in a quick huddle. I told them that even if we won the 4x400 relay, we would lose the meet by a mere two or three points. I told them they'd had such an amazing meet, most of the people in the stands actually thought we were winning. If they won the mile relay, the fans would leave the stadium before the team awards would be given and the last thing they'll remember would be the greatness of Florida. "Let's go out as winners!" They not only won the relay, they set a new school and collegiate record.

Even with the distractions, that particular group of young ladies were the embodiment of determination. Not only were they great athletes, they were great people. They formed bonds that would not only lead them to the top of the charts athletically, but would also propel them to become one of the top academic/athletic teams in the history of Florida women's sports. Athletes like Anita Howard, Kimberly Mitchell, Tasha Downing, Michelle Freeman, Leah Kirkland, Monifa Taylor, Maria Galloni, Dionne Rose, Nekita Beasley, and many others, helped move the University of Florida to the forefront of Women's Track and Field. They made history and created friendships with each other that still exist today.

* * *

As the collegiate season came to a close, I turned my attention to preparing my athletes for the 1992 Olympic Trials and Games as well as on getting a raise for my house. UNLV and the University of Texas both turned up the pressure to persuade me to move to their universities. Never in the history of collegiate sports had a woman created a public bidding war between several universities, especially in the sport of track and field. I had no intention of taking another offer because Florida was my dream job. Getting a house was the only reason I even entertained the other offers. Had Florida agreed to pay me the salary I desired, I would have never been in jeopardy of leaving.

As the pressure mounted, the bidding escalated, with the offers reaching $50,000. By the time it reached $60,000 a year, my women's athletic director made a statement implying that I needed to be loyal to Florida while giving me the impression that it was Florida that had made me so valuable. From her statements, I realized, it was no longer just business, it had become personal. However, I needed to make a business decision not a personal one. Male athletic directors regularly pay their coaches considerably more than their own salaries, but at the time, female athletic directors had trouble paying their coaches, especially other females, more than what they made. I went directly to the men's athletic director who had been instructed by the President of the University and several powerful boosters to not allow me to get away.

Finally, Keith Tribble, who happened to be a great strategist, announced he was going to put an end to the bidding war. I was honest with him and had told him I didn't want to leave the University of Florida. He called back with a final offer of $74,000 per year, more money than I had ever imagined making in my life. He said he would not only pay me as a track coach, but would give me the title of assistant women's athletic director as well. The offer was unheard of among college coaches, with the average track coach, male or female, making around $30,000 a year. Now it was up to Texas and Florida to counter the offer. The pressure was tremendous and I received letters from the alumni and the president of the university asking me to stay. What would I do if Florida refused to match the offer?

My fate was in the hands of two new powerful athletic directors. The newly appointed Florida athletic director, Jeremy Foley, and the newly appointed Texas women's athletic director, Jody Conradt. Jody was scheduled to meet with me at the Olympic trials in New Orleans, and there she matched the offer. Florida had asked that I not make a final decision until we could talk after the Olympic trials.

I had four athletes make the 1992 Olympic team. Two from the United States, Anita Howard in the 400-meters and LaVonna Martin, who had come to train with me in Florida after graduating from Tennessee. Two others, Michelle Freeman and Dionne Rose, had made the Jamaican Olympic teams. We had accomplished more than we could have ever imagined that season and now, back on campus, I prepared myself for the final round of negotiations with Florida in anticipation of getting my house. I wanted to be prepared since negotiation was new to me. I singled out several coaches at Florida to speak with, the women's tennis coach and the men's football coach, Steve Spurrier. They both gave me great advice. I was ready and I had even expanded my request list.

Jeremy, Florida's athletic director, started off by saying how much they wanted to keep me and that Texas had stolen too many of its coaches in the past, but they were not getting me. He asked what I needed and I told him I needed help financing a home. Several of the coaches told me that Florida had assisted them with financing. Florida also had a policy that mainly seemed to affect the Black student athletes, which required pre-college summer courses to be taken prior to enrolling as freshmen in the fall. Not only did it take their last high school summer away but the school did not pay for the classes. I asked for exemptions for some of my athletes who could not afford it. I had already been told that other sports were granted exemptions. He agreed to the request and I agreed, as a show of loyalty to the University, to take a slightly lower offer of $70,000 plus some other non-monetary incentives to stay. I called the two other athletic directors to tell them of my decision and thanked them for their interest. Both were very gracious, but there was something special about my conversation with Jody Condrat at Texas. Her words really touched me. She said, "Texas really wants and needs you. If for any reason, at any time, you change your mind, please let me know. I am going to hold the position open for a while."

Keith Tribble had been the first to up the ante for the salary bidding war. All he asked of me was to not leave him hanging and help him find a great coach. Karen Dennis and I had become lifelong friends and in the midst of the job offers, she had asked if I would recommend her for one of the positions I didn't take. My recommendation to Keith was accepted and Karen began as the new Head coach at UNLV. Years later, Keith moved on from UNLV to become the Head of Athletics and sought my counsel in hiring for his track coach position. I insisted he hire Caryl Smith Gilbert. Again he listened and Caryl not only went on to move UCF among the top schools in the country, she would later go on to become one of the top coaches in the history of the sport at the famed University of Southern California.

My belief starts with creating the most from every opportunity. When blessed with successes, you must pay it forward. If only you benefit from your opportunities, what is the real value of the opportunity?

My decision to stay at Florida was on the evening news and the next morning, it was all over the local and national papers. The local papers spoke lavishly of my accomplishments and emphasized how valuable I was to the university and the community. I received cards, letters, and phone calls from everyone thanking me for staying. Strangely, the night after the decision, I couldn't sleep at all. I tossed and turned all night, having no clue as to why I wasn't happy about my choice. I thought of the older Black coaches who had been around for a while. They had all suggested I take the Texas job because they had never hired a Black coach, and someone needed to break the barrier. For me, I was finally home and even the idea of being the first Black coach at the University of Texas would not change my mind. I had already been through too much as a result of color and wasn't about to break down another door and start all over again.

I made the arrangements to buy my house and took the details to the athletic director. Basically, he told me there would be no help from the University. Strike one. Next, I gave them a list of the recruits I had signed and asked for summer waivers and was told, maybe next year. Strike two. Then I bumped into some of the administrators who thanked me for staying and began to celebrate yet another Florida victory, kicking Texas's butt by winning the battle for me. Strike three. They didn't want me, it had all been about beating Texas.

At the end of the day, I went home and I prayed with all my might. I had been so adamant about not wanting to leave Florida that there had to be a reason I was still not at peace with the decision. Through the night, the words of the Florida athletic director echoed in my head. She had said, "If you leave, you wouldn't be loyal to Florida. Remember, if it wasn't for Florida, no one would be interested in you." I didn't want to leave but now, I wasn't comfortable staying.

All night I thought about Texas as well. It was one of the most visible schools in the country and I had been told that I could make a greater impact if I went there. What stuck out in my head was the warning that if I didn't take the job, it would more than likely be decades before another chance came around for another African American coach at Texas. That night, I barely slept. The next morning, I arose with a sinking feeling in the pit of my stomach. I knew I had made the wrong choice. I was supposed to be in Texas.

The next day, I shocked Jody with a call asking if her offer still stood. I accepted the job without ever officially visiting the campus or knowing the true extent of the program. After accepting the offer, it was time to speak to Florida. It would be one of the hardest conversations I'd ever had, but I had no other options. My soul had led me to Texas. He was gracious in our conversation but skeptical, thinking it was another negotiation ploy. When he asked if there was *anything* they could offer to get me to stay, my answer was simple, "It's not about money. I'm doing what my heart is telling me to do." That was my first official decision that was made beyond a doubt, by the direction of God. Although I didn't know it at the time, this was the beginning of my true purpose. I now know I was never meant to only be a coach.

In July of 1992, I left the University of Florida, and headed to the University of Texas. It was also the Olympic year. There were three athletes from the University of Florida's track and field team who had made the Olympic team that year. As loving and warm as the Gainesville and Florida media had been the day when I announced I'd stay, they were equally as harsh after my subsequent decision to leave. They ate me alive. I went from sugar to shit at the stroke of a pen. Now in the midst of another upheaval, the words of the athletic director at Tennessee rang true—if you are going to succeed in these types of high-powered programs, not only was it important that I be driven, but that I have thick skin.

Florida taught me how to manage young people and stress. Despite the turbulence throughout my stay at Florida, they were the best and most stable five years of my young adult life. They were full of good times that I will always cherish. I had a ball. When you go to battle and both teams refuse to give up until the bitter end, there are no losers. It's history being made. In my career, I have had to battle many things, but there is no victory sweeter than learning not to quit even when you know you will not finish first. Winning is staying in the battle in spite of the odds, obstacles, and the challenges.

Never give up!

By the time I got to Florida, I was no longer a young, naïve coach. I was focused and determined to be the best. I intended to win. I wanted to have the best team in the nation, and to have one of the best academic records to go along with it. I stood through the criticism, the racism, the sexism, and the personal and professional attacks. I had even gotten hate mail in Florida. I was making history and didn't know it. I was so busy fighting off skeptics and focused on winning, I didn't realize how I well I was doing. Florida not only taught me to stand up for what I believed in, but gave voice to my dreams as I began, for the first time, to proclaim unapologetically, my desire to be the best. Declaring my intent gave my goals and dreams life.

I was learning about learning. Every experience contained a lesson and I no longer feared failure or tears, for I began to realize that through my failure, my mistakes, my tears, I had grown stronger, smarter, and a little bit wiser. There was only one way I had chosen to look back on my past experiences and that was to see the blessing of them. I had set out to earn $46,000 a year and now I would be one of the highest paid coaches in any collegiate sport in the country, male or female, at $72,000 a year. God always seemed to go a step or two beyond whatever I thought was possible.

DO IT

"In Believing It, I began knowing my truth. In Speaking It, I began to become my truth. These steps of evolution empowered me to move forward in life with conviction and with confidence. This awareness created action! It was action that brought the three concepts together. Believe It, Speak It, and Do It. The concept promulgated the action needed to see the results of my efforts. It was here that my intuition was accessed at its highest level and I no longer anticipated. Now, I knew!"

CHAPTER 12

I had literally driven through the night, playing music to keep me awake as fatigue and exhaustion overtook me in the wee hours of the morning. The trip from Tampa, Florida back to Austin, Texas was especially grueling, as I knew what awaited me once I arrived. I had been on a Christmas cruise to the Caribbean, having taken it upon myself to overindulge each Christmas in hopes that my daughter Imani, who had lost her mom in a tragic car accident on Christmas ten years earlier, would never dread the holiday. Now I was rushing back to find out the final results of a ferocious and intense investigation into not only a consensual affair with a student I'd had some ten years earlier, but also my own allegations of years of racial and gender discrimination.

As the darkness of night slowly shifted into the early morning light, my thoughts remained hopeful although my spirit felt the heaviness of the past few months of the exhaustive investigation. I'd been hoping for the best but deep inside, I knew the outcome held an equal chance of being favorable and unfavorable. My lawyers, on the other hand, had continuously tried to assure me that everything would be fine. They felt this was simply the beginning of what would surely be brief negotiations between the University and myself. No matter how much I wanted to believe them, somewhere in the depth of my soul, I knew it would not be simple. Throughout my twenty-some odd years at the University of Texas, nothing had come that easy and I had grown to be a little more pessimistic than I had ever imagined possible. I had learned to never underestimate anything or anyone and warned my attorneys repeatedly not to underestimate the extent of the racism that existed, especially in athletics.

As I continued to drive, I mustered all the inner power and faith I could, under the circumstances, to remain optimistic but it had been an uphill battle. During the drive, I hit repeat on two songs so often I think the girls, Imani, Tamya, and my niece, Rheagan, fell asleep early just to relieve themselves of the torture of hearing them being played over and over again. I needed to forgive myself, to heal, to know that God still loved me. I found comfort not only in prayer but in those songs. I played "Good and Bad" by J. Moss and "Bruised but Not Broken" by Joss Stone on repeat for the entire ten-hour drive back to Austin. My mother had always played the blues when she was sad or soul music when she wanted to celebrate and party. My grandmother would simply hum while moving about the house doing one thing or another. I could determine by the sounds of her hums whether she was filled with joy or sadness. I too had learned to use music as an expression of my feelings and now more than any time in my life, I needed those two songs.

Earlier that day, during my drive, I received a phone call from a fellow coach on the west coast asking if I was okay. She told me she had heard my job was in trouble and wanted to check on me. I assured her that everything would be okay. I repeated the words my lawyers had used to reassure me, but even as I spoke, I felt twinges of doubt swell in my gut. My lawyers were both Texas graduates and loved the university just as I did, but for them, the thought of UT being unfair to me, someone who'd given so much, was unthinkable. I knew better. I had gone through too much. Especially over the last eight years, which had felt more like a battle to survive than a fight to succeed. They reassured me the case against me had no precedence of firing and had insisted it was going to be an amicable meeting and everything would be resolved with fairness and respect.

I made it home about 6 a.m. on Friday morning, December 28, 2012. I laid across my bed, too scared to close my eyes, too exhausted to think straight, and too worried to rest. Finally, as the time neared for the meeting, I showered, got dressed, and headed for the University of Texas. Although I had spent the last two decades making the same drive and parking in the same space, it now it felt foreign. I had only been on paid suspension for three months, but the stress made it feel like years.

Thoughts of being fired, of not being able to do what I loved, and not being able to take care of those I loved, brought tears to my eyes many nights during the suspension. I had to shake off the negative feeling before entering the building. I sat alone in my car and prayed. As the prayer came to a close, I said the words that I always ended my prayers with, "Let Your will for my life be done oh Heavenly Father! My trust is in YOU!" With those final words, I stepped out of the car and headed for the building, not knowing it would be the last time I would exit my car from my parking space of twenty years.

My lawyers met me in the athletic offices. There, we were to be given the final results of the months-long investigation stemming from a consensual relationship I had with a student athlete back in 2002. As the President of legal affairs greeted me, she kindly said hello and gave me a hug, which was in stark contrast to the cold greeting of the women's athletic director who spoke without making eye contact. I knew right then it wasn't the type of meeting my lawyers had tried to assure me it would be.

We entered the beautiful, newly renovated athletic administration offices. Usually lively, the halls appeared dark and cold as everyone was still on Christmas break. As my lawyers pleasantly greeted everyone, thinking they were heading into the meeting for the final negotiations of the case, I surveyed those in the room representing UT and I could tell this was not a friendly meeting. In time, my accurate assessment was proven correct. Without hesitating, Chris Plonsky, the Women's Director of Athletics, opened the meeting with the bombshell that the university had decided not to move forward with our relationship, effectively firing me. They were terminating me for having a relationship with a student athlete and there was nothing I could do because I had admitted to the relationship. I looked at her, wondering if she had actually expected me to lie. She went on to say that the message from the President of the University was, "And we are not giving you a dime." Her statement, as directed from the President, seemed very personal which lead me to believe my firing had more to do with my filing another unofficial grievance against the department for gender and racial issues as well as the pay raise I had requested.

I had never been so grateful to be fatigued. I was too tired to fight, to get mad, or to scream. I sat listening from a distant mindset as my shocked lawyers argued facts to no avail. They asked about others who had affairs with students and the administrator's response was that it was not the same. My attorneys sought clarification, asking if I was being fired for failing to self-report the affair at the time, ten years earlier, or for the affair itself. The administrators reaffirmed I was being fired solely on the basis of the affair and nothing else. They continued to argue their case, saying UT's policy stated that affairs were discouraged not banned. Chris countered by saying I had the right to file an appeal, which she assured them I would lose because I had already admitted to the affair. She quickly added, "But there is another option."

Chris, who was noticeably uncomfortable at this point, attempted to hand the conversation off to someone else. She turned to Patty Orlendorf, the head of legal counsel for the University, and asked, "Patty, you remember the options?" It was a painfully obvious attempt at feigning ignorance, desperate for someone else to intervene.

Patty, however, was of no help. Almost stuttering she replied, "No. What options? I don't remember the options." Chris responded, "Yes you do." Now without help, she had to state the options herself, which only seemed to make her more nervous. Reluctantly, she gave us the second option. I could resign and the university would keep the details of my firing out of the press. However, if they had to fire me, they would have to reveal the reason for my termination. After giving me my options, Chris again made the statement that bothered me the most, "Either way, we still aren't giving her a dime."

My leg began to shake beneath the table. I had been staring at Chris the entire time and the more I stared, the more uncomfortable she became. But now, I was pissed off. My mind raced and as it raced, the words didn't leave my mouth, but they played so loudly in my head that surely, she could hear, or at the least, *feel* them. I screamed internally, *You weak, self-serving, trifling ass bitch! I could just jump across this table with my disability and punch your weak ass right in the face.* The stronger the urge got to punch her, the faster my leg shook. Anger toward this vicious, heartless woman swelled within me. The possibility of actually committing verbal or physical harm toward her became less of a thought and more of a reality. For both our sakes, I had to get out of that room. I had to leave before I exploded. Without ever saying a word, I grabbed my cane, stood up, and headed for the door. As I made my way to the door, I heard my lawyers still trying to recover from the shock of the decision and the options provided. "How long do we have to decide on these options?"

As the door closed behind me, I heard Chris say they needed an answer now. *Yep,* I thought to myself as I left the room, *Of all the decisions I made today, the decision to leave the room was the best one.*

Once outside the offices, I paced the hall. My anger slowly turned to hurt. It sounded like a cliché, but in this case, it was simply the truth, I had given The University of Texas the best years of my life, and in return, they had discarded me like a piece of trash. Finally, too physically and emotionally exhausted to pace, I stood looking out the enormous glass window by the elevators. Still too mad to cry, too angry to scream, too hurt and exhausted to think. I glared into nowhere, looking at nothing in particular. I leaned against the wall, coming to terms with my new normal and understanding those minutes as the last time I would ever see the inside of the place I'd called home—the University of Texas Athletic Department.

I wanted to blame someone, anyone, but I was emotionally and spiritually drained. Plus, who would I blame? Not my lawyers. They had been great. But as an older white male and his younger son, they could never understand the levels of racism that Blacks faced on a day-to-day basis. Most whites and even some Blacks thought racism was behind us, but I knew better, and I should have known better. I had felt "the establishment" at the university trying to get rid of me for years. They loved what I brought to UT, what they didn't love was the attention being gained by a Black female. I had fought for the university to create a more diverse administration and as a head coach, I always hired at least one staff member who was female and or Black. My lawyers had greatly underestimated just how far the university would go to defeat anyone they deemed a threat, especially someone Black. I had tried unsuccessfully to warn my attorneys that fairness and legal positions would not matter, and that they should be prepared. But how do you prepare for something you can't imagine?

As they joined me in the hallway, I could tell they were in shock at the decision because no one in the history of the university had ever been fired for having a relationship or an affair with a student. The only guidance in place at UT in 2002 was a fairly new rule requiring that you self-report and I was not being fired for failing to self-report.

When I was first placed on suspension, I knew I would eventually need legal counsel. I had tried to find an African-American attorney but was discouraged after speaking with the legal representative of the Texas NAACP. They warned me that Blacks had little, to no chance of defeating the institution. The university had a history of intentionally dragging cases out for so long, especially for African-Americans, that the litigants generally ended up mentally broken and financially destroyed. I realized then that the NAACP had been beaten up way too many times to take on the public and complicated case I presented to them. Hence, I looked for other alternatives. I had established a great rapport with the elder stateswoman and former State Representative, Mrs. Wilhelmina Delco, who had become my mentor and advisor throughout my stay at Texas. I met Mrs. Delco at the one place in Austin that I could find women who looked like me, the Classy Lady Beauty Saloon, owned by Mrs. Jackie Stewart. Mrs. Jackie's place was the go-to bi-weekly spot for Black women to not only get our hair done but to connect, talk, laugh, and more importantly, find comfort and support. One of the earliest connections Mrs. Jackie had arranged for me had been to meet Mrs. Delco. She was elegant, fearless, intelligent and knew the history of the political system and it's relationships with African-Americans which was uniquely Texas. Now some twenty years after our first meeting, it was she who suggested—no, insisted—I reach out to Derek Howard. She believed he would be my best option. I loved Derek and his son the moment I met them. I felt they were the ones who could best represent me in what started as a basic case and ended up as a major legal battle that would last almost five years.

In the hallway, my lawyers admitted to being blindsided by the university's decision to terminate me. I reminded them of my warning not to expect UT to treat me as they would any other employee of the institution. However, it was a moot point by now. The damage was done, and from all appearances, we were not prepared for the fight. As we entered the elevator and headed back to our cars, they told me I had been given until Monday to make a decision.

Once home, I exploded into a mass of tears. I informed Michelle Freeman and the kids of my termination. Michelle and her eight-year-old daughter, Tamya, had been living with Imani (whom I had legal guardianship of since her mother's death) and me. I then called my brother-like-best-friend, Raymond Coleman, Derick, and Gerettia, telling them of the outcome. Everyone was speechless, unable to come up with any words of comfort. They had all hung up in the midst of deathly silence. What could they say? I too had been left speechless and was glad the conversations had been short. After making the calls, I collapsed, fully clothed, into a fetal position on my bed and cried my exhausted self into a restless nap.

Sleep was not an option as my soul and mind wrestled to make sense of the circumstances at hand. One minute, I was on a stage being honored with the likes of Dr. Maya Angelou and the Tuskegee Airmen, or coaching at the Olympics in Athens, Greece, and now I was disgraced and discarded.

By the time I awoke that afternoon, the severity of the situation had finally sunk in. It felt more like an execution than a termination. Chris had administered the verdict without emotion, condemning me to a professional death sentence with the same energy one throws out the garbage. I contemplated the one decision they'd gifted to me, the method by which I would die. I could choose to fall on my own sword or be publicly beheaded by them. Either way, I was doomed to a humiliating death. I wanted to cry, I wanted to be angry, but the pressure to make a decision outweighed time for self-pity.

Raymond came over to check on me. He had no words to express his hurt so the two of us sat in silence. After much contemplation, he stood up and said, "Trust yourself! Trust God Bev, and you will know what to do. Everything is going to be all right." As he left the room, I knew he ached for me, but it was not a decision anyone could help me with other than the true source of all my strength, God. I thought to myself, *I've always trusted God's direction for my life even when I didn't understand it.* Now, that trust was needed more than ever. I needed God more now than ever. I closed my eyes and I prayed. My heart got heavier and my eyes began to water. I continued to pray through the tears for God's guidance. I don't ever remember feeling so alone. Even when I was homeless and slept in my car during high school, I had felt at peace. The tears flowed and the pain increased. Just as I was on the brink of being broken, it hit me. A moment of pure clarity manifested through the hurt and tears. The answer rang so loudly in my head and heart, it silenced everything else. I could hear it clearly, as though a voice was speaking to me, "Remember your prayer." Louder again, *"REMEMBER YOUR PRAYER!"* I didn't want to think about the prayer I had prayed continuously in the hours, days, weeks, and months following the death of my sister, Cherry.

Cherry had died from a stroke that summer, just as I was headed to the 2012 Olympic Trials in Eugene, Oregon. I had suffered what could have been a minor stroke at that year's NCAA Indoor Championship. I woke up in the early hours of the morning on the final day of the competition feeling disoriented and throwing up all over myself. I had just undergone another internal investigation of allegations levied against me by someone not outside the program but from within. The constant barrage of rule violations and the need to disprove allegations of misconduct started to take its toll. I loved Texas but there were people at UT who definitely didn't love me. I didn't break rules and proving them wrong over and over again did little to impede more allegations. As I drove alone to Oregon for the USA Olympic trials, with those events weighing on my heart and mind, I began a month's long prayer for "peace of mind." I had called out to God, "Give me peace!"

Now as I sat in my mediation chair in the solitude of my bedroom, the answer to my present prayer for guidance and my prior prayer for peace collided, forming one answer. "If you truly desire peace, tell the truth. The truth will set you free, and in your freedom, you will find peace of mind." I rose, no longer exhausted, but committed to truth and trusting in the words that still rang through my soul.

I called my makeshift family of Michelle, Tamya, Imani and Raymond into the room to inform them of my decision and to seek their approval. I was aware that any decision I made would affect them. I had been emotionally and financially taking care of everyone in my home since the car accident in 2002, which resulted in the deaths of both Imani and Michelle's mothers and had left me paralyzed. Raymond, who was in a miracle battle with cancer, had moved back to Austin from Washington, DC with his new wife, Cheryl. They were attempting to recover from the ever present, but rarely discussed, issues associated with someone fighting cancer. I had extended myself in every way imaginable to support my family and now we all gathered for the decision that would impact our lives.

They immediately knew my choice to tell the truth meant everyone would learn about my relationship with a twenty-year-old student athlete ten years earlier. I was most concerned about Imani. After losing her mom in the car accident, she had endured enough and most importantly, I didn't want to cause her any more harm and definitely no embarrassment. She was the first to respond. Surprisingly, her response was one of unadulterated anger. She was only twelve years old, but she was more mature than her years revealed. Even still, her grasp of the situation surprised me.

"After you took her into our house and treated her like family, and after all you have done for the University of Texas, this is how they treat you? Mom, fight! I don't care what people think about you! Fight!"

Michelle expressed what Imani really wanted to say but knew she was too young to verbalize it.

"Fuck them ungrateful motherfuckers Bev! Fight!"

Tamya, the youngest in the room, looked up to her mother and big sister. She echoed their sentiments.

"Fight them Grammy! You've helped a lot people! Fight them, they are wrong." After each of them spoke, they exited the room, leaving Raymond and I alone.

Raymond sat quietly, nodding as the others spoke. I had rarely ever seen him speechless, not since he was with me bedside at the hospital after the accident, and when I was airlifted back to Austin from Florida. He and I were kindred spirits who had once thought we were the perfect romantic match but came to realize, we loved each other but were not in love. It was my close relationship with him that had helped me to conclude I was in fact, gay. He was the perfect man, tall, dark, handsome, intelligent, spiritual, and financially stable. Over time, our relationship evolved into a big brother, little sister relationship and I loved his new wife. She was perfect for him. I think he knew after dating that we were destined to spend the rest of our lives together, though not as husband and wife. His rare form of cancer, from which no other patient had survived, had him heavily medicated over the last year. That, along with my legal battle with Texas, had taken a toll on him physically and emotionally. I watched in silence as he struggled to gather himself to speak. I waited in anticipation for his words of wisdom, which had saved my life after the accident, to save my soul now.

I broke the silence between us and spoke on the burdens my present circumstances had placed on my heart and loved ones. I told him of my prayer, asking God, "Please don't allow anything I have done, or that has been done, or is being done to me, to get in the way of the purpose you have set before me. Please don't allow me to harbor hatred or ill will towards anyone for anything."

As he thoughtfully listened, it gave me the courage to open up about my deepest, darkest fears. We spoke of the accident, we spoke of God, of my Angels, of the university, and how lawyers were intimidated by the power of Texas. Finally, only after I expressed every feeling and fear, did he speak.

He told me the situation was not only hard on me, but on him as well, as he felt helpless. He assured me that all he knew for sure was that I would be okay and that everything would be okay. Neither he nor I knew what "okay" meant in that moment, but I needed to hear his comforting words. I didn't need a lecture or a lesson, just comfort. As he spoke faith into me, I could feel the grips of fear and hurt loosen their hold on my fatigued body and mind. I don't know if he believed it or not, but it was what I needed to hear in that moment, that everything would be okay. His last recommendation was to trust my heart and to rely on my faith, because God was still in control. He reminded me it was the same faith that had propelled me to walk after the car accident when others said I would never walk again.

He later confided that he knew during our conversation at my home, our purpose was one of universal love and what God had intended for us to do moving forward. He had spent countless hours ten years earlier at the hospital reassuring me, praying with me, and providing me with materials to read about universal love and the laws of attraction, in addition to the wonders of leading a love-filled and God-filled lifestyle. Prior to the accident, I had led a life in which I *unknowingly*, yet intuitively, loved and manifested my desires.

After the accident, the insights, language, and affirmations I learned while still in the hospital taught me to be absolutely *intentional* in my dealings with life, and its circumstances, and it had been liberating. The doors to my heart and mind were opened, and I knew for the first time in my life I was not alone nor, would I ever be alone. I had felt alone and lost many times prior to the accident and had even prayed to my mother and grandmother, and ultimately to God, to help me through various situations I had faced. After the accident, my prayers became more focused. I felt the need to give love, but more importantly, I felt safe and loved in the light and love of God's favor. Regardless of the road I now had to travel, or the outcome of it all, it was a *knowing* that I prayed from.

It was my continuous studying after the accident that taught me about God, Christ, angels, belief, faith, and knowing. I had studied all the angels during my recovery and had learned not only about the power of prayer and God, but of the legions of angels available to all of us. I needed to pray specifically to Archangel Michael, who had been noted as the greatest and most revered of all the angels. I prayed for the words and guidance to simply do what was right without hatred or ill intent. My desire was peace and only by standing in my truth, would I obtain the peace of mind that had eluded me.

I called my lawyers and told them of my decision to speak my truth. We scheduled a meeting and I laid across my bed exhausted, but at peace. I continued to seek God's comfort, telling him I knew He had not brought me this far only to allow my demise at the hands of those whose only mission had been to destroy me. If there was a time that faith and knowing was needed, it was then. Before drifting off into a peaceful sleep, my last prayer had been one asking God not to allow something I had done or that had been done to me to cause me not to be able to be of assistance to others. I dedicated my life to God before closing my eyes, affirming my trust in His will for my life. Whatever I had to go through, I knew I would not have to travel the road alone.

As I woke from my short sleep, the need to remember what I loved about Texas preyed on my heart. Rather than dwelling on the hurt and pain of my present circumstances, I reflected back over the last twenty years and I smiled. It had been a beautiful August day in 1992 and Jody, my new boss at Texas, had picked me up for lunch. As we drove down Interstate 35, which ran through the center of Austin, I recalled Jody proudly asking me to look up. There, on the side of the interstate, stood a huge billboard welcoming me, Beverly Kearney, to the University of Texas. I couldn't believe it. A billboard had my name on it! I had never imagined my name on a billboard. Seeing it and being in Texas that day gave me such joy, never assuming it would end in such a disastrous way. My excitement, naiveté, and faith, had led me to trust that this was where I was supposed to be, and that great things lay ahead. The more I learned about the great history of Texas, especially regarding minorities and women, the greater my commitment to meet the levels of excellence and expectations of greatness. I vowed to be a part of the historical greatness of those who had gone before me and lived by the Texas mantra of, "Everything is bigger and better in Texas." It fit my competitive nature like a glove. Now, I couldn't help but laugh to myself as I thought of the other

Texas mantra, which best-suited my present dilemma, "Don't mess with Texas."

CHAPTER 13

Every move I had made thus far in my career had been one of upward mobility, but leaving Florida had been different. The decision was similar to leaving home for the first time and being guided by a greater force. It had baffled everyone, even me. Why was I compelled to move to Texas? Becoming the university's first African-American head coach was a historical honor but that wasn't the rationale. There was more but I couldn't explain it. Aside from the historical significance, there was little else that excited me. Nonetheless, I knew intuitively it was where I was supposed to be. I was thirty-four years old and I longed to find a stable place to call home. Eventually, I would find everything I desired and so much more in Texas.

Falling in love with Texas was more difficult than my love-at-first-sight experience with Florida. During the first few weeks of my stay, I walked the campus alone, experiencing longing pangs from my separation from the University of Florida. I was wanted at Texas and I was making more money than I ever thought to ask for, but the homesickness for Florida dominated my thoughts. I'd shake my head trying to clear my mind, knowing there was no turning back. I had to find a way to make Texas home.

I wondered around for almost two weeks trying to make sense in my head and heart of my decision to uproot my life and move. Jody unknowingly provided me with the answer in a phone call and an invitation to dinner. She had been everything I thought she would be upon my arrival, and having dinner with her and listening to her stories and wisdom would be a welcomed distraction to the doubts that had invaded my heart. I had no idea just how impactful and special that dinner would be as it altered my feelings about being at Texas, for the better.

We met on campus and she drove us through beautiful neighborhoods before stopping in front of a magnificent home. It was the home of one of the greatest orators and stateswomen of all time, former State Representative, Ms. Barbara Jordan. My heart fluttered as she greeted us from her wheelchair. She was no longer the physical presence I had seen on television or in pictures, but even from the chair, she was larger than life. Her energy commanded attention, respect, and reverence. While researching the history of Texas, it was she who had stood out as one of the most intriguing of the current living legends who resided in the great state of Texas. I had hoped to meet her someday. The thought of having the honor of breaking bread with her and engaging in an intimate conversation in her home had been unfathomable.

Throughout the evening, every word and every story was electrifying, filled with the humor, intelligence, strength and courage of the trials and tribulations of these two iconic women, Jody Conradt and Barbara Jordan. Although I don't remember the exact content of the conversation, I do remember feeling inspired by their combined presence. I can't even recall what we even had for dinner because it didn't matter. The meal took a backseat to the moment. As I listened, my earlier apprehensions about relocating to Texas dissipated and I began to comprehend the responsibility and magnitude of being there.

For the first time in my life, I was not reading about greatness, I was sitting in the midst of greatness.

That day, I understood why God had led me to Texas. Even after departing their company, I wished others could have shared the experience with me. It had been a life-altering, awe-inspiring evening of greatness. I hoped to one day be able to provide something similar for others. *Everyone deserves to have a moment in the presence of greatness.*

As with every position I had taken, there was always something greater inspiring me to succeed. If left on my own accord, I had too little confidence, too much fear, too much doubt and I felt I wasn't as capable as others. Surely, with all those inner traits, I was doomed to fail. But I always found something that drove me beyond the self-doubt and fears. That evening, with the power of being in their presence, I found my strongest inspiration and motivation to succeed. I had to live up to their examples of excellence, grace, and greatness. As I reviewed my circumstances at Texas, my first and most important decision was to hire a staff to assist me on the journey.

I wanted to replicate what had worked at Florida by hiring my staff from Florida, but it wasn't to be. My two former assistants, JJ Clark and LaTanya Wynn, had personal commitments in Florida and couldn't afford to make the move. They were in committed relationships and both ended up getting married shortly after my departure. Left short on time and without many options, I hired a former student-athlete on a one-year basis to coach the distance events along with a young man, Greg Sholars, who had been working at the University of Florida as the speed and conditioning coach for football. He was a former Texas high school state champion, All-American track and field graduate, and athlete from Texas Christian University (TCU). He and I had bonded while at Florida and once he found out I had taken the position at Texas, he immediately put the pressure on me to hire him. Greg was full of ideas, passion, life, and energy, exactly what I needed. He called day and night, promising he could and would coach any event on the track, if I'd give him a chance. Texas had been a dream position for him. I knew he loved Texas, he loved coaching, he loved people, and he loved winning. I agreed to hire him and never regretted that decision. His passion and commitment matched mine perfectly and together we set out to rebuild the greatness of the University of Texas.

The team we inherited was left in disarray with most of the former talent having either graduated, gone professional, or failed out of school. The team was a shell of its former self. Of the fewer than twenty athletes who remained, most were on the verge of quitting, in academic trouble, or emotionally and physically burned out. I was told by the administration that the former staff had not been allowed to recruit and thus there was no new talent to develop. We had to work with what was left. I had been told to focus my energy on rebuilding the team and not worry about trying to salvage the talent that remained, which only drove Greg and I to work harder to motivate and nurture the talent and dreams of those who were on the team. I had learned that every person's dream mattered, and I had taken on the responsibility for each person I had been blessed enough to coach.

With my staff set and our focus set squarely on building our own brand of success, we headed for the women's department retreat. The retreat at The University of Tennessee had been held at a beautiful but rustic resort and golf club, which had not been very embracing of me as an African-American and thus I was leery of attending any event held at a golf club. As Greg and I drove onto the grounds of the Barton Creek Country Club, we were in awe and disbelief at the beauty and elegance surrounding us. Greg laughed and said, "I told you everything was bigger and better in Texas." He was right, for as we entered the facility, we were greeted royally as part of the University of Texas family. I let my guard down, embracing my new home.

The retreat was the first meeting Jody would host as the new women's athletic director and the room buzzed with excitement. I had not had the privilege of attending past retreats Donna Lopiano, the legendary, former women's athletic director, had held at Texas. But I knew she had been the one who set the standard of excellence for which Texas was known. Jody had already exposed me to those standards and as the meeting began, she dove straight in with her expectations.

I appreciated every minute of it. I was driven and being in a room full of like-minded coaches, enhanced my comfort level. I was comfortable and found it intoxicating to be surrounded by others with an unapologetic desire for greatness, excellence, and winning. I enthusiastically contributed my thoughts and opinions. We talked about how to help each student-athlete have a great experience and about how to be winners academically and athletically. As the meeting wore on, I noticed, from my periphery, Greg moving constantly. He fidgeted so much, I assumed he had to go to the bathroom. Finally, they gave us a ten-minute break and he looked relieved. But instead of bolting for the men's room, he pulled me aside.

Looking a bit distressed he said, "Bev, what are you doing? This is Texas. You can't speak up like that. Telling them what you think they need to change."

He was right. I didn't know Texas the way he did but I was shocked. I thought back to all the times I had spoken up and this was the one time I had felt most confident in my words.

He continued, "We're new here and we're the only Black people out here. You don't know Texas. You're going to get us both fired." I had no intention of losing our jobs, but I also had no intention of losing on the field of competition either. He and I were on a mission.

"Greg, in life you have only one of two choices. You can either kick ass, or you can kiss ass, and my mama taught me to never kiss ass. I don't know about you, but I ain't kissing nobody's ass. I want to win!"

My words hit him like a brick, jolting the winner in him, and he loudly proclaimed, "Hell, I ain't kissing no ass either so let's kick some ass." We walked back into the meeting and Greg was so on fire, I had to kick him under the table a few times. We bonded through that exchange, and together we set out not to merely rebuild Texas, but to create our own version of greatness.

From that day on, we had an unwritten rule to always do what was in the best interest of not only succeeding and winning, but what was also in the best interest of our athletes. Over the next three or four years, he and I rebuilt the Texas program, set new standards of excellence, and reinforced the foundation of greatness that the program would become known for.

Over years of coaching, I developed the philosophy that if one expects the best, they must give their best and be given the best. I had great expectations for those around me and of myself. Therefore, I intended to give my best. From the hotels we stayed in and the food we ate, to the uniforms we wore and how we traveled, all of it played a part in creating a winning mindset. If given the best, you begin to live and perform up to that standard. As I toured the facilities at Texas, I noticed they were subpar. Texas had always been one of the most stylish and competitive teams on the track and competing teams admired their fierce fighting mentality while simultaneously hating them for it. While looking around the track and field facilities, I was taken aback by the lack of quality for such high caliber athletes.

At the time, the women's track and field locker room was located underneath the football stadium and the space had to be shared with the roaches and rats that had taken up residency. I looked at the paint peeling from the walls and the beaten-up furniture in the locker-room and offices and my heart sank. The move had chosen me more than I had chosen it. I was at UT and committed to excellence. The team and I picked up paintbrushes and cleaning supplies and remodeled the locker rooms ourselves. We brought in new carpet and new furniture. With all the physical and cosmetic changes complete, it was now our desire to create our own version and standard of excellence *within* each athlete. That would be our most difficult challenge.

After creating a clean physical environment, we had to address the negative energy surrounding the team. We held our first official team meeting during which Jody was to officially introduce our new staff. She knew of the difficulty of the program and came into the meeting guns blazing. I loved her style. After listening to Jody in other meetings, I heard her special gift for mixing words with purpose and humor. But on the day of our meeting, I saw another side of Jody, and to be honest, I loved it. She walked in and without hesitation, beelined straight to the front of the meeting room. Within five minutes, she made both her statement and exit. Pointing towards my staff and I she said, "This is Coach Bev Kearney and her staff. She is the new coach here at The University of Texas and if any of you have any problems with that, feel free to transfer." At the conclusion of her statement, she smiled at us, welcomed us, and walked out. You are only effective as the people who manage you, and Jody showed me she was the type of leader who would not only allow, but would also encourage, success. As she left the room, I had no doubt I was where I was supposed to be.

We then gave the team thirty minutes to express whatever ill feelings they harbored toward the old staff, and our new staff for that matter, and after that, it was time to move forward. It was not a pity party. At the end of the session, I told them we had to focus on the next steps and their goals, leaving behind all other baggage as we moved forward with a clean slate and clear purpose. I left that meeting mentally, physically, and spiritually embracing everything about Texas. It was now my new home.

That year we won the NCAA Division I Southwest Conference Indoor Track and Field Championships with about fifteen athletes attending. We also finished as one of the top ten teams in the nation, actually we place tenth, with only two athletes scoring. I had battled to win a national championship the year before, and now I was grateful and cheering as we maintained a spot in the top ten. At the outdoor national championships, Greg and I ran into members of the filming crew who had followed me around for three days when I coached Florida at the championship the previous year. As we passed, they stopped to say hello and before leaving, they wanted to know if I knew where to find several coaches they needed to interview. It was a rude awakening to how far I had fallen in my move to Texas. I told Greg it'd be the last time anyone would ever be able to overlook Texas again. We decided we would never go to another National Championship as a non-factor.

At the end of the first year, we had made great strides towards our goal but still needed to fill voids on our staff. While replacing coaches and staff members, I noted that all the people I intended to hire just so happened to be African-American. It didn't dawn on me until Greg and I looked at the list of names for each position. It would in fact be the first all-Black staff at a predominately white institution. I needed a trainer and wanted to hire University of Florida graduate, LaGwyn Johnson Durden, who was at LSU working on her doctorate degree in sports medicine. I also wanted to hire a former jumper from Texas, Cynthea Rhodes Patterson. Texas had just hired me as its first African-American head coach in any sport, and if I were to hire the staff I needed, it would result in my having a Black staff.

I sought out the advice of others from a cross section of coaches in track and field—Black, white, male and female, all strongly advised me against it. Even warning me the action would ensure I would be fired. I didn't know any Black coaches in other sports, so I asked around and found several of the most successful Black women's basketball coaches in the country and just called them. Only one of them would answer or return my phone call and it was the one I needed. She was the Hall of Fame coach, Vivian Stringer who, at the time, was coaching at The University of Iowa. I explained who I was and why I was calling, concluding with the question of me hiring an all-Black staff.

Without hesitation, Coach Stringer told me, "When you're Black, it doesn't matter who you hire. If you don't win, you will be fired. If you do win, it won't matter to them what color your staff is. Make all your decisions based on winning." She concluded her advice by saying she knew Jody and that she was a fair person, and Jody was the only person from which I needed to seek advice.

I went to Jody and her response was to hire whomever I needed to hire to succeed and not to worry about the color of their skin. I hired the staff I needed at the time. Not only did we succeed, but their professional demeanor and work ethic impressed everyone. This gave me the credibility to talk to the academic director about hiring Ilrey Sparks-Oliver, an African-American who had run for me at Tennessee, as an academic counselor for women's athletics. Initially, the academic department did not fully embrace the idea. They reluctantly agreed to hire her as a tutor, then promoted her to academic mentor and by the end of her first year, hired her full-time as an academic counselor. Together, we rebuilt the foundation of the winning tradition of Texas Track and Field both on the track and in the classroom. They helped set the foundation for the six National Championships the teams would win throughout my tenure. Those teams would also be among the strongest academic teams at the university.

Greatness is not situational. It's a lifelong mindset. That all-Black staff, which also included my volunteer coach, four-time Olympian and medalist Michelle Freeman, went on to accomplish greatness well beyond their stays at Texas. Greg stayed for four years before moving on to become a successful head coach and subsequent businessman. Cynthea was with me for four years, becoming not only an Olympian in 1996, but also a top business executive. LaGwyn came into the program in 1993 and remained with me until my departure in 2012. She would become the trainer for several Olympic teams and then go on to become the director of a historical position created for her at the NCAA national offices. Ilrey was like a daughter to me and her being at Texas was a blessing for me and the student athletes. She, just as the rest of the staff, never saw color or gender. We only saw potential and capabilities. Ilrey worked tirelessly to ensure every student-athlete in her care achieved greatness, and as a result of her efforts, her students experienced unparalleled successes in their academics.

Ilrey died in the car accident that left me paralyzed, but her legacy lives on in her daughter Imani. Furthermore, there was a scholarship established in her honor at the University of Texas and the study center library bears her name. Both Ilrey and Michelle lived with me while they built their careers. They were like sisters, attending every track meet with Michelle coaching and Ilrey there as an administrative representative. Michelle went on to have a historical career as a four-time Olympian, a medalist, and now as a world-class coach. She would eventually marry and have a beautiful daughter, Tamya. Her survival and success in the face of adversity would be put to the test as she was the driver of the car in the accident that resulted in the deaths of her beloved mother and her sister of the soul, Ilrey. She eventually bounced back, dedicating all her success in honor of the ladies who had meant so much to her, her mother Murial, and Ilrey, her sister.

It would be the accident that took the lives of two very special people that would not only change my life forever, but it would touch the lives of people all over the world. It would serve as a catalyst for my life's journey and purpose beyond the boundaries of coaching.

CHAPTER 14

As cold chills moved through my motionless body, I lay peacefully in a dark void, something I had never experienced. However, I could still feel the warmth and light of love within the void. Strangely enough, I transcended into a place of knowing, a place of benevolence. I drifted further into the comfort of the moment. Although I was aware of the chaos surrounding me, all I could see was pure blackness and I felt a sense of peace and love. Disruptive voices of pandemonium engulfed me, and I sensed panicked energies, yet calmness still emanated from deep within me. For some reason, I knew I was being embraced by a higher power, an energy resonating with peace and love. Intuitively, I tried to reassure the strange voice speaking softly into my ear that I was all right. Despite my reassurance, the voice, which was female, kept whispering gently, "Don't worry, you're going to be okay."

I gave up the debate with the strange voice and simply accepted that I was already okay. Despite the chills from the cold, damp ground, which coursed through my body, I felt warmth and peace. No pain, no fear, just an overwhelming sense of benevolence.

Slowly, through the darkness, the sunlight began to appear, touching my body in a way that imported me back to semiconsciousness, making me aware of the physical warmth and the attentiveness I was receiving. While the light wasn't overwhelming, its effects were immediate. I drifted towards its warmth and security, bringing me more into the awareness of the now. In the midst of my awareness, a radiant, glowing figure moved towards me. I attempted to focus intently, to discern what I was seeing. It was Ilrey. She was emitting a peaceful and loving energy. Although I could tell it was her, she was somehow emotionally unrecognizable. She had an undeniable glow and serenity about her. Her energy gave me a sense of peace, reassurance, and love. I felt relieved in her presence. She no longer looked worn and tired from all the pain-filled stress of her worldly years. Her smile was bright and her heart was filled with unconditional love, emanating forgiveness of all the trespasses and actions of her life. This experience was overwhelming to say the least. It shifted me to an altered state of consciousness, connecting me to every single soul that existed. Not only in my immediate circumstance, but every soul in my life's experience.

As we approached each other, her smile lit up every aspect of her being. We met in what looked and felt like air but was called nowhere. She smiled, letting me know she was all right. I saw movement behind her and around her but couldn't make out faces. At one point, I thought I saw my grandmother but shrugged it off. As I gazed, in awe of her presence and basking in the light of love, she began to move away. I called out to her, begging her not to go. As she continued to exit this loving experience, I begged her to let me go with her. I had subconsciously searched throughout my life for this loving, warm, peaceful feeling and I had no intention of being separated from it. I begged her again to stay or take me with her. Ilrey lovingly turned to me and said, "You have to go back. It's not your time. It is my time and Murial's time. You have so many things left to do, so much love to give. They all need you and you have the power to teach and effectuate change."

"Ilrey, remember I'm struggling already to find myself, I'm afraid. I don't think I am strong enough!"

She smiled, seemingly amused at my confusion, before saying, "Yes you are. You just have to believe and trust in your strength. We will give you the words and you will always be surrounded by our love. You have to go back because this is where you're supposed to be."

Again, she smiled reassuringly and began to dissipate, either from my sight or my consciousness. However, words were spoken from this nowhere place, clearly and resoundingly. "Remember this feeling of love and share this with all who walk into your experience. Your love will be tested, but know each test will strengthen you and will bring you closer to this love light we exist in." Finally, I heard, "Take care of Imani and teach her as she moves forward in life and goes through life's circumstances. Trust us and trust yourself."

I winced as everything drifted back into darkness and the chilled air engulfed my body. I found myself shivering, crying out to the voices around me, "I'm cold." The response was immediate, "She's got to be cold, get a blanket." I never felt the blanket being placed on me, only the chills dispel into the darkness. The change settled my heart and I drifted back towards the warmth of the light. As I floated, I could still hear the faint sounds of the stranger's voice reassuring me I would be okay. And then it happened! The most amazing moment of my life. I heard my mother's voice. I felt at peace as I reached out to her and I could feel the loving comfort of her hand as she stroked my face, telling me she loved me, telling me I had to stay, telling me to take care of our family. It had been those rare moments of affection from her that I lived for, and now she loved me in ways I never could have imagined. I found comfort by her and I promised her I would I take care of everyone. As she reassured me, I drifted further into the darkness. The voices of the strangers gently pleaded with me, "Hold on, you're going to be okay."

I was again surrounded by complete darkness and felt the cold wetness of the ground beneath me. I couldn't see anything, but could hear everything happening around me. The peace-filled dream had now dissolved into chaos and darkness and I struggled to force myself from the grips of a beautiful dream that had become a nightmare. I focused on the warmth of the night, moving myself back towards the state of euphoria I had just experienced. As the winds hit my body and darkness turned to light, I heard the sounds of emergency vehicles in the background. More voices joined in as the chaotic scene erupted into screaming commands of action, not of comfort. I kept telling myself, and those around me, that I was all right, but no one was listening.

The gentle light of love I had experienced turned into blaring lights being aimed at me rather than illuminating the scene. The gentle female voice that had comforted me earlier was replaced by a male voice that was firm, direct, and mixed with business and concern. It was flat out noisy now. However, all I could see was darkness and flashes of a harsh light occasionally beaming into my face. Suddenly, the energy directed towards me was different. His voice was alarming. I wondered what was happening around me, not to me because I knew I was, and would always be, okay. But something was terribly wrong. This was definitely not a dream.

Although I could not see, I perceived sounds of what appeared to be a helicopter hovering close by. I heard noise of the engine and felt the force of the wind from the propellers. Then, everything went blank.

My next memory was waking up on what felt like a slab in a hospital emergency room. As I tried to comprehend what was happening, I opened my eyes to see a doctor standing over me. He asked for my name. I told him. He asked if I knew what had happened to me. I paused and hesitantly stated, "I think I was in a car accident."

* * *

As I lay on the table answering question after question, totally unaware of the personal physical damages that I had sustained, or even the severity of the accident itself, one thought came to mind. I immediately asked, "Where is Imani? How is Imani?" For some reason, I didn't think of anyone else but her. One of the medical attendees asked me to be quiet and listen, and that's when I heard her tiny voice cry out, "Ouch, that hurts." Her voice must have comforted me, for it was the last thing I remember hearing as I drifted back off into my euphoric dreamlike state, hoping to re-connect with my mother once again. It would not be my mother who I awoke to, but a room full of medical personnel attending to my body, which now was covered with needles and tubes, a neck brace, and a facemask. I was not in that harmonious place of love and peace, but I had awakened to a sterile intensive care unit at Shands Hospital in Jacksonville, Florida.

I lay in ICU, fighting to remember the moments before the darkness had overcome me. I remembered driving to Orlando and getting sleepier and sleepier. I had consumed multiple cans of Mountain Dew® hoping the caffeine would keep me awake. I played music, talked on the phone—did anything to stay awake, but none of it was working. Although we were within a couple of hours from our destination, I could no longer focus. I couldn't see the road and it had officially become dangerous for me to keep driving. I had pulled the SUV over at the nearest exit and told Ilrey, Michelle, and Michelle's mom, Murial, it was no longer safe for me drive. I suggested we get a hotel room for a few hours, sleep at a rest stop, or one of them should resume driving. Little did I know, that one decision between us would impact, alter, and cost lives.

It was supposed to be a trip of celebration with my housemates, Ilrey and Michelle, both celebrating their newly found independence. Michelle had recently purchased a new condo for she and her mother, and Ilrey had finally been able to afford a new apartment for she and her daughter. They would all be moving in January and no longer living with me. In a way, I was also celebrating the next stage of my life, personally and professionally, as I had finally resolved the inner conflict of my sexuality. I had revealed to Ilrey, among a few others, that I was gay.

We had all in some way found what we thought were loving relationships. Ilrey and Michelle had both found the men of their dreams. I was grappling with the circumstances of my own same-sex relationship. After winning for so many years, my career took a tumble. When it happened, I discovered that I had no meaningful romantic relationships in my personal life. I had finally concluded that I was gay, but still alone. When a relationship did present itself, it *seemed* to come at the right time, but in reality, it was not. As I drove away during the Christmas break, I knew the consensual relationship I was having with a student-athlete had to end. Ilrey, who was in the final stages of her own divorce, and I spoke about the pain of breaking up and my need to break off the relationship she had been encouraging, almost demanding, I end. I knew what needed to be done and although painful, she had ended her marriage and found love again and I needed to end the one I was engaged in.

Aside from that, I had a renewed passion for coaching. Although Jody's stepping down as athletic director had opened the flood gates of attacks against me from within the department, I had decided to focus on winning again and ignored the confusion. The biggest challenge I had now was the new staff. They were great people and good coaches, but paled in comparison to the driven and focused staff I'd had in the past. Aloneness washed over me. They weren't against me but they weren't exactly *for* me. Either they, or I, needed to make changes in order to rebuild a team that was once National Champions and now could barely remain in the top ten. Michelle, Ilrey and I all needed to reflect and plan our next stages in life. The road trip would do that and so much more, just not in the manner any of us anticipated.

We left Austin, stopping briefly in Houston, to see both Ilrey and Michelle's new boyfriends. Unbeknownst to us, Ilrey and Robert had been discussing marriage after her divorce finalized, but that encounter would be the last time he would ever hug or kiss her. After arriving in Mississippi, we spent Christmas day laughing and watching my crazy family play cards, argue, curse, smoke, eat, and drink. It had been a long day and we knew staying at my sister's house was not an option. So, we hit the road, excited to get to Orlando to spend the rest of the Christmas break in warm weather, enjoying the fun of Disney World. I drove because I always did all the driving, but after the first six hours or so, I was exhausted. Michelle and her mom appeared to be wide awake, so Michelle took over. I got in the back seat with Ilrey who'd taken Imani out of her car seat and laid her across our laps. No sooner than Michelle had taken off, I fell asleep.

I remember being awakened by the sound of Michelle's haunting, yet surprisingly calm voice yelling, "Bev help me! Help me Bev!" Unsure whether or not I was dreaming, I slowly sat up, only to see headlights coming straight towards us. I had no time to ask questions. I instinctively leaned forward in an effort to take the wheel to steady the car, while calmly reassuring Michelle.

"Don't panic, it's all right. I got it." Without warning, I felt the jerk of the vehicle and then darkness. Apparently, before I could take over the steering wheel, Michelle jerked it hard in an effort to avoid the oncoming traffic. From there, everything went black. In the darkness, all I could remember was the calming voices, the darkness, the chills, the warmth, but no pain.

Even as I lay in the ICU, I was unaware of how much damage had been done to my body or the fate of the other passengers. I had no idea I had undergone a lifesaving, five-hour emergency back surgery to repair my spine. I didn't even know that staples had been placed in my head or that I was wearing a turban like wrap over my braided hair. I later found out from Derick that he had received a call from my sister telling him of the near-fatal accident. He hopped on a plane that same day from Dallas to Jacksonville. He had actually arrived while I was still in the emergency room prior to what would be the first of three surgeries I would endure. He saw me lying on the gurney, unconscious and soaked in blood. My head and body were so swollen, I was barely recognizable. He witnessed the extensive scarring on my face, arms, legs, and body, causing his eyes to water as he said I looked so badly damaged that there was little hope I would survive. The doctor who spoke broken English had confirmed his greatest fears, there was in fact a good chance I wouldn't make it. He went on to tell him that even if I survived the surgery, there would be little chance I would ever walk again. My brother relayed to me that although he had rarely ever prayed, he stood over me, tears falling from his eyes praying, "God, please help my sister. Don't let her die. Please help her."

I was later told Michelle had swerved to avoid the oncoming traffic and the SUV actually flipped over three times, ejecting both Ilrey and I from the back seat. Ilrey, who was thrown from the vehicle first didn't survive, neither did Michelle's mom. That information was relayed three days later. I was ejected second, landing fifty feet from the SUV. Despite Ilrey's two-year-old daughter not being in a car seat, rather, lying between us, she wasn't thrown from the vehicle. Most people contributed our ejection to us not wearing seatbelts, which may have been true. But Michelle's mom, who *had* been wearing her seat belt, did not survive.

The greatest mystery of all was how Michelle sustained no major injuries. As she watched her mother take her last breaths, she heard the sound of a small voice behind her. When she turned, she found Imani, unharmed, lying on the floor of the SUV behind the driver's seat. She told me she was grateful to find Imani because her presence jolted her back to reality. She unbuckled her seat belt, grabbed Imani and hid her face from the scene within the car and the scene occurring outside. She said she knew when she saw the EMS crew drape a sheet over Ilrey that she didn't survive. When she saw them working on me, she knew, at least for the moment, I was still alive.

Many people came to the conclusion that Imani was in a car seat, but the car seat was actually amongst the other contents of the car, which had been scattered on the highway and the embankment. You can come up with many explanations as to why a child laying between two adults was not ejected, but the reality of the situation—and I know this sounds like a cliché—is some things are meant to be. I mean that from a spiritual perspective.

After my complete recovery, I had the opportunity to assess Imani's survival, and it was with the inclusion of all my spiritual readings and teachings. I may have been her caretaker after the accident, but she was my strength and my teacher. After Ilrey's transition, Imani gave me the tangible purpose of getting back to the world and coaching. However, my spiritual growth would teach me through trial and error *how* to do this. Imani was the cheerleader and my inspiration to keep it moving. I don't know if I would have been so obsessed with standing, walking, and driving if things had been any different. But because of her presence, I was focused. Now you must understand, none of this means raising Imani after her experience of losing her mother was all peaches and cream. We both needed healing and we both needed God's help in moving beyond the accident and our losses. There were many days I saw Ilrey through the words and actions of Imani, and many days I saw myself. My ability to learn and evolve in the way I did was due to her presence. She taught me subtle lessons that a mother normally nurtures into her children, lessons of love and strength. Yeah, I guess you could say Imani and I were destined to be together. It was simply meant to be. It was not our time.

Being isolated in the hospital, I had no idea of the sheer number of calls the hospital had received or that news of the accident had been broadcast all over the world. I also had no concept of the number of people who had flooded the hospital's lobby. The ICU only allowed two family members to visit. To this day, I have no idea how LaTanya, my former assistant coach from the University of Florida, managed to work her way into the room. As I lay in bed talking to LaTanya and Derick, doctors and nurses rushed into the room, almost screaming, insisting that I had to take an important call. Unsure of what to say, LaTanya asked for me, "From whom?"

"The President of the United States is calling for Ms. Kearney." *Oh wow, now I'm Ms. Kearney.* They tried to figure out how to get a phone into the room, but it was Latanya who said, "Nope, we gonna roll her out of here to the nurse's desk. She's gonna take that call." They immediately started unplugging things and moving me. As they wheeled me next to the nurses' desk, my heart fluttered. I was a bit overwhelmed with what outside my room felt and looked like. I looked around in awe as they handed me the phone, and that's when I heard a familiar voice, "Hey Bev, how you doing? This is President Bush. How they treating you?"

I reassured him not to worry, "You know me, I'm fine. I'll be back on the track in no time."

He laughed, "I told my wife you're a fighter and that you'd be okay. If you need anything, you have them to get in touch with me." I thanked him for checking up on me and we laughed a bit longer before hanging up. They wheeled me back into my room and immediately reconnected me to the various devices and monitors. I told them to hold on because it was apparent I no longer needed everything, considering I had survived being unplugged and wheeled into the hallway. They removed the oxygen mask and several other things before settling me back into my room.

After the phone call from the President of the United States, the people at the hospital must have thought I was somebody important. LaTanya told me the rules of ICU and the hospital were adjusted to accommodate their requests and needs, especially about how many and how long visitors were allowed in the room. To me, it didn't seem like such a big deal until an older Black female aide came in. She reminded me of my grandmother. She and a younger Black male were cleaning around me when she leaned in closer to me. Her words made me proud.

"Baby, I don't know who you are, but thank you. These white folks are jumping around here for a Black person and we've never seen anything like it. So thank you honey, thank you." She went on to tell me in whispers how the President had called, and they thought it was a prank and hung up on his office. Apparently, the hospital had been flooded with calls of people pretending to be family so when they got the call from the President, they hung up, assuming it wasn't true. The President's office called back, demanding action.

She laughed and said, "Baby, you should've seen those white folks jumping." I smiled as I lay there thinking back on how often I had seen my own grandmother jump at the beckoning call of her employers. Although my own grandmother was not able to share that moment, that this woman who reminded me so much of her had felt a sense of pride, gave me satisfaction.

To me, I wasn't important. President Bush calling was a friend checking on a friend. Although he and I were on different sides of most political issues, we shared a common bond of competitive spirits and a great sense of humor. He was funny and competitive, and we always had brief but great conversations each time we'd meet in Austin while he was serving as Governor of the State. A year after the accident, he reached out to me again, sending an invitation to attend the Annual White House Christmas dinner. Raymond accompanied me on the trip.

* * *

T he President and the First Lady descended down the stairs as dignitaries and celebrities from around the world lined the hallway to greet them. As he walked down greeting each guest, his face lit up as he neared me sitting in my wheel chair, still recovering from the accident. He leaned in and hugged me before standing up and proclaiming to the entire room that I was his hero.

When it was time for the actual dinner, a military attendant wheeled me into the dining area. The soldier placed me not at one of the far tables, but at the table of the President. That evening, I enjoyed an amazing dinner seated between President Bush and the great country singer, Kenny Chesney. We talked of many things and he knew I wanted to meet my hero, General Colin Powell, who had not only been appointed as the first African-American Secretary of State, but had been unanimously confirmed by the U.S. Senate which in itself, was a rarity. He had been on my bucket list of people with whom I wished to converse. When Governor Bush ran for the Presidency, he informed me that he had planned to have him in his administration along with Condoleezza Rice. I had told him I would love to meet them both. I hadn't known much about Condoleezza but I rushed home that evening and researched her. During the dinner, President Bush apologized to me for the absences of both Condoleezza Rice and General Powell, remembering I wanted to meet them. However, he explained they were unable to attend the dinner because earlier that day, the U.S. military had captured Saddam Hussein. President Bush proudly recalled the accounts of the capture as any great competitor does when victorious in battle.

Somehow the conversation shifted to the negative impact of performance-enhancing drugs in sports. He had asked my opinion and I told him the greatest threat of drug use was that it allowed athletes to bypass the process of becoming successful, therefore impacting their ability to recreate success throughout their life's journey. I really never cared about others using drugs. For me, it had always been a personal decision not to win by cheating. I had to work harder and smarter to beat them. It was from our conversation at the table, and even the contribution of an opera singer who said that in her field, weaker singers used drugs to strengthen their vocal cords eventually causing permanent damage, that led him to create initiatives against the use of drugs in sports.

* * *

My family came to the hospital, including my father and that lady, who was, by that time, his wife. It was LaTanya, who had spent the most time in my room, who first noticed that whenever that lady was in my room, the monitors would sound. After several episodes, she realized it only happened when that lady was around. LaTanya informed my brother of her observation and told him he needed to take care of it. Derick told our father that his wife was no longer allowed in my room. They both left and never came back. I never saw or heard from him throughout my recovery. I later found out it had only been at the urging of my aunt, his sister, that he had even come to the hospital in the first place. I didn't really care. I had already accepted him as my father and had long forgiven him for all the horrible things he'd done to my mother, my sisters, and me. I was at peace and in an effort to not hate him, I decided it was better to love him from afar. It would be several years before I would see him again. By then, that lady had died of ovarian cancer and he was recovering from a stroke in a nursing facility. Even then, he managed to be insulting when he saw us. For the first time in my life, I saw him cry and my heart went out to him. As I reached to hug and comfort him, he said, "I miss Virginia," which was that lady's name. He wasn't grateful that Derick and I had individually driven over a thousand miles to see him in North Carolina. I'm not sure he even cared.

The University of Texas supported me throughout my accident and representatives flew in on a private plane to see me in Jacksonville. The delegation included Jody and Chris Plonsky, who had replaced Jody as the new women's athletic director. I was surprised and happy to see them. I'm not sure how I looked from their end, but from what my brother and others have since described, it was probably shockingly scary. I had bandages all over my head and body, scarring on my face, and tubes and needles attached to my body. I had heard them whisper "paralyzed" but had no idea they meant me. I was also unaware they thought I would never walk again. Despite what they saw, they were supportive and reassuring. Their presence and that of my assistant coach, propelled me back to coaching mode. Everyone was shocked as I began to rattle off instructions for the team. The team had meant so much to me and I had finally reconnected with the joys of coaching. I might have been lying in a strange hospital room bandaged, bruised, and paralyzed, yet I was more alive, more connected, more empowered, more driven, more loving, and more at peace than I had ever felt in my life. Growing up, I had been taught to move on from every situation, but this was different. I was moving on while in the midst of it, not at the end of it. Something inside told me I would be okay.

The three years leading up to the moment of the accident had been emotionally painful years. As a track and field coach, I had spent most of my career working in environments where both covert and overt racist and misogynistic tones existed. I had been blessed throughout my career to have a strong inner circle, which helped protect and support me within those environments, allowing me to have the successes I had experienced. After several personnel changes, I no longer had the connection or protection of my staff. Frankly, they were purely people who worked for me. As a result, in the years prior to the accident, I felt tired, lonely, lost, and exhausted from fending off the constant attacks that came primarily from within the department and my own staff. After winning four straight national titles, the last having been in 1999, the team struggled to remain in the top ten. As I had reflected prior to the trip, my success had caused my current downward trend. I had gotten spoiled by the drive and dedication of my team and assumed that by signing talent, we would remain champions.

By 2001, while I had hired and recruited talented coaches and athletes, they didn't have the same drive needed to overcome the pressure and stress of winning. Many people want to win but they are not willing to pay the price of success. It felt like I was always pushing for everyone to step up to the plate. Meanwhile, resentment had started to build. I didn't know how to *not* be driven to be the best and I had very little understanding of others who were willing to lose. It had been like oil and water or fire and ice. Whichever analogy fit, the energy of the team and staff had become toxic. We were no longer bonded by a common purpose and I had felt like I was alone on an island, leaving me more vulnerable than I had ever been.

I had longed for the years prior to the 2000's. Back to a time when my teams worked to figure out how to win. In 1997 we were one of the team favorites at the NCAA Outdoor National Track and Field Championships trying to defeat the powerful LSU Tigers who had won the last ten or more championships. We were a fairly young team battling for the championship and by the final day of the four-day competition, we had a significant lead. As the final day began, we fell apart, one race at a time. It had been a slow, painful death to watch as LSU methodically closed the scoring gap. As the final event, the women's 4x400 relays rolled around, we were behind by eleven points. We were the favorites to win the event but winning would be worth only ten points. Simple math dictated that even if we won the relay, we would lose the meet to LSU by one stinking point.

As the teams lined up for the final event, the television crews decided to line the LSU team up on the infield of the track prior to the start of the final race. As LSU's team strolled in, cheering across the track, they looked at our relay team waiting to run and gave our young ladies the choke sign. In fairness, we *had* choked under pressure. At the conclusion of the meet, as LSU celebrated another championship, we begrudgingly accepted the second-place trophy for the second year in a row. That evening, as I sat alone in my room, part angry, part shocked at the loss, pondering what went wrong, there had been a knock on my door. In walked members of the team led by Toya Brown, Angela

Vaughn, Nanceen Perry, Kim McGruder, and Susanne Reid, among others. They all sat down waiting for me to either fuss or give them words of wisdom and encouragement, but I was speechless.

Finally, I said, "I don't know what to say. What do you guys think?" I'm not sure who spoke up, but I think it was Nanceen who said, "We already talked about it and we already decided that as long as we are at Texas we will never lose another National Championship. Now I don't know what's gonna happen after we leave, but as long as we're here, we're winning." After they spoke, they left the room. I knew I had to do my part and create a winning staff. As we boarded the plane home, there was no getting around it. I had to make changes.

That summer, I brought in a new staff with a renewed commitment to win. When the team came back, they were introduced to their new coaches, John Rembao and Diane Whorley. Along with returning staff members, Michelle Freeman, Ilrey Oliver Sparks and LaGwyn Durden, their drive to win equally matched mine and together, we went on to win four straight NCAA titles and set records along the way.

Soon John and Diane moved on to other positions and by 2000, the team had started a downward spiral. It had taken me several recruiting classes to rebuild and as I lay in the hospital bed in 2002, I finally had a team to match my tenacity and drive. Their commitment to be their best was now pushing me past the restrictions of lying in a bed in Jacksonville. I needed to get back to Austin. The thought of my team and Ilrey's two-year old daughter, Imani, gave me the inspiration to heal and get back to life and work. Before Chris and Jody left the hospital, I reassured them I would be coaching in no time. I don't know if it was the medication or just being in my own zone but I didn't notice the looks on their faces. Later I was told no one, including Derick, believed I would ever coach again.

I had no concept of time and had no idea how long I had been hospitalized or even what day it was. I just knew it was time to go home to Austin. I informed the doctors and my family that I was ready to go home. They told me that they would elevate my hospital bed to slowly rise, emulating a seated position. If I could rise to level six, I would be okay to be flown back to Texas. I thought to myself as everyone gathered around the bed, *Let's do this.* Surely, I could get to level six and even seven if I had to. As they hit level one I thought, *Okay, I am good.* With level two, I was a bit uncomfortable, but okay. They paused at every level and when they hit level three, the pain hit. I tried to keep a straight face and internally coach myself up, *Come on Bev, you can do this.* Three more levels. They hit the button to elevate the bed to level four and I could have sworn I saw Jesus and all His disciples as the pain catapulted past 100 to 1,000. As grateful as I was when they lowered the bed, I was still disappointed as my mind, body, and that darn pain medication they were pumping into me failed to even get beyond level four. *What the heck!* The doctor said they would have to do another surgery to in order for me to travel, which went well and I was told I could now be flown back to Austin.

On the day I was scheduled to be flown back to Austin, I asked my brother what date it was. That's when I found out I had been in the Jacksonville hospital for almost two weeks. As they rolled my hospital bed outside to an awaiting ambulance to take me to a private plane accompanied by Derick and a nurse, the sun hit my face for the first time in weeks. It both excited and scared me. I became anxious about being outside. I had become accustomed to being in an enclosed room. It had felt safe. Even the fresh air was strange and as they loaded me into the cramped quarters of the airplane to be airlifted back to Texas, my heart settled and filled with joy as I knew I was finally going home.

CHAPTER 15

Being back in Austin, I found myself in a hospital suite, not fancy, but big. As I settled in to my new surroundings, I noticed everyone being quite nice to me. So nice in fact, I told Gerettia, who was staying with me during my recovery, not to say anything, because they thought I was someone important. I thought if they knew I was an average patient, they would take me back to the other room I had been in, and I really liked the new room. It didn't look anything like a hospital room and all of my family knew I had a fear and dislike of hospitals. I had avoided them up until the accident. The room was truly an extension of my personality and I was comfortable in it. I had no idea how long I was scheduled to be in the hospital and it being my first hospital stay, I asked them to make it feel like home.

I was hospitalized in Austin from mid-January 2003 until mid-March 2003. Over the two months, not only did my body go through many transformations, my inner spirit did as well. Although my physical being had atrophied and weakened, my spiritual self grew in strength and power. I might have become a shell of my former self, having gone from 140 pounds to somewhere under 100 pounds, but I had never felt more powerful and peaceful. Something different existed within me but I could not put words to it. People came to see me from near and far, but it had been the visit one day from my friend Raymond that brought me the most joy. He had been to the hospital several times and the room was always full of people. He would kiss my entire forehead and settle in the back of the room watching everyone entering and leaving. I originally asked him to go on that fateful Disney trip with my makeshift family that he had become so much a part of. He had graciously, and in hindsight wisely, declined my offer.

One particularly memorable day, I opened my eyes to see him alone in my room, sitting quietly beside my bed. He shifted nervously in his seat as he wrestled to find the words for a conversation that would forever change not only my life, but his as well. He spoke with caution as if he was channeling the words from somewhere else. He asked how I was doing and I gave him the same run-of-the-mill answer I normally gave well-wishers who asked that question.

Then he asked if I was afraid. I don't really recall what rehearsed answer I gave, but he saw right through it. He leaned in as if his words were meant only for me to hear.

"I've been praying and meditating on you every single morning, trying to come up with an answer or a reason why this is happening. I've been so depressed and guilt-ridden since the accident, and have been trying my best to find some comfort and peace in it all. This may sound crazy to you Bev, but I need you to hear and believe me."

I clung to his words as if I was reading an intriguing novel. He continued, "What I'm about to tell you no one knows but my Dad and he's crossed over. Not even my siblings know. I've always kept this to myself and for my own purposes cause I knew everyone would think I was crazy or full of shit. When I meditate, I actually talk with my angels. I ask questions and listen to their love-filled insights. They've not only guided me through various circumstances, but they've also provided me with insights and direction to all my worldly experiences. I even asked them, prior to you leaving for the trip, if I should I go, since I was still dealing with my father's death. The reply was it wasn't my time yet. As strange as it seems, that's what was said. I didn't give it a thought other than to not go. Besides, I was still in a deep funk with my dad's death and dealing with my siblings. And who would believe me anyway? Hence, my response was no. This all made sense when the accident occurred and that's the reason for the guilt I guess. When I heard about it, that very next morning during my meditation, I asked them why, and what was to be the outcome. Both answers were refreshing and believe me, I'm on team Bev to encourage you along your recovery. But along with the answers came instructions with the insistence that I share them with you."

He took a long pause and I broke the silence by asking, "So what did they say?" He went on to tell me, "First, the angels kept telling me you're going to be okay and you'll walk again. Then, they wanted me to share with you about my meditations and to assist you, through meditation, with your recovery by allowing you to ask questions pertaining to treatments and outcome."

He looked at me timidly and asked, "So what do you think?" This must sound crazy, but for some reason, I knew what he was saying was true and part of the process. What I knew wasn't in anything I had ever read, nor did it come from some intellectual teaching I had gone through. Instead, it came from a place deep within me, as if it was a triggered memory. I looked at him and with all the confidence I could muster, asked, "So when do we start?"

With a look of surprise and confusion he responded, "Well I guess I should start by telling you all that was told to me. First you must know, usually I don't get clear answers to questions about others. Like

I said before, who would believe me? I felt like this experience was just for me and me alone. You see, when I'm close to someone, they don't reveal clear and concise information anyway. When I was younger I would present a lot of ego-based questions to the angels and get what I felt like was a slap on the wrist response as if that was a no-no."

He laughed at the thought of what he was saying, but I thought he was making excuses and not sure of himself. I guess it was harder than he had thought it would be, revealing a secret he'd held within himself for so long. He mustered the confidence to keep going and said, "However, when I heard the news about you, I was dying inside, and I told myself I would never tell anybody about this. I felt so guilty. You can't imagine my pain. So here we are with me spilling my guts."

Reverting back to his timid voice, Raymond stated, "You know, either in one of your prayers, or it could've even been a consistent thought you entertained over and over, you asked for a larger platform or a greater venue to speak from in an effort to touch people's lives, to heal hearts, and to inspire people to follow their dreams and visions. Well, in spite of all that has happened, this was the arena that was given to you."

In retrospect, the only way I could have learned in the manner in which I did was through an unfortunate and deadly set of circumstances. If I could change any of it, I would, but I can't, and it occurred this way. There I was, trying to figure it out. All things happen for a reason.

He went on to say he understood my feelings about Ilrey and Michelle's mom and knew it would take some time for me to move beyond it, but to know they were at peace. He later expressed that he needed me to invest my entire self into my recovery. The investment included my ego and my emotions as well as the tenacity and will to move forward. "As humans we are taught to saturate ourselves in the emotion of our circumstance as opposed to relying on the core of our spirit's consciousness to move us beyond our experience. This can be extremely liberating but it conflicts with what we are socially taught on how to deal with tragedy. The peace you've felt in the midst of all the trials and tribulations you've experienced was because of your ability to heal from within. This was one of the angel's directives for me to share with you."

I have always subconsciously known everything happens for a reason and whether we like what happens or not, we have to learn from it, then move on to whatever it is we are trying to accomplish in our lives. My story is not about the physical or emotional challenges I've overcome, but more importantly, it's about a spiritual awakening. It's about finding your inner will and utilizing the power within yourself to heal yourself of whatever you may face.

It's true, Raymond has some type of communication with Angels/God/Universe, whatever you choose to call it. He even told me about HBO and People magazine before I knew that they were going to call me. He also said, "Whatever this thing is that I do, meditating and communicating with my angels, we all have the ability to do it. It's just a matter of quieting ourselves in prayer, then meditating, and listening to our hearts. This opens us and allows us to be humbly, as opposed to fearfully, vulnerable.

"That is where God and the angels exist." I smiled because it was as if he had triggered a memory of something I had innately known all along. It's how I had unknowingly lived my life. He started recommending books for me to read and even brought some of them up to the hospital to fill the hollow hours when I was alone with my thoughts and memories. We shared countless conversations on spirits, spirit consciousness, and even discussing the social and political attitudes of the world. We discussed the idea of meditation and how to meditate, as well as how to control some of the pain associated with my injury. The many hours long talks I shared with Raymond and the books I read led me to a truth that I discovered about life and love, and this truth became my spiritual awakening. An awakening that would have occurred much later in life I'm certain. However, the accident accelerated my journey. The awakening led me to an inner strength that pulled me from the clutches of the wheelchair to standing. Yes, I will always remind myself that everything does happen for a reason, a God blessed reason.

I had started rehab, which consisted of therapist working to get me into a wheelchair, taking me down to the rehab center, and stretching me as I threw up. In my mind, things were moving along nicely. When I look back on it, things weren't going well but the thought of another surgery never crossed my mind. It had been such a beautiful Saturday, I had told my family and friends to take the day off and not come to the hospital. Truth be told, I had not been alone since the accident and I wanted some time by myself. Of all the days I told them to go away, it was the day the new doctor came in to tell me I would need another surgery. Everyone rushed to the hospital, only to be speechless and cry along with me. No one knew what to say, for in reality, there was nothing *to* say.

As they wheeled me down the stark, white basement hallways of the hospital, I could only see the brightness of overhead lights through the tears that streamed down my face. I asked "Why?" for the first time. I asked God why He allowed this to happen to me. Not why I had been in the accident, but why I had to endure a third surgery. I had screamed out in pure agony as the doctor in Austin told me he had looked over my charts and film and saw it as necessary to redo the entire surgery if I intended to walk again. I didn't hear much he had to say after that because I was stuck at "redo surgery." I screamed, "No! No! God, please no!"

As the tears flooded my face and my screams filled the air, he looked confused about what to do. With his red hair, freckles and small frame, he reminded me of an older Opie Taylor from the Andy Griffith show. He was a matter-of-fact kind of doctor. His bedside manner definitely left something to be desired. He always presented me with the facts. I liked his swagger. He projected a take charge, "I know what I am doing" posture. However, in that second, I needed more than facts and figures and skills. I needed consoling and he wasn't the one. I think he knew as much because he started hitting the call button and verbally summoned the nurses. As they entered the room trying to console me without success, he backed away.

I was scheduled to undergo surgery the following Monday. In the meantime, he sent me down to the labs for more tests to see exactly where the nerves were damaged. He also told me only one relative could accompany me to the lab, which was in the basement of the hospital. I chose Derick. He was always the calm one in our family but even he was shaken by the news. He apologized for not being able to come up with anything positive to say. As they wheeled me down to the lab, Derick realized he left something in the room and ran upstairs to retrieve it. The lab tech wasn't ready, so they literally parked me alone in the hallway, naked under the paper gown and sheets. I lay there on my back looking at the lights, talking to God. I was hurt, scared, and angry. I repeatedly asked God why He was allowing this to happen to me. The answer came through as clear as a conversation, but it came in the form of a question.

"Do you intend to walk again?"

I replied, "Of course."

The next question was, "What are you willing to do to walk again?"

"Anything I have to do."

"Then this is what is needed. Trust us, Trust Me, and Trust yourself, because the doctor cannot heal you without your help in healing yourself." I was told it would be my faith through the surgery that would determine my outcome. My tears dried up and by the time Derick came back still wearing a solemn expression, I was smiling.

The lab tech came out, pushed me up next to the lab table, and told me to slide myself over from the wheeled bed, onto the table. I laughed aloud and reminded him that if I could move myself over there, I wouldn't be down here. He was embarrassed but, in the end, he, my brother, and I had a good laugh together.

I had already survived two major surgeries and now, having thought the worst was behind me, I found myself being loaded into another ambulance and transferred to another nearby hospital for a third surgery. After the operation, I lay in bed awaiting to be transferred back to St. David's Hospital across town. My sister and I had been alone in the room when I caught a cramp in my right leg. I winced in pain. I screamed at her to help me as the pain began to shift from leg to leg before finally settling on cramping pains in both legs at the same time. It felt terrible as I realized my legs were finding life again in the most unimaginable way, through cramping. Gerettia smiled at me while saying over and over, "I am so happy for you."

What the hell! Help Me! I threatened to choke her if she said how happy she was one more time. She smiled and said it again. As I dealt with the pain, I remembered the exchange in the hallway before the surgery. *What are you willing to do to walk again? This is the only way.* Somehow, I found comfort in the pain and even more comfort in the sight of the nurses who my sister finally called in to help. By the time they transferred me back to St. David's hospital, I had contracted a virus and had to be placed in quarantine. My body emitted horrific smells and although my family and close friends had to visit me in what looked like hazmat suites, they still came.

As Raymond and I grew closer spiritually, he became my confidant and guide. His wisdom and insight enabled me to maneuver through all the unfortunate diagnoses from the doctors over the next two months. The first and most terrifying diagnosis was not that I would be confined to a wheelchair for the rest of my life, but that I had a serious case of vertigo caused by damage to my brain during the accident. After exhaustive testing, specialists told me the particular form of vertigo I had could not be treated. Vertigo is the sense of everything spinning when you move, creating lightheadedness and dizziness. I asked Raymond about it and he said it would go away. With that, I never thought of it occurring again. Over time, everyone forgot about me being diagnosed with vertigo, and I never had a problem with it again. Similar to the vertigo, most of my injuries disappeared. I'm not sure if it was a case of mind over matter, but having seen the other side of life, I had a newfound sense of knowing that I had never thought possible. Raymond helped put words to what I had been feeling inside. His presence as well was a constant reminder to stay centered in the promises whispered to my soul as I lay dying in the middle of that highway road.

Raymond and I sat in silence, contemplating the deep conversation we had just had concerning life and spirit, when a doctor I had never met came into the room. He too, had bad news. With every doctor came a new potential fear. This time I was told my most recent blood work showed that I had contracted hepatitis from either one of the blood transfusions or maybe from some undetected internal damage. He wanted to take me in for more testing and possibly for another surgery. As he spoke, Raymond, who was seated behind the doctor shook his head no. I asked the doctor to give me a moment and

I then asked Raymond his feelings. He said as the doctor spoke, he had been told that the symptoms would be gone within the next two to three days. I called the doctor back in and asked if he would kindly give three days to see if things would clear up. He argued his medical points and after each point I simply repeated my request to be given three days before moving forward with his recommendations. He held his ground and I held onto my request. I could see his frustration growing. Finally, he reluctantly agreed to allow me the three days. By the second day, the blood work was clear of any signs of hepatitis, but they kept testing me, drawing blood before 6 a.m. each morning. Eventually, the doctor stopped coming and it was never spoken of again. I went back to focusing on walking and coaching.

Just prior to the beginning of the indoor track and field season, I was told the team had been worried about me and that I should meet with them. The staff selected members of the team and I began to meet with each event group, reassuring them I would be back on the track. We had set high goals that season, and I told them in no uncertain terms, "I was the one in the accident, not you. So there is no excuse for any of you not to achieve your goals." I told them I would be there for them every step of the way and if at any time they felt the need to see me, they had full access. I know they must have been startled by my weakened and fragile appearance, but they were equally inspired by my words and inner spirit. If they knew I had no intention of quitting, neither should they or would they. During that entire indoor season, I coached from my hospital bed. My staff would film the workouts and track meets. I analyzed the tapes and gave the athletes and coaches feedback. As a coach, I was surprisingly sharper now. I could actually close my eyes and envision each athlete and performance and see clearly what was needed. My voice had become my body. Whereas I could no longer demonstrate, I could describe in such a graphic and detailed manner that the coaches and athletes could see my words. I was shocked to hear words coming from my mouth that I didn't even know existed in my mind. My team embraced my circumstances as temporary, but when others approached my room, it was different.

I couldn't figure out why people stared at me when they entered my hospital room or why they whispered as if noise might somehow harm me. I would hear people laughing and joking as they approached but as soon as they'd turn the corner and entered, they looked solemn and sad. They even talked to others in the room about me as if I wasn't there or as though I couldn't answer for myself. Finally, out of frustration, I asked Raymond why people were acting like I wasn't myself. He laughed softly and asked if I really wanted to know the truth. Of course I wanted to know. Still sort of laughing he replied, "Bev, they don't think you're going to make it. Some are coming to show their respects before you die."

I was in shock. "Raymond, what the heck! Do they really think I'm dying?"

He laughed louder now as he nodded his head repeating that everyone thought I was dying. I asked why they would think that. He laughed so hard I thought he was going to fall out of his chair.

"Bev, you look pretty bad right now." He told me if it weren't for my ever-present, big smile, it would be hard to believe it was me lying in the bed. I burst out laughing because I had not bothered to look at myself. The thought that I looked a mess made me laugh even harder. I had no idea what everyone else saw, only what I felt and visualized in my mind. Thus, I looked as if I had always looked. I felt like myself.

After talking with Raymond and frustrated with people whispering to me or about me, I made a rule. If you weren't upbeat, don't come in my room. I wasn't dying. I felt more alive than I had ever felt in my life. We both laughed for a while and then resumed talking about spirits and the books he had given me to read.

I still am not sure how I read the books, but I not only read them, I understood them. I could barely see but hadn't wanted to tell anyone because it would be another issue they felt the need to fix. That didn't bother me as much as what happened to me every evening around 6:00 p.m. or so. I would go from feeling fine to feeling sluggish. To top it all off, I continued to lose weight. I already weighed less than 100 pounds when my primary nurse told me if I continued to lose weight, they would have to place a feeding tube down my throat. I didn't know what a feeding tube was but I knew it sounded painful. I told them there was no way I was going to allow a feeding tube to be inserted. I had my family bring me the biggest burger they could find along with a large milkshake. It took me over an hour to force myself to eat it all and then I promptly became ill and threw it all back up.

Out of pure frustration and fear of a feeding tube being shoved down my throat, I called LaGwyn, the athletic trainer, and my nurse Robert. I had not been able to eat and every evening, I would slump into a zombie-like state. I needed to know all the medications I was taking and the purpose and side effects of each. To my surprise, I was taking so many heavy drugs it was a wonder I could function at all. I had always feared addictions and had stayed away from alcohol and drugs, even over the counter medications such as aspirin. I didn't even take vitamins! Now I was on so much medication that it scared me. As they read through the list of drugs, explaining its purpose and side effects, I decided which ones I wanted to stop taking. The ones of the most concern were the heavy pain medications, anti-depressants, and sedatives.

As the doctor and other nurses reviewed my request, they especially warned me against getting off the pain medication, telling me I needed to take into consideration the severity of my injuries. But after hearing the side effects of the drugs, I knew I needed to get off of them. I had tolerated the severe pain of them pulling over twenty staples from my scalp and back without medication and I figured I could deal with the back pain as well. The doctors and some of the nurses spoke to me about the nerve damage and the huge chunk of flesh, approximately the size of a cup, that had left a gaping hole in my back. They warned that without the pain medication, I would not be able to withstand the intensity of the pain. Finally, after being scared the crap out of, I called Raymond to my room. I didn't know as much about the angels as he did, and I knew everything he told me thus far had come to pass. I needed to be sure I was indeed making the right decision. I didn't ask him if I should get off the medication. I asked how long it would take my body to adjust to the pain. Without hesitation, he said within two to three days the pain would subside but in the meantime I would suffer greatly. I told him I would rather suffer three days of pain than to endure a lifetime of addiction to pain-killers and the zombie-like state I had been reduced to.

Needless to say, of all the decisions I had to make, the one to get off the pain medication was the biggest leap of faith I would ever make. It was decided that I would take Advil or an over-the-counter pain medication but everything else would cease. As the pain meds wore off, the debilitating pain in my body increased. I would stutter, no longer able to speak clearly and eventually it hit so hard, I blacked out. Still, I refused to go back. Not because I was brave or strong, but because being on them was not an option. I had no choice. I had to either move forward, trusting my spiritual self, or be enslaved by the pain, the side effects, and possible addiction to the drugs. By the second day, I could function and by the third day, I tasted food for the first time. I ordered a Pizza Hut personal pan pizza (I ordered the personal pan so I wouldn't have to share). I took a bite and for the first time in months, tasted flavor. I did everything but lick the crumbs from the box. I waited for two hours, praying I wouldn't throw it back up and I never did. It would take years for me to gain my weight back, but it was the decision to endure the pain that allowed me to get my life back.

I had lost movement in my body, I lost weight, I lost the control of my bowels and many other things, but the one thing I lost that impacted me the most was my loss of independence. I had spent my whole life learning how to take care of myself and now I couldn't even turn over without assistance. If I wanted to change positions in my bed, one of the nurses had to come in to turn me. Not only had I lost my freedom, I was rarely ever alone. I had always loved my alone time. I would either sit with a book, or in quiet room, or go for a walk or a jog and simply reflect on my life and the lives of others. Now, in the hospital, all those things had disappeared. Although I had clarity of thinking and a feeling of contentment unlike anything I had never experienced before, I was slowly becoming drained. My nurses were amazing, and I had become their confidant, encouraging them to move beyond their obstacles towards their dreams. Robert was my primary nurse and he and I would have the most amazing conversations. He was also my partner in crime. I would collect money from visitors each night and hide it under my pillow. After everyone left, I would call Tiffany's Treats and place an order for warm, fresh-baked cookies to be delivered. The nurses would make their rounds and end up in my room for conversation and cookies. Robert had aspirations of becoming a country music singer and writer and after our long talks, he pursued his passion for music and acting. He wrote and produced music and served as a consultant for the popular television series, "Friday Night Lights," which was filmed in Austin. As time went on, even the doctors asked for my help in talking with other patients who struggled with their paralysis. I loved helping people and it took my mind off my own circumstance. One night, while alone in my room, I had a moment of clarity for myself.

I glanced around at the posters decorating my walls. My eyes stopped at the large Texas Relays poster. The Texas Relays was a huge track meet, which attracted athletes from all over the country and some international athletes as well. I stared at the poster in my dimly lit room and thought to myself, *I'm going to stand at the Texas Relays.* That night, alone in my room, wide-awake and with fewer than usual interruptions, I repeated the thought over and over until finally it became real. I could actually see myself *standing* at the relays.

As sunshine seeped in through the window and the first nurse of the morning walked in, I proudly announced, "Hey I am going to stand at the Texas Relays!" Every person who entered my room that day, medical personnel and civilians alike, heard the same declaration. It was all I could think of and all I could talk about. No one discouraged me, probably because they didn't want to hurt my feelings. I did overhear one of the nurses mumble rather loudly to herself as she exited the room, "She can't even roll her ass over, talking about standing up." I heard her, but I ignored her. The thought had become so real there was nothing anyone could say to change my mind.

When my physical therapists came in, I told them of my desire to stand at the Texas Relays. They asked when the relays were and I told them in a month. They looked at each other, trying to decide who would break the news to me. Standing was considered a major feat and getting me to that point was expected to take a year or more if at all. They tried to convince me that I needed to learn to use the sliding board to transfer myself from the bed to the wheelchair, and then I needed to master life from the wheelchair. I refused to go to rehab unless they agreed to help me learn how to stand. Eventually they agreed, but I know it was a ploy to get me to go to rehab. They insisted

I learn to use the sliding board and the wheelchair in order to get to the rehab room to learn to walk. "Deal," I agreed. With that, I used the sliding board and wheeled myself to the rehab room. I held them accountable for everything we did and how it applied to me standing. Without the drugs, my mind was clear and focused. I had a goal.

The speed at which my body healed itself surprised everyone. It didn't surprise me because I had seen my mother go through horrendous injuries sustained from fights and car accidents. My body healed so quickly that as soon as they ordered one back brace, I transitioned out of it and they would have to order a new one. One day, I was finally able to sit in the shower as opposed to being wheeled down to the wet room in a big blue plastic tub. There, they would grab a large handheld shower head and family and friends would take turns bathing me. That day, as I sat in the shower with my sister bathing me, the brace I had been wearing fell off. I knew right then that I would stand and within no time, they placed me in a machine that allowed me to stand upright for the first time.

My dream of standing at the Texas Relays had given me new purpose for being in the hospital. It had helped to ease the internal pains of my loss of independence and quiet time. During the week, I focused on standing, counseling, and coaching. On the weekends, I looked forward to the calls from my coaches and the team who had been competing at various meets across the country.

My breaking point came on a Sunday evening as my sister and I sat alone in the room watching television and getting updates on my team which was competing in the 2003 Indoor Big 12 Conference Championships. At the conclusion of the meet, they called excited, announcing their victory. But for some reason, along with my elation came a strange sense of sadness. I felt as though I would break down and cry. I had not cried much because it was painful and worried my family and friends so much that I held all my emotions in. This was different. The tears would come any minute so I asked my sister to help me to my wheelchair. I needed to get out of the room for a while.

I never left my room. In fact, they had sent a psychiatrist to see me out of concern, thinking something was wrong. One afternoon I had been taking a short nap only to wake up to this strange slender, older white guy with facial hair and wire-rimmed glasses sitting next to my bed with a pen and paper. He talked in whispers, introducing himself and telling me he had come to speak with me. I figured out from his demeanor and conversation that he was a psychiatrist or something. He spoke about life in the hospital and how I was coping but I never said a word. Finally, he asked if I had any questions. I said, "Yes I do. I just have one question. Am I paying you? Because unless you have something you want to talk to me about, I'm fine." He told me everyone was concerned because I never wanted to leave the inside of my room. I told him that sick people were in the hospital and I had never been able to handle people being hurt or in physical pain. Therefore, it felt safer in my room. There was no way anyone could have ever known the amount of pain I had witnessed my family go through, and the thought of seeing others suffering was unbearable.

Despite my apprehensions about going outside, that night I had to get out. As I wheeled myself down the hall, I could feel the tears beginning to fall. I had remembered the solitude of the hospital basement and knew no one would be down there on a Sunday evening. I hit the elevator button, got off on the underground level, and wheeled myself into a corner facing the wall. I broke down crying. Just as the crying was getting good, I felt a tap on my shoulder. It was my weekend nurse. I told him I just felt the need to cry, that nothing hurt or was really wrong. For some overwhelming reason, I just felt the need to cry.

The next morning, every nurse who walked into my room asked

if I was okay, which frustrate me. Finally, I asked, "Why do you guys keep asking me that and looking at me with pity?" Nurse Robert told me my crying breakdown was noted on my chart and everyone was concerned. *So I'm not even allowed to cry without it being over analyzed or negatively impacting my loved ones?* It was time for me to go home. My tears had not been tears of pain. Instead they had been tears that served to empower me to have the courage to move on from the safety of my hospital room and go forward.

* * *

That Monday, I started a rumor about myself. I greeted everyone who entered my room that day, visitors and medical staff, not with a hello but with, "You know I'm going home on Friday." By the following day, even my doctors began to prepare me to go home. I guess they all thought that the other doctor had cleared me to leave. Everyone was excited and finally on that Wednesday, someone asked Gerettia who had authorized my release. Gerettia, being Gerettia, could not wait to spill the beans as she proclaimed with a smirk on her face, "Shit, I've been waiting for someone to ask me that damn question. Hell, Bev started that shit herself. Nobody told her ass she could go home." Then she had the nerve to laugh. But by this time it was too late. Even the press knew I was going to be released that coming Friday. My physical therapist was furious, telling me not only was I not ready to go home, but I would prove to be a burden to my family if I did. She demanded I be able to tie my own shoes before she would sign off on my release.

My back had been broken but not my spirit. Although I could barely sit up, let alone reach my own feet, I was going home. It took me almost an hour to figure out how to tie just one shoe. Exhausted, I looked at the second shoe, trying to gather the strength to begin to tie it when the therapist was called away. As soon as she left the room I turned to nurse Robert and pleaded with him to tie my other shoe and make it look like the same horrible way the one I had tied looked. When she walked in and saw both shoes tied, she reluctantly gave her approval. I was going home.

On Friday, as I loaded up to head home, it dawned on me that I was not going to have around the clock care like I had in the hospital. I had to shake off my fears, but as we approached my house, and they wheeled me to my room, I knew my life would be different. I was not the same person who had left there on December 23, 2002. I was now returning home March of 2003 a physical shell of my former self, but not weaker as a person.

While I adjusted to my new surroundings, my team laced up to compete at the NCAA Collegiate Indoor Track and Field Championships, finishing fourth. It was time to get back to doing what I loved, coaching.

As Derick wheeled me onto the grassy infield area of the Mike Myers Stadium at the Texas Relays, I could feel the rush of energy throughout my body. We were accompanied by hospital staff, friends, family and various University of Texas staff and administration. This was it. This was what had driven all those nights in the hospital. My desire to stand at the Clyde Littlefield Texas Relays. I had declared my intention to stand and the moment was now at hand. With my wheelchair in place, I glanced at those around me, seeing both excitement and nervousness on their faces. I knew it was their moment as well. Their success and failure had been attached to the dream and I had no intention of letting them or myself down. I still weighed less than 100 pounds and my journey to that moment had not been as easy and successful as I had anticipated. All the failed attempts behind me, I zoned in on my dream, barely noticing the media personnel and cameras who had followed my every move from the moment I entered the stadium.

The stadium was filled to capacity with over 20,000 people in attendance. The commentator introduced me to the crowd and I lowered my head in a moment of prayer, focused on the dream of standing. A walker was placed in front of my wheelchair and everything went silent. I could hear nothing, nor could I see anything other than the walker. I was in in the zone, that place that exists before every great moment. As the power surged through my body, I stood and spoke words that I don't remember saying. And then I instinctively did what I had been clearly warned not to do. I had been warned to keep both hands on the walker at all times for stability. However, in the zone I had not only stood, but I raised my hand, waving it in celebration of what God had accomplished through me.

I lowered myself back in the wheelchair and as Derick pushed me off the infield, I pulled him close to me and whispered, "Derick, no one clapped for me." He looked startled and said, "Are you kidding me? Twenty thousand people went crazy!" I had been oblivious to it all. I guess I had been so far in the mental zone, I saw nothing beyond the rim of the moment of standing. As we rolled off the field, I shifted my thought from standing. Apparently, I told the crowd that I would in fact, walk again. The words whispered in the middle of the highway on that cold December 26th morning resonated within me, "Trust Us. Trust Us!" and "All is Well."

* * *

During the transition from the hospital to home, the scope of the damage of the accident set in. Michelle was now pregnant, married, taking on all my coaching responsibilities, caring for Imani, and the most overlooked task she had at hand was dealing with the hidden grief from the accident that had consumed her. In the hospital, I had seen the levels of pain in her eyes and she dove into taking care of Imani, the team, and myself in an effort to outwork the pain. She was slowly dying on the inside. She hid it because to allow any emotion, she would be consumed by guilt, anger, and the burden of having been the driver at the time of the accident. Everyone flocked to me with compassion because they could see the scars, but they rarely comforted Michelle whose inner turmoil ran deeper than my physical injuries. It would be easier for me to heal my body than for her to heal her heart. It would be easier for me to adjust to my physical losses than it would be for her to deal with the loss of her mother and her best friend/sister, Ilrey. My eyes became brighter with healing while her eyes became sunken and dark. She was dying from the inside out and I was healing from the inside out.

One day, I pulled her close to me and whispered so others couldn't hear, "Michelle, it's not your fault. It was an accident." I held her tighter and whispered it over and over. As I held her, the tears streamed. She managed to mutter, "I'm sorry! I'm sorry! I'm so sorry! I hurt you. I killed Ilrey and my mother. I'm so sorry!" I tried, with all the love I had, to convince her it was not her fault and that it could have happened to any of us. It had been an accident. I went on to tell her I had seen her mother and Ilrey and they were at peace. They had told me to look out for both Imani and Michelle and they had told me it was their time. I assured her they were at peace and looked happy and content. I released her, wanting her to feel the love that God had given to me. I hoped that someday she would heal and grow to understand that it was an accident. I prayed most nights not for myself, but for Imani and Michelle. I vowed to step in the gap and be a mother to both of them.

Being outside the confines of the hospital was harder than I predicted. Not so much the physical aspect but retaining my spiritual connection. While inside, I hadn't realized how much people keep from you. They don't want to be a burden, so they only bring you good news. I had stopped watching anything dramatic or violent on television and the few times I did watch TV, it was something funny. By keeping my environment clear of negativity, I unknowingly accelerated my healing process both internally and externally. Yet, outside the boundaries of the hospital, it was not possible to avoid the negative chatter.

From the moment I had awakened on that damp asphalt, I had been surrounded by a warm, comforting, powerful love. I saw love in everything and everyone my entire stay in the hospital. But in the real world, especially the work world, things were different. I couldn't maintain as tight of a grip on love. I'd discerned the purpose of the accident was to show people that no matter what we go through in life, we can not only survive, but thrive. Our ability to succeed, I discovered, was based not on our efforts but our beliefs and our capacity to love.

Coaching had been my life for so long and I had grown weary. But now it had new meaning. Besides winning, I was driven to deliberately empower people to believe and pursue their dreams. I looked at life differently and only saw the possibilities of how much better things could be. As I settled into my life with my disabilities, newfound visions, and a very talented team, there was no doubt great things were going to happen. And they did. After arriving home that March, I coached my heart out from my wheelchair with the help of my staff, particularly my team manager and Michelle. I had been unaware of how many people had been touched by the accident until I was asked to do a press conference while still in the hospital. I hadn't realized how unusual my reaction to the accident had been until HBO's Real Sports and People magazine did international segments on me. Both included coverage of my recovery, my attitude, and the successes in regards to walking again and winning. Next, awards came from all the over the country accompanied by requests for me to speak to various organizations. The press coverage was fun but the most impactful and fulfilling opportunities came when I was asked to speak to organizations, corporations, and youth groups. The ability to inspire people to move beyond their challenges was an even greater feeling than winning. All the major networks had done specials on me and as we headed into the Olympic season of 2004, the future looked much brighter than the past. After the team finished second in the nation, with me coaching from my wheelchair, several of our athletes went on the have international success. A number of coaches, including a coach on the men's side of track and field, began to attack my program and me. That's when I knew I was back!

Word had gotten back to me that the men's coach at Texas had interviewed replacements for me while I was in the hospital, telling people he was going to take over the women's program. It must have been shocking when I rolled onto the track still coaching. As the season rolled around, I was using a walker and the wheelchair equally, but my vision and instincts for coaching were clearer than ever. The team was incredible, breaking records and dominating in almost every event, but things were not as good as I thought they were. I had been so blinded by my desire to maintain that spiritual presence in my life, which had given me peace and purpose, I failed to see what was happening around me. I couldn't blame anyone when the team fell apart at the 2004 Outdoor National Championships or when the sports agents, parents, athletes, coaches, and shoe companies drove wedges between us all. I held myself responsible for our demise and it was me who needed to make the changes within me and the environment to ensure each athlete had the best opportunity to be successful in future seasons.

I wrestled with my desires to be spiritually grounded in the ego-driven, male-dominated world of sports. As time went on, I found myself farther from my center of love and fighting to survive, literally fighting. I cursed out the head of a major shoe company, I cursed out several of our sport agents, I took crap off of parents and administrators, and I battled to fire one of my staff coaches who'd shown little commitment to me or how I wanted to run my program. In fact, he was working more with the men's coach who opposed me than with me. When I approached Chris about firing him, she told me I didn't have the authority to fire a coach. I explained to her why it was so damaging, and she basically told me she didn't care, he was staying. I calmed down, looked at her and asked, "So who's going to explain to the press why I'm no longer the coach at Texas?" She looked puzzled and asked what I was talking about. I told her it was either him or me and it was apparent she had chosen him. She relented and allowed me to release him. He then went after her. I had the impression they were all having conversations behind my back. I might have been physically challenged, but I was beginning to tap into my survival instincts again. I would not survive if the people close to me didn't like me. I replaced two coaches, not because they couldn't coach, rather we were not unified in purpose and focus. A team divided against itself would fall and we were failing to live up to the expectations the levels of talent demanded we achieve. To prove my point, several years later, the men's coach hired that same person to coach his men's team and I think it surprised everyone except me. The crazy thing is, the coach that I fired and I are friends to this day and have a mutual respect for each other.

Eventually, he was fired again by the other coach and understood what I had been trying to teach him about coaching.

I not only changed coaches, I needed to find a way to balance spirit with reality and stay centered and focused on producing the winning outcomes we all wanted. I hired two high school coaches because I thought they could and would relate to the student-athletes better. One worked out and the other was a train wreck. As we entered the championship season of 2005, we were not slated to be among the contenders to win the title. Most of the talent had left after the disastrous 2004 season.

I had made changes within myself and started studying the art of deliberate manifestation. So much of what I had accomplished had been a result of instinct. I saw it was possible, but hadn't been sure how I'd done it or how I could teach others to do it. I studied, and read, and had the most amazing conversations with some of the most successful people in the world. I was learning to move effortlessly through all the confusion, trusting in the goal I had in my heart and pouring positive energy into it despite the negative things happening around me and to me. It all played out at the 2005 NCAA Outdoor Championships. Every moment of crazy drove me deeper into the positive visions of success. My team actually got into a fist fight with each other at the conference championship. My athletic director called screaming and cursing at me during my practices. Agents and parents clamored to get major contracts for some of my most talented athletes and I decided to sit still, always focusing on the outcome of winning.

At the 2005 NCAA National Championships, with a team of only seven athletes and facing teams with as many as twenty, I rode off into the darkness of the practice field to have a moment alone. We were about to compete in the final event, the women's 4x400 relays and it was slated to determine which team would be crowned national champions. I looked up towards the starry sky and I immediately felt Ilrey's presence. It brought a smile to my face and a comfort to my heart. I smiled because I knew we would not only win the meet, but we would win it because of her.

She was my guardian angel. As I turned the scooter to return to my team, I could see South Carolina, the favorites to win the entire meet. They were jogging and chanting while wearing celebratory pink and white tennis outfits although we were at a track meet. I smiled at the sheer power of their numbers, knowing that although we weren't strong on paper, you couldn't measure the strength of our willpower to win. We won both the relay and the championship.

Along with winning, I had a desire to fulfill my promise to God to use the platform with which He had gifted me to send the message that all things are possible if only we believe and trust in those beliefs. I accepted a ton of speaking engagements aimed at encouraging people. I also restarted the minority mentoring program and re-named it, "An Intimate Conversation with Greatness," in honor of the conversation that had changed my life, the one that took place with the Honorable Barbara Jordan and Hall of Famer, Jody Conradt. I met with several people who helped me elevate the program, from local professionals to a national and international list of speakers. Conversations with, and efforts by, The UT's former Director of Relations for the Department of African and African Diaspora, Brenda Burt, Mister Mann Frisby, Amber Nobel, Angela Vaughn, Raymond Coleman, LaTanya Wynn, Cynthea Patterson, Karen Taylor-Bass and Ms. Jackie Stewart helped create the platform and talent needed to create one of the most powerful and effective mentoring programs in the country. We created conversations from the heart and encouraged each speaker to have a conversation, as opposed to speeches with the audience, which consisted of both male and female college students from several universities and student-athletes from all sports.

The most important aspect of the program entailed connecting our efforts beyond the University and into the community. This portion of the program was spearheaded by the efforts of actress LeToya Luckett, celebrity make-up artist Keesh Winkler Smith, celebrity stylist Jason Griffin, Walmart, media specialist Paula Goins, and Olympians Carlette Guidry, Cynthea Rhondes, and Tamala Saldana, all of whom worked tirelessly with children in foster-care, the battered women's center, and the Ronald McDonald House. The programs were quite successful and even award-winning. However, the greater the successes, the greater the visibility, and therefore, the greater the attacks.

* * *

By the time I headed into the 2012 season, I'd recovered from some of my physical challenges, by walking with a cane, but emotionally and spiritually, I was worn and bruised. I was the go-to person in athletics for administrators who felt lost and abused, still within that department, I had nowhere to turn for help. With Jody having retired as athletic director and without a staff who constantly watched my back, I was weary. I did what I had done most of my life. I rolled up my sleeves and headed into the 2011-2012 Olympic season ready to pray and muscle my way through it. I laugh as I think back on all the times certain white female administrators would close my office door and cry to me seeking advice. Then, after their promotions, would become part of the problem and not the solution. The University of Texas is an amazing place full of life and opportunity, but it was also full of deceptively racist and misogynistic employees who deny their prejudices as they exert them. You can't blame the university itself for the attitudes and actions of a few, but they did impact the culture in which we had to work. As I became more visible, the attacks became more aggressive.

As the team prepared for the 2012 NCAA Indoor Championships, Chris asked me to meet her in the parking lot of a fast food restaurant. She exited her car and entered mine, handing me a handwritten note containing a list of allegations lodged against my program and myself. The allegations had come from within the program. I asked if they were from men's track and field department and she confirmed they were. They had declared several of my athletes ineligible until they could clear them. When I spoke to the head of compliance, it was obvious, they weren't looking to clear but to convict. She had been one of the women who had sat on my sofa and cried for help, and now I felt she was attacking me. She was not only the head of compliance, she was sport administrator for men's track, clearly a conflict of interest. I voiced my concerns about her investigating allegations against me by the sport she supervised, and she actually told me they had turned me in out of concern for the program. She claimed they had my best interest at heart. I wasn't sure if she was stupid or if she thought I was. Either way, I didn't trust her to be impartial and I told her as much.

Although every allegation proved to be untrue, the damage had been done. At the Indoor National Championships held at Texas A&M University, I was worn out. My body still suffered from the damages of the accident and I had tolerated countless hours of excruciating nerve pain over the past ten years but nothing prepared me for what happened the morning of the finals of the 2012 National Championship. I had awakened in the wee hours of the morning, disoriented and vomiting all over myself. I called the trainer, Michelle, and my manger in to help me. They cleaned me up, and in my weakened state, insisted I go to the hospital. I refused and told them to get something to help me sleep and to make sure to wake me up by 4:00 p.m. because the championship finals started that evening. I had made it to the meet that evening too weak to stand and was confined to my scooter. Despite my diminished physical state, I felt strong inside and was able to coach from a place within. We pulled a huge upset and by the grace of God, we finished second in the nation after barely being ranked among the top ten teams. When I saw the administrator who had led the investigation against me, she had the audacity to smile and pat me on the back saying, "You see, we knew if anyone could handle this, it would be you." Again, I wondered, *Is she stupid or does she just think I am?*

As my popularity and visibility grew so did my opposition. With each win and with every award, life became more unbearable for me within the athletic department. I became the first African-American, the youngest inductee, and only the second female in the history of Auburn University to receive their Lifetime Achievement Award. I received honors that I would never have imagined possible as I was inducted into the Women's International Foundation Hall of Fame, The United States Track Coaches Hall of Fame and The University of Texas Women's Athletic Hall of Fame, among others. I was even honored as one of Women's Day Magazine's "50 Women on a Mission" along with the likes of Michelle Obama and Angelina Jolie. It wasn't until I was honored at the "2012 BET Legends Honors" along with Dr. Maya Angelou, Stevie Wonder, Spike Lee, and the Tuskegee Airmen that things at Texas took its worst turn.

After returning home from the 2012 Indoor Championships, where I had literally passed out from the stresses of the attacks, I went to see one of my elder mentors from the community, former State Representative Mrs. Delco. She told me how proud of me she was and that now, of all times, I needed to be careful. She said I would become a target, because as an African American, too much recognition was not embraced at Texas. The BET Legends Awards, along with my winning record and my political and corporate contacts, would surely make them uncomfortable with me. I left her home confused. I had figured the better I did, the prouder of me they would become and the safer I should be. I didn't know what else I could do. I left feeling more broken and alone than I had felt in my entire life.

That summer, I loaded my car and drove alone from Austin to Eugene, Oregon for the 2012 Olympic Trials. While on the trip I received a call informing me of my sister Cherry's death from a stroke. I had lost my mother, grandmother, and three sisters. My older brother and my father had also been weakened by strokes and I could feel the stress levels rising within me. If things didn't change, I too would die soon. I cried and prayed the entire drive to the trials and following a disastrous meet in Eugene, cried and prayed all the way back to Austin. I asked for peace and for God's guidance for myself and for others. I prayed that God would resolve all my issues and I would live my life in peace and with purpose. I didn't just pray, I begged. I implored God to not forget about me. As I drove, the answers became clear. I had to stand up for myself. I had to demand something be done and that I be given a raise.

With fall 2012 approaching, there was only one year left on my contract. I needed to start discussions for renewal. This year was different. I had not received a major raise since Jody's departure and Chris, as our department head, had always managed to come up with an excuse as to why my raises were so small. I reasoned to her that while football and baseball and I had all won championships in 2005, I had won again in 2006. As I looked at their salaries in 2012, they had been given raises that amounted to over fifty percent increases while my salary had barely been raised by fifteen percent throughout that same time. I had been in the top ten the majority of the years since the 2006 victory, yet the disparity in raise percentages was unequal when compared to our successes and visibility.

As I engaged in the negotiations, I received another warning to be careful. Several white male coaches had warned me to watch my back as the men's coach had allegedly bragged that he was finally going to get me out of Texas. I went back to the Human Resources department and expressed the stress of my present situation. "It's like successfully heading a huge corporation, being praised publicly during the day and going home and being beaten by your spouse each night. Then getting up the next morning and going out into the world as if nothing happened." I was being beaten up at the university while being honored throughout the country. I felt overwhelmed, helpless, and abused. My faith had been weakened but at the same time, I was empowered by the prayers of that summer. I was determined to stand up for myself. The representative from Human Resources believed me and followed up with a meeting with the President's office. In no time, we hammered out a salary increase and a five-year extension that would almost double my present salary. I also requested a written clause be included in my contract to ensure that if the time came and the men and women's track teams were combined under one leadership, I would be the head coach. I wasn't sure if the rumors were true that the men's coach was pushing to combine the two programs but nonetheless, I needed to protect myself.

In the end, none of it would be enough to protect me. I had not figured that the relationship I had ten years prior would be used to destroy me but it was. I was placed on administrative leave and summarily fired. Now I had to decide whether to tuck my head between my legs and hide, or to stand against the injustices of how I had been treated. I chose to stand. I stood not because I thought the ill-advised, consensual relationship I had with a student athlete was a good decision but because my punishment was harsher than anyone else in the same situation had ever received. Discrimination is not just about being rewarded equally, it is also about receiving equal disciplinary action as well.

CHAPTER 16

Imani and Tamya stood in the doorway to the garage as I spoke with the driver who had come to pick up my car. I had to sell it, but I had not expected it to sell so quickly and neither did the girls. I looked over my shoulder as I handed the driver the keys to my Porsche Panamera only to see the tears falling from Tamya's eyes. She, unlike Imani, was experiencing her first loss of anything she valued, and although she had tried to be strong, the sale of the car somehow made her understand what my firing had actually meant. Imani had lost her mother when she was only two years old and now at thirteen, she understood loss. I turned to Tamya and asked if she was okay. She nodded, then asked if she could sit in the car one last time. The three of us had taken many weekend trips in that car, blaring our music and singing at the top of our lungs. Imani and I watched as she sat behind the wheel and eventually moved to the back seat, in the spot she had always claimed as hers. After a minute, she jumped out of the car, said her goodbye, and announced, "Okay Grammy, he can have her now."

As we watched the driver speed off, Imani and I laughed at the expression on Tamya's face as she broke out into a full sprint chasing the car down the street. We laughed so hard at the sight of her tired little body standing in the middle of the road, waving goodbye as if she was saying goodbye to an old friend. We laughed so hard that she started laughing at herself and soon her pain-filled tears turned to tears from laughter. We hugged and walked back into our near-empty home to watch the movers pack what little remained of our personal items into boxes.

After everyone had gone, I returned to my now empty house for the last time. The next day, I would hand the keys over to its new owner. I stood in the doorway of my empty bedroom whispering to myself, *Wow, what a beautiful house but I know everything will be okay.* I stood there, remembering just how excited family and friends had been when they had seen this magnificent house, complete with a swimming pool in the back, for the first time. I had meticulously picked out every component of the home, creating that dream house I had always promised my grandmother. She never got to live in it, but I knew she had looked down from the heavens with a smile on her face. I had named the home's movie theatre after my mother and grandmother, the Triple B for Brady, Bertha, and Beverly because they had always been the force behind my every success and my every dream. I would have been nothing without them.

As I stood in the empty room, I knew they had forgiven me for making a decision a decade earlier that cost me my career. But I was having trouble forgiving myself. The thought of disappointing others made my knees buckle and I slumped to the floor and cried. I could not care less about standing in an empty room or losing a house. The thought of crying over the loss of material things broke the flow of tears. I was reminded of the countless times as kids we had come home from school only to find a moving truck parked outside. My mother, for one reason or another, would up and move. Everything you loved about wherever you were would disappear into the background as we drove off to who knew where for who knew what.

I looked at the empty room and chuckled remembering the rental home I was now moving back into. I laughed thinking of the time I had to do a combat crawl up the stairs because Gerettia had come in and announced she was leaving and returning to Mississippi. I had hired her as my primary caretaker after getting out of the hospital and she traveled all over the world with me. After a particularly long day, she got so mad at me and yelled, "You've got to be the busiest cripple person I have ever seen. Why don't you sit your ass down somewhere? I can't keep up with you." Within days she was gone, leaving me and four-year-old Imani to be taken care of by Michelle, who had recently had a baby. Her husband had gone back to Houston for work and Michelle had taken ill. Imani came downstairs to my room to tell me Michelle was crying. We were both shocked because Michelle rarely, if ever, cried especially over pain. I remember she once cut off the tip of her finger while cooking. We had to literally beg her to go to the hospital as the blood squirted everywhere. She was a different kind of tough but now she was in tears. I had not been able to go upstairs in over a year but that time, I combat crawled up the stairs along with Imani who fell into a combat crawl behind me. I whispered for her to sneak in and get Michelle's cell phone. I took the phone and crawled to the guest room to call Michelle's sister, Yvonne, who lived in California to come and help us. As I entered the upstairs guest room to make the call, the room was empty. My sister had not only taken every piece of furniture, she even took the pictures off the wall. I had no idea she was leaving. She had taken the big check I had given her, thinking she would stay longer. Instead, she hitched a U-Haul to her truck, kissed me on my forehead, and never came back.

I chuckled harder as I glanced around the empty room and remembered going to visit Gerettia in Mississippi and saw all of my furniture and pictures on the wall of her mobile home. Still laughing,

I closed the door to my now empty dream home, built in honor of grandmother, and headed into the uncertainty of my new beginnings.

Texas had been true to its word. They did not intend to give me a dime. Without a steady income I had to downsize as quickly as possible. Having grown up in an unstable environment peppered with uncertainties, I found security in numbers. As soon as I could afford them, I always had two or three cars and two homes. Now, I sold as much as I could as quickly as I could. I had not been financially prepared to go from making hundreds of thousands of dollars a year to nothing. There had been so many family and close friends who depended on me financially that I not only worried about my own well-being but theirs as well. My first instinct had been to downsize, and my second thought was wondering how my brothers and sisters would survive without my financial assistance. To ensure they would be all right, I took money from my retirement to repair my rental property and paid off all their bills. I had no idea what the future held for me but I wanted to guarantee they would be okay.

After being fired, I went into crisis mode, preparing for the worst while hoping for the best. During a crisis you go though many emotions and the most damaging is fear. Throughout the crisis of my accident, I had managed to avoid fear. My hospital stay had been a period of spiritual evolution. I evolved from a place of belief, to a place of faith and eventually awakening to a spiritual space of knowing. I didn't depend on others. I instinctively trusted what I believed to be true and I was able to manifest my reality by knowing, which became my outcome. In the hospital I had seen myself standing at the Texas Relays, hence I began to work on my vision without negative distractions. No one voiced or created opposition, which in itself produces doubt. As a result, no one or no thing could impede or turn me away from my outcome. The hospital became my bubble, protecting me from the naysayers who were doubtful, reluctant, or cautious in their pursuits in life. Not only was I learning, I began to actualize what Raymond meant when he casually said one day, "Bev, don't figure out how to create magic, you got to *be* the magic." This had been my mantra throughout my stay in the hospital. It was through discovering the magic that existed *in* me that I defied the odds *against* me by standing and actually walking again. What most had deemed a tragedy, I knew was an opportunity to do greater things and impact more people, helping them believe in their own greatness, their own magic. It would allow me the ability to help others move beyond their circumstance and see the greater possibilities of life.

In the hospital it had seemed effortless to manifest because I had come to trust that all I had to do was ask and then allow. Oh, but things really changed once I left the confines of that hospital room and returned back home and into the world. I couldn't figure out for the life of me how and why things had change so drastically. I had gone from a place of knowing to doubt, and at times, even fear. What people thought and said mattered and altered my direction. What I knew to be truth still existed, but I no longer controlled the magic that existed in me. The world around me did. I couldn't figure it out. Then it came to me, I was back home. I was back in the world of competitive stress, jealousy, naysayers, people who thought from a practical perspective and who refused to dream big. My dreams had been so big while in the place of knowing, that as I entered back into the world, I had tried to taper them. As I spoke to people, I unwittingly thought from a place of practicality rather than from a place of magic. When it came to real world circumstances, I had become more susceptible to the ideas and fears of others. As a result of my shift in thinking, I became somewhat dependent on the input of others and their truth became my truth, which became my reality. The only place I was able to sustain the inner magic to believe in greatness was on the track. On the track coaching, things were different. I was Aladdin with the lamp. I believed so much in others, my faith could not be tested or shaken. The team was succeeding, and the magic was real, but I couldn't see magic for myself. I was full of doubt and when people warned me to watch my back, I didn't shake it off and trust that I would be okay. I became fearful and my belief in myself suffered the most. My prayer became, "I don't want to lose my job," and guess what happened...I lost my job. Along with it, I lost not only material things like money, houses, and cars, I also lost friends and people who I thought were part of my inner circle. However, none of those things bothered me as much as losing sight of who I was and what I was driven to do. They say when we take a leap of faith, there is a moment when we are suspended midair right before we land on the other side. I felt permanently suspended midair, knowing I couldn't go back, but not sure what was on the other side once I landed.

I hadn't realized how lost I had been until about three years into the lawsuit and I still found myself without a consistent source of income. I had been driving alone trying to clear my thoughts. As I drove, I felt a tightening in my chest and the pounding of my heart. Realizing I couldn't breathe, I headed for the nearest medical facility. It was just my luck to be near a clinic not an actual hospital. They offered to call an ambulance, but I couldn't afford it, so I drove myself to the nearest hospital. My blood pressure had sky-rocketed and they wanted to admit me to confirm I had not had a stroke. Instead, I convinced them I would be okay and they released me after I signed the paperwork. I knew Imani and Tamya would be coming home from school soon and I needed to be there for them. As I drove home, I took an evaluation of my life and knew if I intended to find my purpose and passion, I had to turn to the only source who could help me. I had to turn within, and I had to turn to God. I had been discouraged from seeking God only because so many in the religious community who had praised me during my recovery now distanced themselves from me, effectively making me an untouchable. Only Archbishop Sterling Lands stood in the gap for me. He hugged me each time he saw me, and we'd prayed together. He encouraged me through my roughest days. It didn't matter who was for me or against me if I no longer believed in myself.

Once I returned home, seated in my meditation room, I prayed for guidance. For the first time since my termination, I heard the whispers again. I quieted my mind and reconnected to the whispers. I could hear the voice lovingly whispering to me, "When you lost your physical abilities, you were still in my service. Now I ask, if you lose all your money and possessions, will you still serve me? If you no longer have a resume, if you are no longer honored in various arenas, if all you have accomplished goes away, will you still serve me?" My answer was *"Yes. I will serve. I will do what I can whenever I can."* I understood then what Raymond meant when he preached both while I was in the hospital and after I had left, saying I needed to be void of ego. I had thought he was accusing me of being egotistical, but he wasn't. I now understood. He had meant I was not to identify myself by what I did or what I accomplished in the past, but to stay present and focused on the task at hand. I made the decision to begin the real process of divorcing myself from my ego. It would not be easy because that's all we know. We are judged based on what we have done. I called Raymond and told him of my decision and in the midst of a difficult legal and public situation, I took on a purpose that would challenge me more than anyone or anything on Earth would or could ever do.

I considered the unfolding events and fallout from the lawsuit. Administrators and coaches were being released, retired, or reassigned at Texas. It went up to the highest levels and trickled back down to the lower workers. No one was safe. I would often ponder what made them go to such extremes to remove me. They had to have known I would stand up for myself. That's what they both loved and hated about me, my fight. I had fit Texas like a glove. I was dedicated, driven, and tough. Even the men's coach retired after he had self-assuredly bragged that he would oversee both programs.

I watched from afar and most would think I found pleasure in seeing those who were part of my professional demise have their own struggle. That wasn't the case. Through my own difficulties, I learned to be more compassionate and empathetic. I prayed that as I moved through the process, notwithstanding the outcome, asking God to remove anger, fear, hatred, or a desire for retribution. So as Chris appeared to have been the only one to survive the fallout unscathed, I had to seek God, because if anyone deserved to be removed, it was her. I needed to find something to love in her and after months of prayer, I realized that she too had been a victim. She was in survival mode and anything she had to do professionally to survive it all, she would, and she did. It wasn't personal for her. It was survival. I smiled internally as they announced the hiring of the University of Texas's first Black head football coach. In fact, I believed, in some way, my sacrifices had contributed to the growth of a remarkable and powerful institution.

As the lawsuit continued for over four years, it took a toll on everyone, including The University of Texas and the attorneys. It was during that time, I started my consulting business and committed myself to assisting others in discovering and manifesting their own levels of success and greatness. Although I couldn't coach athletes at the collegiate level, I needed to find a way to utilize my knowledge and passion to support others. I was still one of the most passionate, intuitive, knowledgeable, successful magical coaches in the country and

I used that magic to help others find the magic in themselves and in their visions. I have worked with individuals and groups at all levels of sports as well as in the entertainment, corporate, political, and higher education levels on creating the successes they desire. Throughout the lawsuit, I slowly developed into one of the best-kept secrets to achieving success. Often, I did not receive public acknowledgement for my contribution of guidance and assistance. However, people felt more at ease being open about my involvement after the lawsuit was settled. For me, it didn't matter whether credit was ever given. I would rather have something to give than nothing and getting recognition had always been secondary to actually seeing the joy of another's success. Heck, I don't even own a trophy, but I possess every memory of the joy of others.

As the suit dragged on and I continued my mission of advising others in finding the magic and power within, I had a conversation with a friend and it totally altered my entire energy. While engaging in what I thought was a casual conversation, he unknowingly planted a seed in my heart. He told me as if he were empowering me, "Yeah, I heard that a few of the powerful Texas boosters knew they were going to have to pay you eventually, but in the meantime, their intent is to break you financially and emotionally." He went on to tell me how he couldn't reveal where he'd heard the information but assured me he told his source I would be okay because I was one of the smartest and toughest people he knew. Well there it was, that seed.

From the moment I heard about their desire to break me guess what I thought about? Them breaking me! I even began each prayer with, "Oh God, don't let them break me." What a dumb thing to focus on! I sunk so far into doubt and fear that I had literally handed them the hammer to break me. As opposed to being steel, I had become a thin sheet of glass, which broke on first contact. I had gone into mediation with Texas full of fake confidence, you know the kind where you're scared but you give yourself the pep talk. That "Go Team – Fight - Win" kind of inner dialog that not even *you* believe. I didn't stand a chance. I was filled with such an abundance of uncertainty, fear, and negative emotions, even during mediation I had excused myself from the room, ran down the hall, found an empty corner, squatted down and cried. Only through the grace of God was I able to gather myself and re-enter the room and finish the session.

By the time I returned to Raymond's house, I was a mess. I got out of my car in the driveway and never made it inside. I collapsed in their front yard. His wife Cheryl rushed outside, sat down beside me, placed my head in her lap, and stroked my face trying to assure me that everything would be okay.

Raymond and I sat alone in my bedroom of his house and prayed. As we prayed and talked, I comprehended what had happened. It wasn't about the mediation. It was about focusing my energy on what I had wanted *not* to happen. It was about me. It would be a costly financial lesson, but a lesson that would prove more valuable than any lesson I could have ever hoped for.

Within days, my lawyers called with an offer and immediately tried to convince me that although it wasn't a large sum, I had in fact won. I cut the conversation and told them I had prayed about it and it was over. I had no hard feelings about it all and whatever they thought was fair was it. I was told that everything would be confidential and even had to sign paperwork stating as such but to my surprise, the very thing I was told not to speak on showed up in the paper. I know my lawyers didn't release the information and it was probably Texas's way of showing how little they had to pay as a means of "winning." By now, none of that was important because I had learned a lesson that I could now teach with an even greater conviction. I had reaped many benefits throughout my career with my method of manifestation, *"Believe It, Speak It, Do It"* and now I had paid the ultimate price in misusing its power.

My last experience with the lawsuit would be my permanent transformation back into the magic and truth of who I was designed to be. Through trial and error, I had now learned how to knowingly live and how to teach the art of unlocking the magic that lies within each of us.

EPILOGUE

Throughout life's journey, we all encounter circumstances and have experiences that challenge us. It is through those challenges that we find and define who we are and our intents in life. Through my own experiences, I have learned that facing fears, challenges, and shortcomings will teach, empower, and strengthen us. Yet when avoided, they eventually distract, defeat, and weaken us. No one wants to admit to being fearful because we are taught that fearlessness is a strength and fear is a weakness. Neither is true. Our greatest strength is not in being fearless, it is having the courage to face and examine our fears and move beyond them.

At times, our fear shows up in the form of unworthiness or when we are diminished by the greatness of others. It is our challenge to move beyond the negative ego of self-doubt to the positive spirit of value in *knowing* you belong and you are worthy. I have been challenged with that type of fear throughout my professional career. I had to know that what I did had value, what I said held value, and what I created was of value and through this learned process, I found my worthiness. Now, there were times when, regardless of how hard I tried to find a sense of belonging, I fell short. However, it was always through prayer and my knowing of God that I discovered my worth.

"Hello Coach Kearney...Coach Kearney! Could you please move forward to the stage," I could barely hear my name being called and sat motionless overcome by sheer elation and excitement. I had never felt like this before. Paralyzed, unable to hear or move, I sat as my name was called several more times. I thought to myself, surely they are not calling my name. Then my brother said, "Bev, they're calling you."

We rose, still stunned from having just witnessed the greatest moment of our lives. There I was at the rehearsal for the 2012 BET Legends Awards in Washington, DC with my brother and the legendary "Queen of Soul," Ms. Aretha Franklin, sitting directly behind us. What an equally exhilarating and intimidating moment. Even though Derick and I were in our fifties, we kept elbowing each other with excitement, taking turns shifting around to sneak quick glances like school-aged children. For a minute, I was no longer a fifty-six-year-old woman, instead I was transported back to a time when I was a little girl sitting with my family jamming to her songs. Now, I find myself in the same auditorium with the Queen. When they repeated my name, as he and I rose from our seats, my legs became wobbly and I felt a little faint. However, I held my ground and continued to move towards the stage. As we exited our seats, we turned and ever so respectfully greeted the Queen, "Good afternoon Ms. Franklin." She smiled warmly and nodded her head hello before resuming her conversation with the people seated with her. Inside I just knew I'd died and gone to heaven! I strolled down the aisles towards the front of the theater savoring my moment of meeting the legend.

As we walked towards the front of the stage in the nearly empty auditorium, which normally held in the 1000's, with only about one hundred there for rehearsal, people began to recognize and greet me saying how much I had been an inspiration to them. As we got closer to the front of the theater, I read the many names on the tags attached to each seat. It read like a Who's Who of Black Entertainment, and with every name, an overwhelming sense of nervousness grew within me. As the usher continued to guide us to where I would be seated for the next day's event, there it was, my name on a seat amongst such notables as Spike Lee, Stevie Wonder, Dr. Maya Angelou, Jill Scott, Queen Latifah, and so many more. My brother and I shook with excitement combined with a sense of nervousness and I was beginning to feel a bit unworthy to be among the list.

It had all been a blur up to that point from the moment the lady from BET reached out to me informing me I was to be honored as one of the 2012 BET Legends. Kelli Richardson Lawson, a very successful business executive who owns her own business, The Joy Collective, had nominated me for the award. She and Louis Carr, President of Media Finance for BET, submitted my name amongst the hundreds of nominees. I knew they had done it but never in a million years did I think I would be given such an honor. I had been recognized at many events in my lifetime but being honored by my community—my culture—was the highlight of my career. I could not believe I was actually going to share a stage with people I admired like the Tuskegee Airmen and Dr. Angelou. Seeing my name in black and white on the seat in the front row of the theater made my heart drop to my knees but not in a good way.

By the time Derick had assisted me in walking up the steps to the stage, that sense of unworthiness had taken full control and I was now filled with alarming fear. If I had told anyone who'd known me for any length of time that I was scared, they would not have believed me. I had always been applauded for my strength, courage, and fight but none of that existed in that moment. As the director of the event led me to the taped spot in front of the mic, he pointed into the arena at the large monitor, which projected the speech I had been asked to prepare months prior. As he stepped back to allow me to practice my speech, I gripped my cane, which I used to balance myself but no words would come out. I stood there awkwardly in silence until he again approached me, speaking into his mic rather loudly which echoed throughout the theater, "Coach Kearney, can you see the monitor?"

I nodded and began to read what was written as if I were a sixth grader reading in front of the class for the first time. I stumbled so badly that again he approached me asking, "Coach Kearney, is there a problem?"

I answered stammering now in what had to be my third-grade voice, "Yes, I don't want to read that. I don't even know why I wrote it. I don't want to say that." He walked away clearly frustrated when Kelli, who had been sitting in the audience, gently asked if I would like them to turn the monitor off just as Derick, who had been standing on stage with me told the director, "She doesn't need a monitor, she will be just fine without it."

So when asked if I would like for them to turn it off, I nodded, signaling yes. With that, the monitor went black and so did I.

I again attempted to speak from my heart but my heart was no longer available to speak on my behalf for it was preoccupied fighting off fear and tears. So my head took over and I said the stupidest thing stumbling through two barely audible sentences before proclaiming in my preschool voice, "I don't wanna practice! I don't want to do this anymore. Can I please not practice?"

As the silence grew in the theater, you could hear a pin drop. I was now a five-year-old completely lost struggling in quicksand trying to save myself. I said the next stupidest thing I could have ever thought of to say, "Don't worry about me, I will be okay tomorrow. I promise I will be all right." With that, Derick, who had been standing next to me, gripped my arm to help me off stage. He looked at me and tried to reassure me that he knew I would be fine for the speech tomorrow but no amount on consolation could penetrate the amount of fear I had accumulated in that short period of time. His smile gave me the courage to do the walk of shame back up the aisle of the theater where I could see people doing everything to avoid eye contact with me. Each person turned away so as not to acknowledge just how embarrassing the moment had not only been for me, but for them having to watch it.

I asked him why he wasn't embarrassed by my rehearsal mishap. He told me he'd witnessed me inspire and motivate people through speeches and I didn't need to practice so it was not a concern to him. Knowing he had such confidence in me soothed my anxiety and I walked out of the theater not feeling totally destroyed.

Back in my hotel room, I met up with Raymond and Cheryl. I relayed the details of my disastrous rehearsal and Raymond smiled while trying not to laugh. After composing himself, he told me I was going to be all right. That was good news because I was scheduled to attend the honoree pre-event dinner that evening and would have to face people who were at the rehearsal. As more people piled into my room, I soon forgot about what happened at rehearsal and when I did think about it. I managed to make a few jokes about it.

Later that evening, I got dressed and met Derick in the lobby of the hotel to depart along with several of the other honorees for the big dinner. I saw Spike Lee and excitedly spoke to him but I think he thought I was tripping, hence he barely acknowledged us. After what happened earlier at the rehearsal, when I had the opportunity to actually meet Ms. Franklin, I made up my mind to embrace the moment.

Even with the best intents to stay composed amongst greatness, as we entered the art museum ballroom where the dinner was being held, we again nudged and elbowed each other with excitement. Neither of us could believe two kids born in Meadville, Mississippi would be dining among our heroes and sheroes. Roughly 100 finely adorned tables filled the room. An attendant escorted us to our seats towards the front of the room. I was both stunned and excited as she pointed to our table. Just like the White House Christmas dinner in 2003, with me seated next to the President of the United States and country Legend, Kenny Chesney, once again I was blessed to sit between greatness. This time it was The Queen of Soul, Aretha Franklin, and the President of BET, Debra Lee. As I took my seat next to the Queen, it hit me that she had been at the rehearsal earlier that day and I prayed with everything in my being that she would not remember meeting me. As we laughed and talked, I let my guard down assuming she had not remembered me until she looked at me puzzled and asked, "Have I met you before?"

In a very respectful southern voice I lied, "No ma'am." Yep, I sure did. I flat out lied to Ms. Aretha Franklin. She glanced at me again for a moment but I didn't change my expression. We resumed our meals and enjoyed the company of the table. That night, my brother and I enjoyed a magical evening. I awoke the next morning both excited about the awards ceremony and nervous. *What if I panic like I had done in rehearsal?*

I tried to shake off my fears as my hotel room filled with people. Deitra Kearney, a cousin on my father's side from Washington or Virginia, had driven in for the day to meet Derick and me. I didn't know anyone from my father's side of the family and she was a warm and loving distraction. Rose Brimmer, my assistant coach at Texas, had not only flown her high school daughter Bria to the event, but also a hairdresser from Houston (whose name I can't remember), and our stylist from California, Jason Griffin, who now styles for the popular and successful show, *Empire*. Kelli made arrangements for my make-up and Jason secured an amazing dress from a designer in California on loan and over $20,000 in jewelry from a jeweler in New York.

As we all scrambled in my hotel suite to get make-up and hair done, my nerves would not settle. As time drew near to depart, my nervousness had evolved into fear. To address what was happening, I politely asked everyone to clear the room with the exception of Raymond. As we sat alone, I told him I was fearful and to be honest, I had felt unworthy to be honored among the legends and such greats. He listened as I explored my inner fears and finally, I asked, "Raymond, why was I chosen to be here in this moment?"

Raymond's tone and volume required me to lean forward and for some reason, that small act anchored our conversation deep within my subconscious.

"Your story of survival from your childhood to adulthood needs to be felt and heard. Remember when I asked you to speak at the awards banquet for my department at the University? You were scared shitless."

I sort of chuckled because only Raymond could make me laugh at myself with his cursing and bluntness.

"You got even worst after the coach before you spoke. I told you then and I say it once more, this is your destiny. You are supposed to be here in this time and place called now and you are worthy or why the hell would they ask you to come in the first place. Bev, you have the ability to connect your energy of love to the heart chakra with all those you come in contact with. That is truly a gift from God. I saw that when you first stepped behind the podium that night. That's a God gift. Now don't get it twisted, it doesn't mean everyone will fall in love with Bev but it does mean people will find meaning in the words you speak. People who have this gift can do good or they can do harm.

You, my dear, have a heart and a conscious hence you are destined to do good. Sometimes, the power of words comes from the energy of the speaker, which connects and touches at a level that's difficult to explain. Speak from your heart tonight and allow the energy of God and the many angels you have around you to take over. Trust and know that the God energy is with you but first, trust yourself. Be humble and remember you are worthy. Believe me Bev, everyone at some point in their life feels unworthy for whatever reason, however not everyone sees the blessing in the experience. Know that you are blessed."

We ended our conversation and prayer with a hug. Once he left the room, I remained in the quiet of the moment. I spoke to God as if He was sitting beside me.

"God I know this moment is not about me. I ask that you use this moment, my voice, my presence, to speak through me and move through me. I ask for your strength, guidance, and love."

As I ended my prayer, peace set in and the chatter in my mind dissipated. Once again, the whispers arose from deep within telling me I was worthy to be heard not because of anything I had done, but as a representation of Me. God informed me to be allowing of the moment and to trust. The exact words that had comforted me through the car accident were guiding me beyond my fears. "Trust Us! Trust You!" Calmness overcame me and I smiled knowing everything would surely be all right.

That night, I sat in the front row with Derick and we witnessed one of the most magical nights of our lives. We both thought about how proud our mother and grandmother would be. The start of the show was interrupted by the appearance of an unannounced guest. It was a surprise arrival by the First Lady of the United States, Michelle Obama. It got better because in the middle of the show, we were ushered to the stage for a group picture. As we took pictures, the First

Lady stood proudly watching from the side. Soon, I began to lose my equilibrium as standing in one place for too long caused me to experience a small degree of unsteadiness. I swayed, trying to maintain balance, and a distinguished gentleman, one of the famed Tuskegee Airmen, noticed my dilemma and told me to hold onto his shoulder. I looked at his petite stature and grew concerned that placing my weight on him would cause us both to tumble to the floor and I was not about to take a legendary tumble at the BET Honors. Just as I was about to speak, Spike Lee, who stood on the other side of me, grabbed my arm and said, "I got you."

After we took what we thought would be the last pictures of the evening, it was announced that Mrs. Obama wanted to join us for one last photo. As she strolled down the line of legends, I kept waiting for her to wedge between some of the more noted honorees but she stopped in front of Spike Lee and me and said, "I am going to stand between you guys." Spike gripped me even stronger telling her I needed support. Graciously she said, "I have you Coach, just hold on to me." They then asked us to take three steps forward, grateful for the sturdy person to hold on to, I took the three steps with the assistance of Mrs. Obama. Then they said to take one step back. However, going backward for me was a problem. Before I realized it, I said, "Oh shit!"

Mrs. Obama looked at me and said sternly, in support of me, "We really don't have to back up for no one."

Wanting to be a team player, I looked at her and said, "I can do it." With that she said, "Let's do this then," and we took our step back. Holding onto not only the steadiness of the First Lady, and sensing her loving, gentle energy, peace filled the air around me. As we exited the stage, I was certain all was well and I would be all right. I had not battled my fear but acknowledged its presence and as a result, I had refocused on *why* I was there and not only on being there.

As we took our seats and the show resumed, I knew her being there was God's (the Universe) confirmation of a divinely-inspired moment. As the pre-recorded video of my bio played, one of my former athletes, Sanya Richards, who was a noted multiple Olympic Gold medalist, took the stage to introduce me. Wow! I was overwhelmed with humility.

Once I approached the microphone and opened my mouth, I spoke, no longer contained by thoughts of fear or unworthiness. My words were from the heart and not controlled or memorized. To this day, I do not remember what was said. However, I do remember giving a shout out to Imani and Tamya.

As God would have it, my brother gently and proudly escorted me down the stairs and as I moved off of the last step, I came face to face with the impossible. I had not seen him or his name on a seat but there he was, General Colin Powell. I had studied him and all he had accomplished and grown to love him in my heart and mind. He had always been on my bucket list to have a conversation with and now I was face to face with him. He smiled at me shaking his fist saying, "Yes, Yes, Yes!" My heart stopped at the sight of his approval for whatever I had said. Just as I was about to move towards him, someone instructed Derick to lead me towards the First Lady who was seated nearby on the first row. She embraced me and whispered how she had never heard a speech like that and stated, "We need you." At the time, I had no idea what I had said or what the reaction of the audience had been.

As she released me from the warmth of her hug and as I made my way back to my seat, I felt the presence of the angels who spoke to me as I lay dying in the middle of a lonely highway in 2002. My mother and grandmother were happy but mostly, I felt at peace with the moment. God had guided me through and utilized everyone around me to assist in moving beyond, not only my fears, but what could arguably be considered one of the most embarrassing moments ever. I was later told the audience had stood in approval throughout my speech and it was the first time an audience of that caliber had ever stood for an entire speech. I thought to myself, *Look at God*. For when what we are assigned to do is greater than our fear of failing, great moments happen.

We are all faced with uncertainties and sometimes seemingly unbearable embarrassments in our failures but each leads us to our greatest successes. If we are blessed not to be consumed in the opinions of others and embrace our flaws, we allow ourselves to self-correct and continue to move forward. We are not weakened by our challenges but strengthened by them. We are not broken because of our tears but freed by them. We are not rendered powerless by our fears but empowered by them. We are not destroyed by our mistakes but taught by them. Throughout my life's journey, I have faced many challenges, cried many tears, made more mistakes than I care to admit, and failed too many times to count. Fortunately, through the process of living we hone our skills, learn our lessons, strengthen our resolve, and discover the magic within us. We discover our power through our failures and our humility through our successes. For the greatest lesson I learned was it was not the powers outside myself which determine my successes or failures, but the power from within.

When what we desire becomes greater than what we fear, we succeed. What we focus on internally and what we harbor in our hearts will always manifest itself in our reality. We can say the right things, have the right resume, be very talented, and even take the right actions but all will be derailed if we harbor negative thoughts and beliefs. Throughout my passage on this Earth, my truest power has come in discovering the magic within me. It's the ability to stay focused on the present task at hand, being my best in the moment and allowing myself to trust in the process, no matter the challenges along the way.

All of my mistakes are not behind me as I will likely make many more as I continue to grow. With that thought, I must end with the following message. Often times institutions, governments, and corporations have high expectations of its citizens, employees, and members, but do not hold themselves to the same level of expected growth and excellence. We, as a society, must continue to self-evaluate and grow. When we make a mistake, we are expected to own the errors and correct them. But institutions will spend millions upon millions of dollars to defend their mistakes and crush anyone who challenges them to improve. If we are to grow as a society, it has to start from the top and include honesty, trust, forgiveness, and a strong commitment to equality and greatness.

It is with love that this story has been told. It honors my greatest hero, my history. I come from a long line of greatness and people who have overcome obstacles, abuses, fears, and dangers to achieve unparalleled levels of success in all walks of life. As a human being, an American citizen, an African American, a woman, a person with a disability, being Gay, and as a person with a strong spiritual foundation, I stand on the shoulders of all whose sacrifices have allowed me to be the greatness of who God designed me to be. I thank you and hope in some way, my story will inspire you to live your story and journey to the fullest.

ABOUT THE AUTHOR

BEVERLY KEARNEY, affectionately known as "Coach Bev," is one of those rare visionary stars who believes greatness exists within everyone. Her passion and gift for coaching, consulting, and mentoring has inspired individuals in various professions to achieve their greatest successes. Recognized as one of the most successful coaches in NCAA history, Bev has been inducted to various halls of fame as a sports legend including the prestigious International Women's Sports Hall of Fame and the United States Track and Field Hall of Fame. Her record of seven national championships is the second highest among female coaches and African-American coaches in all collegiate Division I sports. In 2012, she was honored with a BET Legacy Award for Education alongside the likes of Maya Angelou, Stevie Wonder, Spike Lee, Mariah Carey, and the Tuskegee Airmen. Throughout her career, she has received several additional awards including the Lifetime Achievement Award for Auburn University, marking only the second time in history that a woman has received the award and the first African-American in history to receive the award.

Woman's Day magazine named her one of their "50 Women on a Mission" along with such notables as Michelle Obama, Hilary Clinton, and Angelina Jolie. The Buoniconti Foundation honored Bev as a Great Sports Legend. She joins other alumni legends like Michael Jordan, Dean Smith, and Muhammad Ali. Bev has served as Head Coach of the University of Texas and the University of Florida, and as an Assistant Coach at the University of Toledo, the University of Tennessee, and Indiana State University. The men and women she coached throughout her thirty-year career stand out as America's best athletes with over a 95% graduation rate, 15+ Olympians, several World, Collegiate, National, and American record holders, and more than 250 All-Americans. Bev's many titles do little justice for her ability to motivate, empower, and realize matchless goals repeatedly and consistently.

High expectations and uncompromising faith in people could result in her being viewed as tough. But Bev believes in love first, both tough love and self-love. Her mantra is, "Believe it, Speak it, Do it." She believes intensely that one must commit to and become fully invested in one's own dreams and the realization of one's personal, cultural, spiritual, and physical goals.

Bev has shared her winning principles nationally and internationally as a speaker and consultant on all of the major television networks including HBO and ESPN. She has been featured repeatedly in magazines and journals including People, USA Today, Black Enterprise, and Women's Health. Bev has also been an honored guest at The White House. Beyond her work as a coach, Beverly founded Mirror of Magic & In Pursuit of Dreams Performance Consultants, which is a results-based consulting firm specializing in the development of extraordinary leaders by assisting individuals and organizations in achieving greatness. The company allows Bev to draw on her philosophy and use her skills to expand beyond the athletic arena. The program has assisted those in athletics, business, education, politics and entertainment to discreetly and seamlessly promote winning cultures, successful solutions, and superior focus for the creation of nothing less than greatness.

Bev has devoted her life to helping people who want to help themselves, discover their own goals, and dig deep to achieve. She believes passionately that everybody can be successful. She lives this model every day through wins and losses, triumphing gracefully through obstacles of all kinds.

Beverly Kearney is a living example that greatness is still possible despite extreme obstacles. Through the development of inner-power, laser focus, excellence of leadership, and proven methods, she has come to realize and teach that a positive focus can outweigh and outlive the most impossible circumstances.

SPECIAL ACKNOWLEDGMENTS

My deceased grandmother, Brady Bracy Buie, and deceased mother, Bertha "Christine" Buie Kearney, were two of the wisest, toughest, and most resourceful, powerful, yet loving women I have ever known. Through their individual choices and journeys, they taught me not only what to do, but equally as important, what not to do.

I also acknowledge my three deceased siblings, Alice, Ernestine, and Cherry, along with my three living siblings, Howard, Gerettia, and my little brother Derick. Our family has endured many forms of abuse, self-imposed as well as at the hands of others. Yet with all of our crazy experiences, we have loved, laughed, fought, and always stood as one. Each of you taught me the essence and importance of forgiveness. My prayer is that you all know just how much you have touched my life.

This book has been a work in progress for 10-15 years and after much prayer, I knew it was time to tell this story. I prayed for the right guidance and assistance and God answered my prayers, not only through inner guidance, but with earthly Angels who assisted me on this journey.

Raymond Coleman, thank you for your honest feedback and invaluable contributions, as well as for clarifying content and helping shape the story around my spiritual evolution. Thanks for your continued guidance throughout my journey.

Mynd Matters Publishing, your staff has truly blessed this project. A special thanks to *Kelli Richardson Lawson* for making the connection and being a blessing.

Marilyn Batchelor, thank you for assisting in the editing process and providing me with feedback every time I needed it.

Imani Sparks, thank you for reading the manuscript and providing clarifying blunt, but loving, suggestions throughout the process.

A heartfelt thanks to *Derick Kearney, Gerettia Buie, Michelle Freeman, Tamya Flenoy, LaTanya Wynn, Cheryl Coleman, and Dr. Tracy Shaw,* for without each of you, I could not have finished this book. Your love, encouragement, and feedback saved me more than you will ever know.

Lastly, I dedicate *Believe It, Speak It, Do It* to my history, for my history is truly my hero. For all who braved the odds to create pathways for us to follow, I thank you. I thank foremost God for guiding me through my life's journey and the writing of this book. I thank my heroes who gave of themselves in life and death so that I might have the freedom to walk my journey. Christ, Buddha, Sojourner Truth, Gandhi, Dr. M.L. King, Malcom X and so many other known and unknown servant warriors who throughout history, made personal sacrifices to blaze trails for us to follow. I could never become me without recalling and relying on the courage, perseverance, strength, and love of your journeys.

CPSIA information can be obtained
at www.ICGtesting.com
Printed in the USA
LVHW030240191022
731045LV00001B/85